FEB - 2000

PHOTOSHOP FOR THE WEB

D1530415

PHOTOSHOP FOR THE WEB
SECOND EDITION

Mikkel Aaland

O'REILLY®

Beijing · Cambridge · Farnham · Köln · Paris · Sebastopol · Taipei · Tokyo

Photoshop for the Web, Second Edition
by Mikkel Aaland

Editor: Richard Koman
Production Editor: Melanie Wang

Printing History:

April 1998:	First Edition.
November 1999:	Second Edition.

ISBN: 1-56592-641-2

CONTENTS

PREFACE

Photoshop for the Web was the first book focusing specifically on using Adobe Photoshop for web production. In this, the second edition, you'll learn about the latest release of Photoshop, Version 5.5, and its companion product ImageReady 2.0, which is included free when you upgrade to or purchase 5.5. With this new release, Adobe has finally created a Photoshop for the Web.

Some of 5.5's more notable web-friendly features that are covered in this edition are:

- A long-overdue Save for Web plug-in, which makes creating optimal GIFs, JPEGs, and PNGs a snap.

- New erase-to-transparent tools, including Magic and Background Erasers and the Extract command, which make it easier than ever to prepare graphics for GIF or PNG transparency.

- New, improved indexed color options that let you control dithering, adjust the color table, and assign background transparency. In addition, a new, interactive Color Table lets you assign transparency to a specified color in the image.

- An improved contact sheet maker that helps you organize your images better, and a Web Photo Gallery that automatically creates interactive web pages from a folder of images.

- New JPEG Save options that let you control the appearance of originally transparent areas, compress file sizes further, and preview the size and download time of the file when saving as JPEG.

- An improved Type tool that gives you control of anti-aliasing and provides faux bold and italic styles.

- A new Color Picker with a web-safe color option and a new color palette that automatically shifts non-web safe colors to web-safe colors.

ImageReady 2.0 features that are covered include:

- Powerful slicing capabilities that enable you to divide a document into sections, making it easier to selectively optimize sections of a document. HTML tables are automatically created as well.

- Automatically generated JavaScript that allows you to display images (or parts of an image) as a GIF animation or as a rollover state.

- New layer effects, including pattern and gradient fill effects, as well as all the layer effects available in Photoshop—drop shadows, glows, beveling, embossing, and solid color fills.

- Styles, which are sets of useful layer effects that you can save and reapply.

In addition, you'll learn step-by-step techniques for creating web type, navigational devices, and backgrounds. You'll even learn the best way to convert vector graphics to bitmaps and how to use Photoshop as a web layout tool.

Photoshop for the Web, Second Edition draws on my 10 years in new media production and 25 years as a professional photographer, as well as the generous advice and wisdom of 25 full-time web producers whose tips and techniques grace the book. It's my hope that you'll find each chapter literally bursting with new and relevant information.

What you need to know

This is by no means a basic Photoshop book. Nor is it a comprehensive guide. In order to get the most out of the information provided here, you should have a working knowledge of at least Photoshop 4.0. While you don't need to use Photoshop 5.5 to create web graphics, I do recommend it. As you'll see throughout the book, this new release makes web designers' lives easier in a number of ways. If you haven't upgraded yet, don't worry. Where Photoshop 5.5–specific techniques are discussed, I also include ways to do the same thing in Photoshop 4.0 and 5.0.

For more comprehensive guides to Photoshop, I recommend *Photoshop in a Nutshell, Second Edition*, by Donnie O'Quinn (O'Reilly & Associates) and *The Photoshop Wow! Book* by Linnea Dayton and Jack Davis (Peachpit Press). If you're interested in the inner workings of graphic file formats, try *The Encyclopedia of Graphic File Formats* by James D. Murray and William vanRyper (O'Reilly).

How this book is organized

This book falls loosely into three main areas of organization. The first two chapters deal with general issues of image processing for the Web. Chapter 1, *Making Photoshop Web-Friendly*, explains how to set up Photoshop to accommodate the rules of the Web. Chapter 2, *Improving Photos for the Web*, focuses on preparing and optimizing photographs and other continuous-tone art for the Web.

The next section covers in detail the Web's two most important graphic file formats, GIF and JPEG. Chapter 3, *Making Great GIFs*, and Chapter 4, *Creating GIFs from Scratch*, show how to convert existing graphics to GIF and how to create browser-safe GIFs from scratch. Chapter 5, *Special Effects with Transparent GIFs*, explains the ins and outs of transparency, including how to avoid the dreaded halo effect. Chapter 6, *JPEG: All the Color You Want*, gives you the lowdown on JPEG, the 24-bit format of choice for photographs.

The next three chapters give step-by-step instructions for creating backgrounds (Chapter 7, *Creating Background Tiles*), graphical type (Chapter 8, *Photoshop Web Type*), and navigational devices (Chapter 9, *Creating Navigational Graphics*). Chapter 10, *Importing Vectors into Photoshop*, shows you how to avoid some of the pitfalls that are associated with importing Adobe Illustrator and Macromedia FreeHand vector-based files into Photoshop. Chapter 11, *Laying Out Pages in Photoshop*, goes into detail describing how web producers are using Photoshop as a web design tool. Finally, Chapter 12, *ImageReady 2.0*, shows you how to use ImageReady 2.0 to slice, animate, and create rollover effects.

In the appendixes, you'll find information on PNG, a new file format that is gaining widespread support, as well as more details on useful Photoshop plug-ins and filters that extend the capabilities of Photoshop. You'll also find more information on the contributors featured in this book.

Version differences

Photoshop 5.5 consists primarily of additions and enhancements to Photoshop 5.0; the base program remains unchanged. Therefore, when referring to features common to 5.0, 5.02, and 5.5, I have referred simply to Photoshop 5. Similarly, "Photoshop 4/5" means the description is applicable to all versions of Photoshop 4 and 5.

Platform differences

Photoshop works similarly on Macintosh and Windows. The only important difference for our purposes is the use of modifier keys. When you use the Command key on the Mac, you use the Control key on Windows. When you use the Option key on the Mac, you use the Alt key on Windows. In this book, we've indicated both modifier keys together. So where we say Command/Control, you should press Command if you're using a Mac and Control if you're using a Windows PC, and likewise for Option/Alt.

A reminder on copyright

As you'll see throughout this book, it is very easy to download and "borrow" images and graphics from the Web. With Photoshop it is tempting to incorporate others' work into your own. I just want to remind you that much of the material that you see on the Web is copyrighted. Behind most images and graphics is a person, company, or institution that owns and controls the copyright to that image. It's one thing to download an image or graphic from the Web for personal use, and quite another to possess the legal rights to actually use the image for one of your own projects.

The law is very clear: if you use a copyrighted image without permission, statutory damages can be assessed against you and copies of the infringing work can be ordered destroyed. If you have any doubts about your rights to use work you find on the Web, especially if your work is commercial, don't take chances. Either contact the artist directly to request permission or consult a legal expert.

How to contact us

We have tested and verified all the information in this book to the best of our ability, but you may find that features have changed (or even that we have made mistakes!). Please let us know about any errors you find, as well as your suggestions for future editions, by writing to:

O'Reilly & Associates, Inc.
101 Morris Street
Sebastopol, CA 95472
800-998-9938 (in the U.S. or Canada)
707-829-0515 (international/local)
707-829-0104 (FAX)

You can also send messages electronically. To be put on our mailing list or to request a catalog, send email to:

nuts@oreilly.com

To ask technical questions or comment on the book, send email to:

bookquestions@oreilly.com

Acknowledgments

The original version of *Photoshop for the Web* grew out of a 1996 lunch with Richard Koman, the editor of this book. He said two words, "Photoshop" and "Web," and I was hooked. During the next year, Richard gave me his full support, as we shaped, molded, and otherwise brought his good idea to life. For this new version, which took shape the minute Photoshop 5.0 was released in 1998, Richard's support has been immeasurable. Once again it's been a pleasure to work with such a smart and gracious editor.

I'd also like to thank David Rogelberg, my agent, for introducing me to the fine folks at O'Reilly and for giving me wise counsel throughout this project.

For this second edition, I'd like to give special thanks to Sean Parker, Valerie Robbins, Doug Meisner of Adobe, Tara McGoldrick of O'Reilly, Laura Levy, Tom Kennedy, Jane Menyawi and Mark Hill of washingtonpost.com, Karen Gauthier, Daniel Brown, and Marc Pawliger of Adobe.

I'd also like to thank Beverly Scherf; Michael Rogers, Newsweek Interactive; Michael Foldes; Ken Phipps; Paula Savage, Savage Design; Doug Frohman, Digital Frontiers; Marsha Weiner; Paul Foldes; Jessica Gould, CorelDRAW!; Heather Dittmer, BoxTop Software; Heather Heller, Heller Information Services; Russell Brown, Adobe Systems; Dennis Poon, IDEO; Fredrick Helmstrand, Icon Media Lab; Andrea Jenkins, Microsoft Sidewalk; Chris Vail, New Century Network; Kristin Keyes; Fred Shippey; Laurie McEachron, PhotoDisc; Kevin Connor, Adobe; John Leddy, Adobe; Sonya Schaefer, Adobe; Lori Barra, TonBo designs; Mark Holmes, National Geographic Online; Fred Sotherland, c|net; Ellen McNeilly; Susan Klemens, Discovery Channel Online; David Spitzler, Adobe; Taylor, HotWired; Cotton Coulson, c|net; Scott Highton; Rudy Burger; Susan Dunsworth; Jennifer R. Melnick; Julie Coburn, SF Gate; John Caserta, Chicago Tribune; Edie Freedman, O'Reilly & Associates; Dan Marcolina, Marcolina Design; Graham Hamilton; Donna Mann; Valerie May, National Geographic Online; Jim Irvine, SF Gate; Alice Kreit, Washington Post.com; Sherry Rogelberg, Studio B; Michael Borek; John Nay, AAA; Lisa Waltuch, Discovery Online; Gary Hokke, PhotoDisc; Mary Anne Koopman, Newsweek Interactive; Sam Merrill, Photo District News; Anders Ottosson, Icon Media Lab; and Diana Rathe.

Many thanks also to the designers and web producers who contributed their valuable tips and techniques to this book. Their willingness to share is largely what made this book possible. (In Appendix C, *Contributor Notes*, you'll find them individually noted with a short bio and an email address.) I'd especially like to thank Brian Frick of MSNBC and Gregg Hartling of earthlink.com.

Finally, I want to thank my wife, Rebecca Taggart, who not only gave me encouragement and moral support, but applied her immeasurable skills as a writer/editor to the manuscript as well.

—Mikkel Aaland
San Francisco, 1999

MAKING PHOTOSHOP WEB-FRIENDLY

P hotoshop has long been the image manipulation and processing tool of choice for photographers, designers, printing prepress operators, fine and commercial artists, multimedia designers, and many others. Photoshop is also the tool of choice for those of us designing web pages and creating images for the Web.

But while the program is a fantastic tool for web designers, it's set up for print, not for the Web. The first step in using Photoshop as a web design tool is to prepare it for web work. This includes customizing preferences to reflect the needs of the Web and calibrating the display monitor to establish some sort of objective reference for viewing work. If you are using Photoshop 5, you'll want change the way the program handles color to avoid unwanted color shifts.

Photoshop 5 color preferences

Starting with Version 5.0, Photoshop comes with the ability to embed International Color Consortium (ICC) color profiles and to work in the sRGB color space. In theory, embedding an ICC color profile is a good thing. It makes it possible to maintain color consistency between platforms and external devices, such as scanners and printers, and ICC-compliant applications, such as Adobe Illustrator and InDesign. However, for anyone producing for the Web or working with older Photoshop files, the feature can become a major headache. Furthermore, when a Photoshop 5 file is created with the ICC color profile option turned on and opened in Adobe Image-eReady 1.0, huge color shifts result. This is largely fixed in Photoshop 5.5 and ImageReady 2.0.

If web work is your primary focus, it's best to avoid the confusion and turn this embedding "feature" off. Thankfully, it's not that hard to set color preferences. If you are using Photoshop 5.02 or higher, Adobe includes a Color Management module (Help → Color Management) that walks you through the procedure. The Photoshop 5.02 upgrade is available free on the Adobe web site.

The Color Management module presents you with several options, as shown in Figure 1-1. It's tempting to choose "Optimize for web use" but this isn't necessarily the right choice. If you choose this option, ICC color profiling will be turned off, but Photoshop will also select the sRGB color space, a limited color space that Adobe claims is good for web work. sRGB has a narrower gamut than Photoshop's original RGB color space and represents more faithfully the color capabilities of most commonly used display systems. The difference between sRGB and RGB is very slight. However, many other applications such as Macromedia Director, ImageReady, and Flash don't support the sRGB color space. You'll be able to open your files in these programs, but you may find some distressing color shifts.

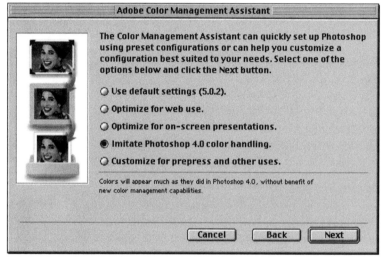

Figure 1-1. *The Color Management module allows you to easily set color preferences in Photoshop 5.02 and higher.*

I suggest you choose "Imitate Photoshop 4.0 color handling." This option will turn off ICC profiling and select Apple or monitor RGB (they are the same). The gamut of this color space is slightly wider than sRGB, which means there is a very slight possibility that some color banding may occur when your work is viewed on some monitors. (Banding occurs when you create a graphic in a color space and then view the same graphic on a device that displays a narrower gamut. With less gamut, colors are squished or banded together.) But for the sake of simplicity the trade-off is worth it.

If you wish, you can always set these color preferences manually.

To manually turn off embedding preferences:

1. File → Color Settings → Profile Setup. See Figure 1-2.

2. Under Profile Mismatch Handling, choose Ignore for the RGB option. (If you don't want Photoshop messing up your older CMYK files, you can choose Ignore for the CMYK option too.)

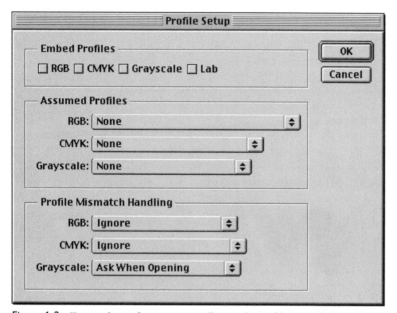

Figure 1-2. *To set color preferences manually, use the Profile Setup dialog.*

To manually set your color space to Apple or monitor RGB:

1. File → Color Settings → RGB Setup. See Figure 1-3.

2. Select Monitor RGB.

To minimize color shifting when you toggle between Photoshop and ImageReady, deselect the "Display Using Monitor Compensation" checkbox.

Stop wasting bytes

Creating images for the Web is a constant struggle to reduce file size. Because the Web is a bandwidth-challenged place, and because we're competing with thousands of other sites for audience, it's crucial to minimize graphics' file size. The last thing you want to do is to waste bytes. But that's what happens if you accept Photoshop's default

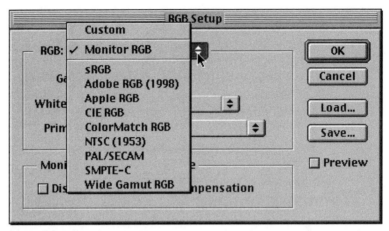

Figure 1-3. *The RGB Setup dialog lets you specify a color space for your monitor.*

preferences. In this section, you'll learn how to shrink your files by
changing Photoshop's default preferences.

Turn off image previews

Unless you change your preferences, Photoshop always creates an
icon and thumbnail version of your image when you save it. This
makes it convenient to identify images from your desktop or a dialog
box; however, it increases the overall image file size anywhere from a
few kilobytes to 30% of the file's size.

To turn off image previews in Photoshop, select File → Preferences →
Saving Files. Whichever version you're using, you'll see options at the
bottom of the dialog box for Image Previews and Thumbnails, as
shown in Figure 1-4. You can choose between Never Save, Always
Save, and Ask When Saving. When you choose Ask When Saving, the
Save, Save As, and Save a Copy dialogs let you choose whether to
save the icon and thumbnail previews. The Ask When Saving option
gives you flexibility but can be a pain if you're working primarily on
web images.

Turning off image previews may or may not dramatically affect the
size of your files. It depends on how you plan to use the image, what
computer platform you are working with, and what format you've
saved your work in.

For instance, when you upload a GIF file to a web server, the process
actually strips all extraneous data—including thumbnails—from the
file. So, there's no harm in taking advantage of the convenience of
previews and thumbnails when working on GIF files for the Web.

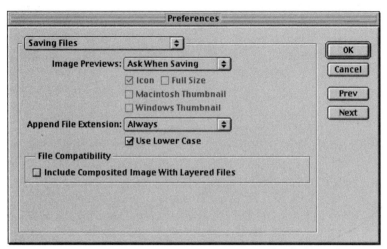

Figure 1-4. *Save space by turning off thumbnails and image previews.*

A word about
Debabelizer

Debabelizer will open a
Photoshop 3.0 or higher
file *only* if the 2.5 option is
turned off *and* the layers
of the image have been
flattened.

It's a different story when creating JPEGs on a Macintosh. In this
case, uploading the file doesn't strip extraneous data, so there is
always a penalty of a few kilobytes if you leave previews and thumbnails on. If you're using a PC, though, don't worry about it;
extraneous data will be stripped.

If you happen to process your images through Equilibrium Debabelizer, you're off the hook, because Debabelizer takes care of stripping
out the preview data.

Many web designers maintain that it's good practice to turn off
thumbnails and icons regardless of how much space can be saved.
Not only does this save hard drive space, but it also speeds up the
transmission of images as you send these files around a work environment and upload them to servers. You can always compensate for
not having a visual representation of the image by descriptively
naming your files.

Turn off 2.5 compatibility

Photoshop 3.0 marked the appearance of layers, probably the most
popular enhancement to the program. The addition of layers resulted
in a new file format, one that couldn't be read by the baseline
version, Photoshop 2.5. (Adobe rewrote the software from the
ground up for Version 2.5.) 2.5 is the Photoshop format supported by
other programs like Adobe PageMaker and Debabelizer. So, in Photoshop 3.0 and later, Photoshop files can be 2.5-compatible, which is
the default setting. To accomplish this, Photoshop actually creates an
entirely new file that contains a layer-flattened version of your image.

By turning off 2.5 compatibility, you can significantly reduce your file size, which is especially important if you are sending files between workplaces or want to save hard disk space. This option affects only Photoshop files, not GIFs or JPEGs, so leaving it on doesn't affect the size of your web images. The option is found under File → Preferences → Saving Files.

Avoid unwanted colors

When you resize or transform an image in Photoshop, it uses one of three complex mathematical formulas to carry out the task:

*   *Bicubic* is the most complex and therefore time-consuming method. It actually analyzes all the data inside and outside the area to be resized or transformed and then "intelligently" adds pixels and color values when needed. (It is also the default method.)

*   *Bilinear* is similar to Bicubic, but analyzes data from a smaller sampling area before adding color values. This method is less accurate but faster than Bicubic. In practice, Bilinear is rarely used.

*   *Nearest Neighbor* doesn't use any intelligent guessing to determine what colors should be added or subtracted when an image is resized or transformed. As the name implies, it looks to the nearest pixel for color information, never adding color data that isn't already present in the image.

Most people use Bicubic because it results in the highest quality by actually adding data when needed. But this is not always the best method for web production. For example, say you have a graphic that you have carefully indexed and applied specific, browser-safe colors to. You save it as a GIF, and later want to touch it up or add a specific detail. You open it in Photoshop and convert it to RGB mode. Now, because of the way the Bicubic algorithm interpolates data, if you even slightly transform or resize the image, you'll be inadvertently adding new—and probably unwanted—colors to the graphic and increasing its file size.

To avoid this, you might consider changing your preference to Nearest Neighbor. This is the least precise and fastest form of interpolation, but because this method doesn't introduce new colors to an image, it is sometimes the most desirable. A major drawback to this method is that it often creates jagged edges; in some cases, such as a small graphic, this may not be noticeable. Although the quality is lower with Nearest Neighbor, you can sometimes improve it by applying the Unsharp Mask filter when you are finished.

To change the way that Photoshop interpolates data and to possibly save kilobytes, choose File → Preferences → General, as shown in Figure 1-5. When you choose Image → Image Size, you are also given a choice of interpolation methods.

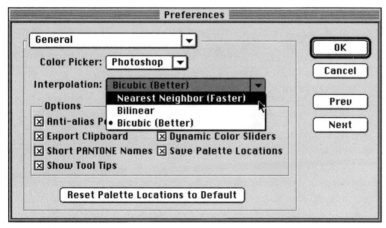

Figure 1-5. *Avoid color contamination and larger file sizes by choosing Nearest Neighbor.*

Other web-friendly preferences

Here are some Photoshop preferences that won't result in a smaller file size but will save you time and make Photoshop more web-friendly.

You must use the proper file extension when you save a file to use on the Web. For example, JPEG files must end in *.jpg* or *.jpeg*, GIF files must end in *.gif*, and PNG files must end in *.png*.

Photoshop 5 and 4 for the Mac can automatically add the appropriate extension to the filename, as shown in Figure 1-6. (This is not an option in Windows because Windows requires all files to have extensions.) Unfortunately, Photoshop 4 adds these extensions in capital letters, an unrecognizable format for some Unix servers, so you'll have to change the suffix to lowercase. Since you have to retype the extension anyway, and you may already be in the habit of adding file extensions, this option could be more of an irritant than a time-saver. Photoshop 5 adds the extension properly, in lowercase letters.

To set the file extension option on the Mac, select File → Preferences → Saving Files. Look for the Append File Extension option and select Never, Always, or Ask When Saving.

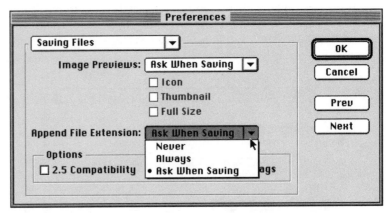

Figure 1-6. *Photoshop 5 and 4 for the Mac can append file extensions automatically.*

You can also command Photoshop to add an extension when you select a format from the Save or Save As dialog by simultaneously pressing the Option/Alt key when you select a file format.

Units and rulers

Pixels matter in the bitmap world of the Web, so it's a good idea to set your Units & Rulers preference to pixels rather than inches, picas, or centimeters. (Since screen resolution is 72 pixels per inch and there are 72 points to an inch, either *pixels* or *points* are acceptable.)

To change your measurement units, choose File → Preferences → Units & Rulers and change the Rulers setting to pixels (or points), as shown in Figure 1-7. You can also bring up this dialog by double-clicking on the rulers in your Photoshop window.

Alternatively, you can change your preferences by following these steps:

1. Display the Info palette.

2. Click and hold the icon to the left of the XY field.

3. Select a unit from the drop-down menu.

Guides and grids

Many web designers are using Photoshop as a layout tool since Photoshop 5 and 4 include guides and grids, as shown in Figure 1-8. It's easier than ever to align type, graphics, and images with a web page in mind. The Guides & Grid preference, found under File → Preferences → Guides & Grid, allows you to control the colors, width,

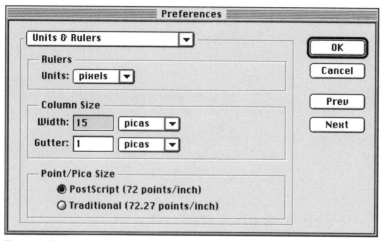

Figure 1-7. *The Web is a bitmap world, so set your units to pixels.*

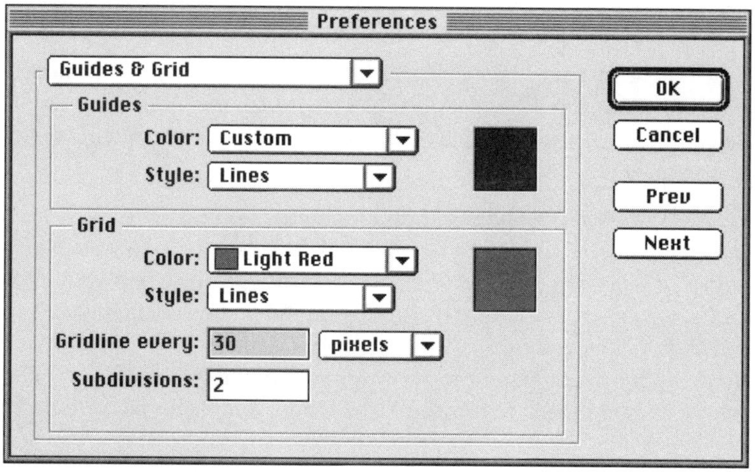

Figure 1-8. *With guides and grids, you can use Photoshop as a web layout tool.*

and frequency of the guides and grid lines. See Chapter 11, *Laying Out Pages in Photoshop*, for more information on setting up guides and grids.

Changing Photoshop's default background color

Many web designers like to see what their graphic looks like against the color of the web page. Here is a simple—but generally unknown—way of changing Photoshop's default gray window into any color of your choice.

Figure 1-9. *Select Web Color Sliders to limit 5.5's Color palette to web-safe colors.*

Figure 1-10. *5.5's Info palette can display both hexadecimal and RGB values.*

In most versions of Photoshop:

1. Open a file and expand the window so the gray area is visible.

2. Choose the paint bucket tool.

3. Choose a new foreground color.

4. Position the paint bucket in the gray area, and click while holding the Shift key.

The Foreground color will replace the gray. This color will remain the default color for all your files until you change it to something else. Figure C-1 (see the color pages) shows a file with a new canvas color.

Selecting web-safe colors

To prepare for working on a web graphic, it's very helpful to have the 216 web-safe colors in one easily accessible place. In versions prior to Photoshop 5.5, the best way to do that is in the Swatches palette. Photoshop 5 and 4 come with a web-safe color swatch. In the Swatches palette, choose Replace Swatch from the pop-up menu, select the Web Safe Colors swatch (it's located in the Goodies → Color Palettes folder), and click OK. The Swatch palette now contains only web-safe colors. See Figure C-2.

Most 5.5 users will want to switch to the new Color palette for picking web-safe colors. You can limit the Color palette to web-safe colors by selecting Web Color Sliders from the palette's pop-up menu, as shown in Figure 1-9. When you move the sliders, only web-safe colors will be available. In addition, the color ramp at the bottom of the palette can show either the full RGB spectrum or only web-safe colors; toggle the Make Ramp Web Safe option in the pop-up menu.

When Web Color Sliders is selected and you choose a non-web-safe color from an open image or from the color ramp, a cube icon appears in the lower left of the palette. Clicking on this icon shifts the color to the nearest web-safe color. Another key advantage is that the Color palette in 5.5 displays hexadecimal or RGB values for selected colors—something unavailable in the Swatches palette.

In 5.5, you can also view hexadecimal values for RGB colors in the Info palette, as shown in Figure 1-10. To view these numbers, select Palette Options from the Info palette's pop-up menu. In the dialog box, choose Web Color as the mode.

The Color Picker itself can also be limited to web-safe colors by checking the Only Web Colors checkbox. In this mode, only web-safe colors are displayed and available, as shown in Figure C-3. Note that hexadecimal values are also displayed. In full RGB mode, selecting a non-web-safe color displays the cube icon next to the color swatch. Clicking on the cube shifts the color to the nearest web-safe color.

> ### Actions, actions
> You can find many useful prerecorded Actions at *http://jmc.mit.edu/photoshop/*.

Using Actions for web production

The Actions palette is one of the most useful features in Photoshop 5 and 4. Actions can be used to automate many of the tedious tasks required for producing web graphics. For example, you can automate converting RGB images to Indexed Color mode, resizing batches of images, simulating an animated effect, and applying a consistently used filter. This book highlights several tasks that are best carried out with Actions.

Some web designers use Actions for even the simplest tasks. Designer Steve Jablonsky keeps his Actions palette open and accessible whenever he creates web graphics. Steve has created Actions for such tasks as creating a new layer, adding an adjustment layer, flattening an image, and using the Save As command.

Keep in mind that not everything can be recorded as an Action. For instance, you can't record work done with the various drawing tools or record changes in Preferences or color settings. You can, however, insert a command for these nonrecordable acts with the Insert Menu Item command found in the Actions palette.

Calibrating your monitor

Ah, CRT monitor calibration—what a snake pit! Everyone talks about it, but few do it. The reality is that it's quite helpful to have some sort of objective standard in which to view your work. How else will you know how much contrast or brightness to add to your otherwise carefully crafted image or graphic? How will you know when your colors are saturated enough?

Your monitor is your canvas, and you should take a moment to ensure that it is at least in the ballpark when it comes to color and brightness display.

Of course, you don't have to get it perfect. Web designer and long-time new media producer Tom Walker points out that the human visual system is very forgiving. When most people look at a monitor, their expectations are lower than when they look at a printed page. Most display systems are backlit, creating an illusion of quality comparable to a slide. Also, in general, our brain quickly compensates for slight color shifts; for example, it makes an image with an overall bluish cast seem normal.

Photoshop provides a rudimentary method for monitor calibration that relies mostly on subjective visual interpretation, so it's not particularly accurate. If you're really serious about precisely calibrating your monitor, you need to use a color calibration device such as the OpticalCal or Daystar's Colorimeter 24 system, or you'll need to purchase a display system such as Barco or Radius that contains built-in hardware calibration.

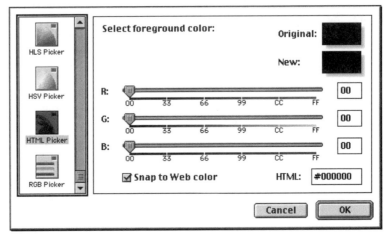

Figure 1-11. *In Mac OS 8.5, an HTML Picker is available for picking web-safe colors.*

Using Photoshop and Mac OS 8.5's color picker

If you use a Macintosh with System 8.5, you'll have access to a very useful HTML color picker. This color picker allows you to choose browser-safe colors visually or via hexadecimal numbers. You can even snap a non-browser-safe color to one that is safe. A total of six color pickers are possible, including a standard RGB picker. See Figure 1-11.

To enable the new Color Picker, change the Color Picker from Photoshop to Apple (File → Preferences → General → Color Picker → Apple).

Now, whenever the Color Picker is chosen (by clicking on the foreground or background color box, or in Photoshop 5, when you click on the type tool color box), you can select the color picker of your choice, including the HTML Picker. (Remember, you can always pick a color outside of the dialog box by holding down Option/Alt, which turns the cursor into the eyedropper tool. Colors can be selected from anywhere on your monitor, not only from an open Photoshop file.)

Photoshop 5 includes easy-to-use software that roughly calibrates your monitor. Called Adobe Gamma, it is found under Control Panels on both the Mac and Windows or via Photoshop's Color Management Assistant (Help → Color Management). It's available as either a control panel (see Figure 1-12) or a self-explanatory, step-by-step process. Before you use it (or any monitor calibration software) be sure to let your monitor warm up for at least 30 minutes to give it time to stabilize.

If you are using older versions of Photoshop's monitor calibration software you'll need to follow these steps:

1. Manually adjust the Brightness/Contrast settings on the monitor itself until you are satisfied with the results.

2. Adjust the background color on your computer to a neutral gray. Turn off any desktop patterns. *For Macintosh:* From the Control Panels in the Apple menu, open the Gamma control panel (see Figure 1-13). If Gamma is not there, look in the Goodies folder that came with Photoshop, install the file in your System folder, and restart your machine. *For Windows:* Access the Gamma control dialog box by selecting File → Color Settings → Monitor Setup.

3. Click on White Pt. Hold a piece of true white paper under daylight-like conditions and adjust the three sliders until the monitor white matches the paper. (Sliding the Red pointer will add or subtract red to your monitor, sliding the Green pointer will add or subtract green, and sliding the Blue pointer will add or subtract blue. It takes a little work to get a clean white.)

4. Set your Target Gamma to 1.8. Slide the Gamma Adjustment slider until the patterned gray area at the top of the Gamma window becomes a solid gray.

5. To adjust color balance visually, click on Balance and drag the three slider triangles one at a time until the gray areas in the strip below the slider become a neutral gray.

6. To adjust the black point, click Black Pt. and drag the three slider triangles until no color tints appear in the shadow tones in the lower strip and you can see a distinct gradation between each pair of swatches.

7. Save these settings in a folder named Monitor Settings inside the Photoshop folder.

Calibrating a monitor for a Windows machine using Photoshop's older calibration software is very similar to calibrating it for a Mac. However, instead of finding the Gamma control panel in the Controls Panels folder, it is accessed by selecting File → Color Settings →

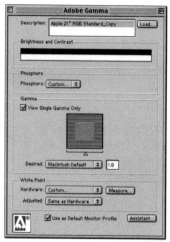

Figure 1-12. *The Adobe Gamma control panel in Photoshop 5, available on both Macintosh and Windows.*

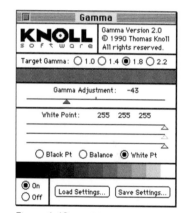

Figure 1-13. *Calibrate your Mac monitor with the Gamma control dialog box.*

Monitor Setup from the Photoshop menu. Once this dialog box is open, follow steps 3 through 6, typing a target gamma of 1.8 into the window rather than selecting it.

Regardless of which calibration method you use, if your monitor has the capability, be sure to regularly degauss it to remove the effects of magnetic pulls that make the images on the monitor look wavy.

Gamma correction

Once you've calibrated your monitor, there's still the issue of the gamma differences between Macs and PCs. In general, what looks right on a Macintosh will look dark on a Windows machine. What looks right on a Windows machine will look washed out on a Mac. The culprit is gamma.

Gamma is the mathematical measurement used to describe a monitor's contrast and brightness. Gamma can be corrected or adjusted in several ways: in the image, in the operating system, and on the monitor itself. When you use GIF and JPEG image formats, there is no easy way for the end user system to determine if you've applied any gamma correction to the image, and if so, what value was used. Some file formats such as PNG contain gamma source declarations that automatically compensate for any variations between display systems.

There are a couple of things you can do to minimize this problem. Assuming that your monitor has been calibrated:

- When you create an image on a Mac system, make the image at least 20% brighter.

- When you create an image on a PC system, make the image at least 20% darker.

- Include a grayscale target on your site so users can calibrate their systems to match yours.

- Use the PNG file format, which automatically adjusts gamma to match different display systems (see Appendix A, *The PNG Format*).

The common wisdom is that since most web viewers are using PCs you should optimize your graphics for them. If you are using a Mac to create your files, you might therefore consider setting your Photoshop gamma to 2.2 when you calibrate your monitor so you can get a better idea of how your work will appear on a PC. However, with Photoshop 5.5 this not necessary. Included in 5.5 is a gamma preview capability that allows you to see what your image will look like on either platform (View → Preview → Macintosh RGB or Windows RGB or Uncompensated RGB).

Take the time

It pays to take a few moments to set your preferences, load a set of browser-safe colors, and calibrate your monitor. Not only will you benefit in terms of smaller file size, but you'll also focus on web-specific issues that will put you in the state of mind to produce images and graphics that look great and download quickly.

PNG

Learn everything you've ever wanted to know about PNG from *PNG: The Definitive Guide* by Greg Roelofs (O'Reilly & Associates, 1999).

CHAPTER TWO

IMPROVING PHOTOS FOR THE WEB

Photographs destined for the Web can benefit from Photoshop's powerful image processing capabilities: contrast control, color optimizing, image sharpening, and elimination of dust, scratches, and electronic noise. When Photoshop's tools are applied properly, the best qualities of an existing image are enhanced.

What happens if a photograph is not properly prepared and processed? Just look at Figure C-4, a *Web Review* article about a World Wide Web Conference. Some of the photos look washed out. In others, you can't see the faces because they are too dark. In short, because these photos weren't properly prepared before they were put on the Web, they decrease the effectiveness of the entire page.

This chapter shows you how to use Photoshop to fix many of the problems illustrated by this example and more. You'll also learn a couple of tricks to optimize images taken from digital cameras. (Preparing images or graphics for a particular file format is the subject of later chapters.) Figure C-5 shows a makeover of the *Web Review* page using techniques discussed in this chapter. Much better, no?

Let's go through the various corrections I made to these images:

* In the first photo, the colors are washed out. The background is full of electronic "noise," and there is a glare in the glasses caused by the digital camera's flash.

  To fix it, I adjusted the curves (Image → Adjust → Curves) by clicking on the Auto button. I used the Clone tool to spot the glasses to reduce the glare. Then I applied an Unsharp Mask (Filter → Sharpen → Unsharp Mask) set at a radius of 0.4 pixels and 100%. Then I applied the Dust & Scratches (Filter → Noise →

Work from copies

Whenever possible, work off a copy of your original high-resolution file and keep your original for other purposes, such as creating new images at different resolutions.

Dust & Scratches) filter with a 1-pixel radius to the selected background. I applied a Gaussian blur (Filter → Blur → Gaussian Blur) with a 5-pixel radius to the blue channel. And finally I applied an Unsharp Mask with a 0.3-pixel radius to the entire image.

- In the second photo, the foreground is too light. The people in the background are out of focus.

  Again, I applied auto curves and an Unsharp Mask, this time with an amount of 150% and a radius of 1.1. The picture still appears slightly out of focus. Not much I could do about that. I used the Burn tool set at 50% and Midtones to selectively burn in the highlights.

- In the third photo, the person in the foreground is too dark.

  I applied an Unsharp Mask (100%, 0.6-pixel radius) to the entire image. Then I selected the text areas and applied another Unsharp Mask at the same settings. I tried to use auto curves, but it didn't help much. Instead, I selectively applied the Dodge tool to the face to open up the shadows.

- In the fourth photo, the colors are flat and the person in the foreground is too light.

  I selectively burned in the foreground person. I increased the overall saturation of the image by 14% (Image → Adjust → Hue/Saturation). Then, using the Sponge tool, I selectively added saturation to the faces.

Although the procedures discussed in this chapter can also be applied to illustrations or other digitized art, we have chosen photography as our main focus. This is because viewers are less forgiving when there is something technically wrong with a photograph. For the most part, they know what a photo should look like, and if their expectations are not met—for example, if a supposedly realistic portrait looks green—they'll probably question the quality of the page and your skills and ability as a web designer.

There is no such thing as a typical web photograph. The content of each photo varies, and photos come from a variety of sources, such as digital cameras, video frame grabs, and scans from prints or slides. Each source can technically affect the way a photo looks.

Because every photo is different, each one requires individual attention before it is placed on the Web. It's helpful to think of this activity as an art in itself rather than just a technical procedure. With the help of Photoshop, you can intelligently peel away the grime and dirt to reveal the masterpiece beneath. (OK, there's not always a masterpiece beneath, but you can almost always improve a photo with the techniques described here.)

In this chapter, we've organized the techniques of improving a photograph into three main areas: global corrections, selective corrections, and enhancing acquired images such as scans and digital photos. We conclude the chapter with information on Photoshop's contact sheet and web gallery features.

Global corrections

Global corrections affect the entire image. In this section, we'll cover the following techniques:

- Removing dust and artifacts
- Sharpening a blurred photo
- Adjusting contrast and increasing dynamic range
- Adjusting tint
- Global color correction
- Resizing and cropping

Giving images the eagle eye

At Second Story, Brad Johnson is keenly aware that each photograph requires individual attention. His company has created web sites for such photograph-centric institutions and companies as the National Geographic Society and Kyocera (makers of Yashica and Contact cameras). Figure C-6 shows the impact of photography on a National Geographic page designed by Second Story.

Brad and his partner Julie Beeler have worked with every imaginable type of photographic image, ranging from corporate product shots to action-filled snaps of white-water rafting. The images are digitized and sent to him on Kodak Photo CDs or Zip disks.

His evaluation of each photo actually begins before he looks at it on his monitor. At the onset, he inquires about any special rules or restrictions placed on a particular image. For example, some National Geographic and stock agency photographs cannot be cropped or altered in any way except for minor color correction and resizing.

Initially, he looks at the image for problems such as dust and artifacts, lack of contrast, ugly color casts, and blurred images. The digital files he gets from National Geographic have already been cleaned up and are nearly flawless—there are no scratches or electronic noise to speak of, and the colors are correct—but files from other sources often need work. Photographs from digital cameras, he has learned, will almost always be flat and need increased color saturation. He doesn't make any generalizations about Photo CD images since they all vary depending on how they were scanned and who scanned them.

After he determines what needs to be done, Brad jumps in and starts to work. For him there is no particular order to follow. However, he always waits to resize images until the end because this action throws away data that can't be retrieved.

Removing dust and other artifacts

It's a rare digital photo that doesn't contain either dust marks or a stray pixel or two caused by electronic "noise." If these flaws are present in your digital file, they will be quite apparent when you open up your photograph. With Photoshop, there are several different ways to rid your photo of these distractions.

Using the noise filters

Under the Filters → Noise menu there are three filters useful for eliminating flaws that are sprinkled throughout a large region of your photograph:

- *Despeckle* diminishes noise by subtly blurring an image. However, some detail is preserved because this filter blurs everything except the edges in an image, where significant shifts in color occur.

- *Median* blends the brightness of pixels and discards pixels that are radically different from adjacent pixels. Adjust the Radius slider to determine how much variation in brightness values the filter looks for. A value that is too high causes a blurred image.

- *Dust & Scratches* is the filter that gives you the most control. Use the Radius and Threshold sliders in this option to set the removal size of dust or scratches.

You can quickly see that in order to get good results with any of these filters, your photo invariably blurs (see "Sharpening a blurred photo" later in this chapter). For this reason, it is best to apply filters only on regions of your photograph lacking important detail, such as the background. Fix the flaws that exist in areas of important detail with the Rubber Stamp tool (found in the Toolbox), which duplicates the pixels surrounding an offensive scratch or unwanted mark and "clones" over it.

The Smudge and Blur tools, also found in the Toolbox, usually are not good alternatives to the Rubber Stamp tool because they smear and blend pixels and create an unrealistic effect.

Cleaning up photos with Gaussian blur

Brad Johnson generally avoids using any of the filters mentioned previously to clean up his images since he doesn't like the way they blur his pictures. Most of the time he uses the Rubber Stamp tool, but when the noise is widespread throughout a photo, he's discovered a method using layers that he much prefers.

Lines of distinction

There are times when the lines of distinction between image processing and image creation blur. Take, for example, the work of Brad Johnson shown in Figure C-7 in the color insert. What looks like an ancient, time-weary photograph is actually created mostly in Photoshop. Brad used a photograph he took of the Mexican site of Chichen Itza and then applied many of the image-processing techniques described in this chapter to produce a stunning effect. By looking at each layer, shown in Figure 2-1, you can see exactly what he did:

- *Layer 0* is the original photograph that Brad took at Chichen Itza in Mexico.

- The next layer up is a copy of *Layer 0* with a Gaussian blur applied to despeckle the original image. Opacity is set at 58% and the blending mode is Normal.

- The *antique 1* layer is a scanned painting that Brad added for effect. Opacity is set at 23% and the blending mode is Soft Light.

- The next layer contains some faint lines or "scratches" that give the photograph an aged look. Opacity is set at 21%, and the blending mode is Soft Light.

- The next layer contains a black border.

- The final layer contains a light orange "glaze" (Red = 255, Green = 204, Blue = 102). Opacity is 58%, and the blending mode is Color Burn.

If you try to duplicate this effect, be sure that you work with an appropriate photograph, one that lends itself to this "turn-of-the-century" look.

Brad cleans up his photos by following these steps:

1. He creates a duplicate of the layer containing the photograph or image that he wants to work on (Layer → Duplicate Layer).

2. He applies a Gaussian blur to the new layer (Filter → Blur → Gaussian Blur), setting the radius to 2.0 or less, but sometimes higher, depending on the effect he wants.

3. He leaves his blending mode on Normal but adjusts the opacity to 30–70%.

4. Finally, he merges the two layers.

Brad applied this method—and other useful methods described elsewhere in this chapter—in the *scratches* layer of his Chichen Itza image (Figure C-7), as described in the "Lines of distinction" sidebar.

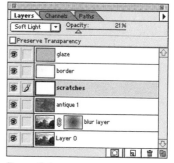

Figure 2-1. *Layers palette for the Chichen Itza image.*

Sharpening a blurred photo

A blurred photo can be a result of many things, such as camera or subject movement, improper focus, imprecise scanning, or too radical resampling. With Photoshop you can sharpen a blurred photo to a degree; however, there is no substitute for a properly shot or scanned photograph.

Keep it authentic

Many historical photos and other images have scratches. If you want to keep the authentic historical look and feel, don't apply the techniques for removing dust and scratches.

Photoshop's filters and tools for sharpening include:

- The *Sharpen* filters (Filter → Sharpen or Filter → Sharpen More). These filters globally increase the contrast of adjacent pixels, with Sharpen More equivalent to applying Sharpen several times. You can control the amount of sharpening by repeatedly applying these filters.

- The *Sharpen Edges* filter (Filter → Sharpen → Sharpen Edges). This filter sharpens only the areas of major brightness change and leaves smooth areas untouched.

- The *Sharpen* tool found in the Toolbox (toggles with Blur), which sharpens soft edges in an image.

- The *Unsharp Mask* filter (Filter → Sharpen → Unsharp Mask), which creates a blurred negative version of the image and averages this copy with the original. You can control the percentage of sharpening, the number of pixels surrounding the edge pixels affected by the sharpening (radius), and how much brightness difference exists between two pixels before they are considered edge pixels (threshold).

Undoubtedly, Unsharp Mask is the mostly widely used sharpening filter by web producers. Through your customized settings, Unsharp Mask selectively applies sharpening only to the areas that you specify.

How do you know which settings to use? It depends on both the resolution and type of image you are working with. You'll have to experiment on your own, but assuming that your image is destined for the Web and is therefore 72 dpi and no larger than 640 × 480 pixels, here are some suggestions:

- For images that contain lots of detail (such as architectural photos), try setting your percentage at 100% and your radius at 1.5 pixels. (I always leave threshold settings at zero.)

- For images that contain expanses of similar color and tone (such as a portrait), try setting your percentage to 100% with a radius of 0.6 pixels.

Keep in mind that the higher the resolution, the less pronounced the effect of the Unsharp Mask and the higher the settings you need to apply.

Adjusting contrast and increasing dynamic range

A low-contrast photograph is like a meal without spice—the picture might be good, but without contrast it's dull. A high-contrast photograph is, well, too spicy. The true flavor and content are lost. For the most part, you can determine whether a photograph has contrast problems simply by looking at your photograph on the monitor. The photo in Figure C-8 of a Japanese Shinto priest taken at sunset clearly has too much contrast. The photo in Figure C-9 has a good dynamic range.

If you're more comfortable getting a precise mathematical rather than visual interpretation of your photograph, you should use Photoshop's histogram (Image → Histogram). The histogram graphically represents tonal distribution in an image. High-contrast images show up as two peaks on the graph at either end of the brightness area. Low-contrast images show up as a mound in only one region of the graph. A wide distribution shows a large dynamic range, which for the most part is desirable (see Figure C-9).

If measurements show pixels falling between a small portion of gray values and none in other areas, there is a small dynamic range present, which for the most part is undesirable, and you'll need to apply the following corrections.

Once you have determined that your photo's contrast needs adjustment, you can select one of Photoshop's several tonal control commands found under Image → Adjust. For our purposes, the more useful tools are *Levels*, *Curves*, and *Brightness/Contrast*:

- *Levels* allows you to set the highlight, midtone, and shadow values.

- *Curves* provides a visual graph that allows you to adjust not only the highlight, midtone, and shadow values, but also any value at any point on the graph.

- *Brightness/Contrast* provides a slider that affects the relationships between pixels: for example, making an adjacent pixel brighter while making another darker. The Brightness slider affects all the pixels equally.

Photoshop 5.5 includes a new Auto Contrast command, Image → Adjust → Auto Contrast, that maps the darkest and lightest pixels in an image to black and white. This causes highlights to appear lighter and shadows to appear darker.

Most web producers work with either Levels or Curves. Although Brightness/Contrast and Auto Contrast are easy to use, they offer only limited control over an image.

As you experiment with these tools, watch as they apply their changes to the image on the screen in real time. Don't think only in terms of keeping detail in the shadow and highlight areas; consider

Don't forget your borders!

If your image contains a black border, be sure to either remove this border or work only on a selection within the black border. The border fools Photoshop's auto-correction tools into thinking the image is darker than it actually is.

the overall look and feel of the image. Sometimes a high-contrast image where the highlights are burned out works. Also keep in mind that Photoshop can improve a poorly exposed or scanned image only up to a point, which is why the original quality of the image and scan are so important.

Tinting to make the photo pop

Brad Johnson immediately saw particular problems with the photograph shown in Figure C-10. The silvery surface of the camera looked flat when viewed on a monitor. Increasing the contrast didn't help because the smooth look of metal disappeared. To correct the problem, Brad pulled a trick out of his large hat—he actually tinted the photograph. The tint isn't noticeable, but it gave the silver the pop that he wanted. This is how he did it:

1. He created a new layer, called *color burn,* where he placed a copy of the selected camera.

2. He filled this selection with a bright violet color (Red = 153, Green = 51, Blue = 255). He set the blending mode for this layer to color burn and set the opacity at 5%. Figure C-11 shows the effect of the tinting.

3. He then created an Adjustment Layer above the original photograph (from the Layers palette, select New Adjustment Layer), using Levels to set the tone and contrast.

4. He added a drop-shadow and a white background. The web page with this final image is shown in Figure C-12.

Getting the color right

Color casts can be a result of poor scanning, or they may be inherent in the original image. In either case, it's an issue if you fall short of a realistic look. (Potatoes, for example, are not very appetizing when they are presented with a sick greenish cast—an effect that can be caused by shooting color film under fluorescent lighting).

Photoshop's color tools

Photoshop provides several commands—both automatic and manual—for removing colors, and increasing or decreasing color saturation. These commands are all found under Image → Adjust.

The quickest auto-correction is Auto Levels, but you can also auto-correct with Levels or Curves. Auto-correction not only attempts to create pure white and pure black and adjust the color range, but also attempts to balance the color cast by adjusting the RGB components of the image. Remember that by using selection tools you always have the option of applying color changes to specific areas of the image or to the entire image.

Manual correction can be applied using the tools under Image → Adjust. For quick, global color correction, use the Levels and Curves commands. With Levels, you simply adjust the sliders until you get the results you want. Using Curves is more awkward because you don't work linearly. The best way to use Curves is to find the midpoint of the curve, click, and then rotate the point in a circle until you get the color correction you want.

To remove unwanted colors, use Color Balance, which adjusts the balance of colors in the image. Hue/Saturation makes global or selective color changes to the color tint (hue), purity of color (saturation), or the lightness of the color. Replace Color and Selective Color allow for even more selective and precise color correction.

Keep in mind that a color image is made up of red, green, and blue layers of color. With Levels and Curves, you can select and control any of one these colors, affecting the entire image.

Variations is another handy option, although it isn't as precise as the other methods described in this section. With it, you can visually adjust an image's color balance, contrast, and saturation. As you click on small color-correct previews, the original image changes accordingly. Optional sample corrections are also included.

Finally, you might consider that color correction can be likened to a black hole—you go in but don't seem to come out. It's so easy to overdo color corrections, especially when you consider that color is subjective and everyone perceives colors a bit differently. Remember, on the Web, your results will vary from monitor to monitor anyway, so don't spend too much time on this step. Fix the obvious problems and then move on.

Removing a blue tint with Variations and Levels

When Discovery's Brian Frick received a digital file containing several photos from the Dominican Republic, he was told that the person using the digital camera forgot to set the white balance. All the frames contained a blue tint. Brian rid the photo of the annoying color cast by using Variations (see Figure C-13) to pick the image with the least amount of blue tint. Then he applied Photoshop's Levels and improved the photo even more. He gave the colors a final tweak with Hue/Saturation. Figure C-14 shows the final image on the web site.

Resizing

Resizing or resampling images is a common task for web producers, and deceptively simple.

To resize an image in Photoshop, follow these steps:

1. Select Image → Image Size.
2. Enter the desired dimensions under Pixel Dimensions.

Unless you want to distort your image, be sure that Constrain Proportions is checked. For the best results, keep the interpolation method set at Bicubic, the default setting. (In Photoshop 5 and 4, you can set the sampling method in the Image Size dialog. In other versions, set the sampling method in Preferences.)

It is tempting to just enter the desired values and leave it at that. However, if you start with a 640 × 480 pixel file and resize directly to, say, 100 × 100 pixels, you are making a huge mistake. You will likely create a smaller image that looks "soft" or mushy, that no amount of sharpening will help. Instead, reduce your file size no more than 50% at a time and apply the Unsharp Mask slightly after each step.

Your Unsharp Mask settings will depend on the quality of the image you are working with, but for the resolution of this example, I suggest you start at 75%, with a 0.4-pixel radius and 0 threshold, then continue to reduce the percentage and radius as you resample. Also adjust your Unsharp Mask settings for each resolution, starting at a higher setting for the larger file and then reducing the numbers as the file gets smaller.

For a 640 × 480 pixel file, you would start by resampling to 320 × 240 pixels, then going to 160 × 120 pixels, then to 100 × 100 pixels, applying Unsharp Mask after each step. If you have a batch of similarly sized images that need to be resized, you can create a Photoshop Action to resize in increments.

Cropping your images

The most simple and effective way to reduce an image file size (short of resizing) is to crop the image down to its most important parts. Figure 2-2 shows an image before and after cropping. The cropped image is 20K smaller than the original.

The actual work of cropping a photograph (or any other web graphic) is easy with Photoshop's Crop tool, found in the Toolbox. In Photoshop 5 and 4, you'll find it on the pull-out menu from the Marquee in the upper-left corner. Select the area that you want to save, then crop. You can also specify the size and resolution of the cropped area with the Crop tool's options by double-clicking on its icon in the Toolbox.

I have observed that many web producers use the Fixed Target Size option found in the Crop Tool option palette. By selecting this option and typing in width, height, and resolution parameters, it's easy to create a consistent batch of thumbnails. However, if you are reducing a large image to a tiny one, I recommend caution when using this method. Resizing in one big step, as this method does, will not produce good results. It's much better to resize in increments. See the previous section, "Resizing," for more on this.

Another way to crop is to use the Crop command. This command, found under Image, discards areas outside of a rectangular selection and keeps the original resolution of the image intact. Just select the area you want to retain with the Marquee and then select Image → Crop.

Once the Crop tool or Crop command is applied, areas outside of the selection will be cut. The result is a smaller image, and a smaller file size. Cropping irretrievably throws away data unless you immediately Undo, so be sure of your decision or save a backup copy of your uncropped original.

Figure 2-2. *Cropping away the unnecessary areas created a file more than 30 percent smaller.*

Selective corrections

Selective corrections affect localized parts of the image. In this section, we'll cover the following techniques:

- Getting rid of red-eye

- Getting realistic results with Photo CD images

- Using the History Brush to improve digital photos

Getting rid of red-eye

Red-eye is caused when a strong source of light, usually a strobe flash, is aimed directly at a dilated pupil. It's a common occurrence when a picture is taken with a flash in a dark room because that is when the eye's pupil is at its widest and the light reflects back from the pupil itself, giving that all too familiar demonic look. It's easy to fix in Photoshop:

- Use the Sponge tool to desaturate the red (click and hold the Dodge or Burn tool to access the Sponge tool).

- Select the red area using the Lasso selection tool, and replace the red with another color drawn from the surrounding area with the Eyedropper + tool. You can also desaturate the selected area by choosing Image → Adjust → Saturation and moving the saturation slider far to the left.

Whatever method you use, it's best to magnify the area containing the red-eye to its maximum before you start.

Getting realistic results with Photo CD and masks

The following method, provided by Steve Jablonsky of Imaginary Studios, is a great way to increase the dynamic tonal range of your image. However, this method is not for everyone. You must use Eastman Kodak's Photo CD process to digitize and store your images. If you aren't using this process, you might consider doing so after you read this section.

Steve knew he could use any number of ways in Photoshop to improve a photograph he took of two detectives that he wanted to include in "Homicide: Second Shift," an online series that complemented the now-canceled television program, *Homicide*. As shown in Figure 2-3, the detectives' legs were nearly invisible because their trousers blended into the dark background.

He could have worked on the problem with the Curves or Levels tools, for example. But, since the original photo was shot on normal film and transferred to Kodak's Photo CD, Steve realized he could use a better way—one that gave him more precise control over the final outcome.

When a photo is digitized and saved on a Photo CD, it can be opened in a variety of resolutions. It can also be opened using different gamma settings, each of which gives a different result. For example, if a photo is opened using a gamma of 1.4 and then opened a second time using a gamma of 1.8, the shadows in the second version will be less pronounced.

Figure 2-3. *In the original photograph, the legs are too dark.*

You can achieve more realistic results with gamma because it is a nonlinear way of applying tonal and color correction. In order to acquire an image from Photo CD in this way, you'll need to download the Photo CD Acquire module from Kodak's web site, *http://www.kodak.com*. It's free. Be sure to download Version 2.2 because older versions don't allow you to specify gamma.

This is what Steve did to give his detectives the legs they needed:

1. He opened one file at a gamma of 1.4 at 512 × 768 pixels, as shown in Figure 2-3. At this setting the legs were too dark, but the rest of the picture was fine.

2. Then he opened a second version at a gamma of 1.8, where the pants were perfect, but the upper bodies were too light.

3. He cut and pasted this version onto a layer above the first version.

4. Then he masked out areas of the 1.8 gamma version that he didn't want, including most of the upper parts of the body, as shown in Figure 2-4.

5. When he combined the two layers, he got exactly what he wanted.

Figure 2-4. *Steve Jablonsky created a mask of the detective photo that allowed only the best parts of each image to show through.*

For the final image, shown in Figure 2-5, he cut and pasted the detectives onto a realistic looking set.

Using 5's History Brush to improve a digital photo

Photoshop 5 includes the History palette, which is one of the most useful improvements to date. Each time you apply a change to your image, its state is remembered and recorded in the History palette. It is then possible to jump to any recent state of the image and work from that state. This has almost the same effect as multiple undos. You can work without saving different versions and go back in time to a given version. By default, 20 states are remembered, but if you

Try it with Adjustments

Photoshop 5 and 4 includes adjustment layers, one of the most important Photoshop features to date. In the Layers palette, select New Adjustment Layer from the pull-down menu. This option allows you to apply color and tonal corrections to a specific layer, and then, if you decide later not to use the correction, to discard the adjustment layer with no change whatsoever to the original layer. (In other versions of Photoshop, when you apply a tonal or color correction, you are stuck with the changes unless you Undo immediately.)

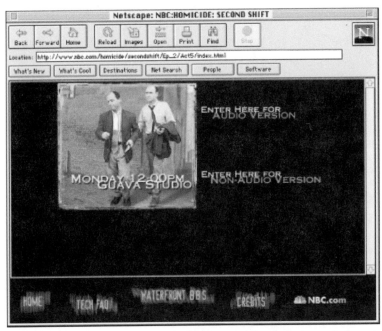

Figure 2-5. *The results of Steve's work: the pants, and the whole picture, look great.*

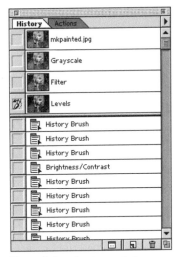

Figure 2-6. *The History Palette.*

have enough memory you can increase this number in the History palette under History Options. Figure 2-6 shows the History palette.

The History palette is what makes the History Brush—located in the tool palette—possible. If you make a snapshot from the History palette drop-down menu, freeze a state in time, you can then use the History Brush to selectively brush in portions of an earlier version. You'll even have the advantages of using different blending modes as well. You don't have to make a snapshot to use the History Brush; you can click on the box to the left of any state you wish to paint from. However, by taking a snapshot, you can be assured that the state you wish to use won't be purged.

Photoshop 5.5 extends the capabilities of the History Brush tool with an Art History Brush tool. This new tool—accessed by clicking and holding down on the History Brush tool icon—allows you to simulate the texture of painting with different colors and artistic styles. It's a nice feature, but if you are serious about digital painting I suggest using MetaCreations' Painter program, which gives you much more control.

I've used the History Brush to selectively apply contrast, color, and filter effects to a photograph. In theory, I could use adjustment layers and masks to achieve a similar effect, but by using the History Brush and palette, I avoid adding layers which increase the file size of my image. I also like the feel of "painting" my effects. It gives me a satisfying sense of control.

This is what I did:

1. I opened a photo taken with a digital camera and desaturated it (Image → Adjust → Desaturate). See Figure C-15.

2. I made a snapshot of this version, called it Grayscale, and then selected the original photo from the History palette.

3. I then applied a brush stroke filter globally to my original, made a snapshot of the results and called it Filter (Filter → Brush Strokes → Sprayed Strokes).

4. I selected my original image again and applied Levels (Image → Adjust → Levels) to increase the contrast and color saturation. I made a snapshot and called it Levels.

Once I created and saved three states (Grayscale, Filter, and Levels), I selected and began painting with the History Brush:

1. With the Grayscale file selected, I clicked on the box to the left of the state called Filter and painted the effect on selected parts of the image.

2. Selecting the state called Levels, I increased the color saturation and contrast of selected parts of the image.

3. I then went back and forth between states, using the History Brush to achieve the effect I wanted, as shown in Figure C-16.

When I was finished, I choose File → Save a Copy and gave my creation a new name. Then I went back to my History palette, reverted back to my original version and choose File → Save. This way I kept my original file intact for future uses. (Keep in mind that when you close your Photoshop file, all the History states, including the snapshots, are lost.) For the sake of this demonstration, I applied fairly radical effects. In reality, I often use the History Brush for more subtle effects such as adding selective color saturation, contrast, and brightness.

You don't have to paint the history states on your image. You can also "fill a selection" from a state. To do this, find a state within the History palette. Click in the box to the left of the state. A brush will appear in the box. Select another state by clicking on it. Make a selection within the contents of that state using any selection tool. Now choose Edit → Fill and choose History. The state with the History Brush icon will fill only the selected area of your image.

Be consistent

If you are processing a batch of photos that are destined to be shown together on the same web page or site, be consistent. Stay in the same ballpark with contrast, tone, and saturation.

Figure 2-7. *Moiré patterns result when printed images are scanned.*

Figure 2-8. *Moiré patterns were removed by scanning this printed photograph at twice the needed resolution.*

Enhancing acquired images

Acquired images—such as scans, video grabs and digital photos—often have unique problems. This section shows how to deal with such problems as:

- Moiré patterns
- Low quality in video grabs
- Crooked scans
- Limitations of digital photos

Eliminating moiré patterns

Moiré patterns result when you try to scan a picture containing half-tone dots, from a newspaper, magazine, or book, as shown in Figure 2-7. Steve Jablonsky of Imaginary Studios has found that by scanning the pictures at twice the resolution he needs, then resizing them in Photoshop, the moiré pattern virtually disappears, as in Figure 2-8.

Another way of ridding a photograph or other scanned art of the moiré pattern is to alter the position of the printed photograph on the scanner and, if your scanner allows, scan slightly out of focus. It also helps to apply the Despeckle filter (Filters → Noise → Despeckle) afterwards in Photoshop.

Getting better video grabs

Moving video, such as a VHS tape and broadcast television, contains up to 30 frames (or 60 interlaced fields) of still images per second, with each frame containing about 640 × 480 pixels at 24 bits of image information. Any one of these frames can be "grabbed" directly from a VCR, a television broadcast, or a camcorder by the use of special equipment.

The actual quality of this still image varies, depending on the quality of the videotape, the quality of the broadcast, and the quality of the equipment you use to grab the frame. With a little help from Photoshop's image-processing capabilities described in this chapter, the frame is usually suitable for the Web.

SF Gate's webmaster Steve Kruschwitz recommends grabbing video frames at twice the resolution of the final size that they will appear on the Web. He does this regularly with frames he grabs from the San Francisco travel show *Bay Area Backroads*, as shown in Figure 2-9.

Steve uses a Super VHS deck and an Apple video player card to grab the frames he wants. Although he ends up using about a dozen images for the site, he starts out by grabbing about 30. Since the images run at 160 × 120 pixels, he sets his player to grab a frame at 320 × 240 pixels. After he has grabbed the frames he wants, he adjusts the color and contrast visually, using Photoshop's Levels (Image → Adjust). Depending on how much time he has, he goes in and plays with the Hue → Saturation controls as well. Occasionally, when he has time, he uses the Burn and Dodge tools. Steve admits that he feels there is always more he can do to improve a particular image, but he's usually constrained by time.

When he's finished, he applies the Unsharp Mask (Filter → Sharpen → Unsharp Mask). Then he uses the Crop tool to reduce the image to 160 × 120 pixels. Finally, he applies Unsharp Mask a second time.

Time lags with grabs

Grabbing a frame from a video is like shooting a camera with a sticky trigger. There is a lag between the time you "click" the shutter and the moment the frame is grabbed. Luckily, if you don't get the frame you want, you can just rewind and start over. Nothing is lost except your time.

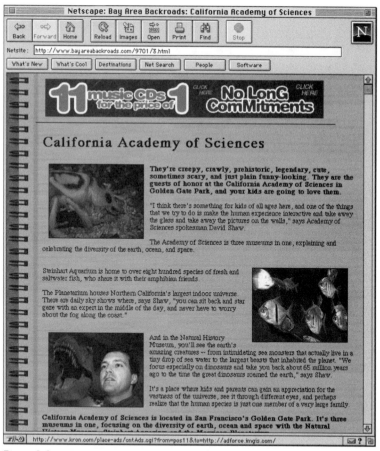

Figure 2-9. *These "photos" were grabbed from the TV show Bay Area Backroads.*

Straighten a crooked scan with 5's Measure tool

Another tool new to Photoshop 5 is the Measure tool, found in the
Toolbox. With this tool, you can calculate the distance between any
two points. Values show up in the Info palette dialog box. You can
also use the Measure tool to straighten a crooked scan. This is what I
did to straighten the photo shown in Figure 2-10.

Figure 2-10. *A crooked scan of a crooked tower.*

To do this:

1. Scan your photo or artwork.

2. If your image is on a background layer, either copy the layer or rename the background layer by double clicking on the background layer in the layer palette. (This process won't work on a background layer.)

3. Select the ruler tool in the tool menu.

4. Create a vertical line on the edge of the image by holding down the Shift key while dragging.

5. Now create a horizontal line that parallels the skewed edge of your scan. (If you look in the Info palette, you will see that Photoshop has calculated the angle between the vertical and horizontal lines. In this example, the angle is 104.9 degrees.)

6. Select Edit → Transform → Numeric. At the bottom of the Numeric Transform dialog box, make sure that Rotate is selected as shown in Figure 2-11. Notice that under Rotate, Photoshop has calculated the amount of rotation needed to straighten your image. In this case, it is 14.95 degrees.

7. Click OK, and Photoshop automatically straightens your scan, as shown in Figure 2-12.

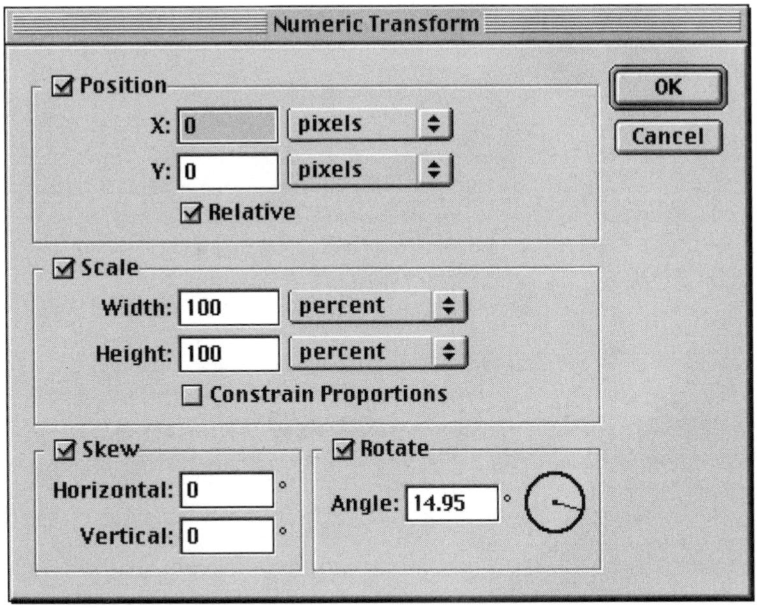

Figure 2-11. *The Numeric Transform dialog.*

Figure 2-12. *A straight scan of a crooked tower.*

Be sure to leave enough room around your image. If you don't, parts of your image will be clipped after the transfer. To expand your canvas simply enlarge your canvas size (Image → Canvas Size).

Improving digital camera photos

Digital cameras and the Web are a match made in heaven. With digital cameras, you don't need film, chemical processing, or time-consuming conversions from analog to digital formats. Photos produced by these cameras can be instantly put on a web page from anywhere in the world—a riverboat in the Grand Canyon or the most desolate corner of Siberia. Best of all, because the destination of the image is a relatively low-resolution electronic screen, almost any of the plethora of digital cameras—including the inexpensive ones—will meet your needs. However, because of the way that digital cameras capture data, they often need help from Photoshop.

Making skin tones look better

Most digital cameras rely on electronic sensors called *charge coupled devices* (CCDs) to capture color information. In general, CCDs do a good job of capturing red and green colors but have trouble capturing blue. The more expensive digital cameras are equipped with better sensors and more sophisticated electronics and do a better (but still not perfect) job with blue.

You can see the problem by looking at Figures 2-13 and 2-14. The photo was taken with a consumer-level digital camera. Figure 2-13 shows the blue channel. Notice how blotchy the image appears. These blotches will also be evident in the final RGB composite, degrading the overall effect of the image. If you look at Figure 2-14, you'll see the green channel isolated. The green channel looks much smoother due to the sensor's ability to capture this color better.

To compensate for the degradation caused by poor blue capture, follow these steps:

1. From the Channels palette, isolate the blue channel by clicking the eye icons for the other colors.

2. Select Filter → Blur → Gaussian Blur. Apply as much of this filter as necessary to diminish the chunky look. Don't worry if it seems like you are over-blurring the image. The other channels are not affected, and the blurring in the blue channel will not be noticeable in the final image.

3. To view the composite effects, from the Channels palette, click the far-left box at the RGB level to turn on all the eye icons. Notice that the chunky effect caused by the poorly sampled blue channel is gone.

This method is especially effective on skin tones, where the adjustments are most noticeable, but it can also be used to improve just about any image taken with a digital camera.

You can similarly improve results when you apply this technique to images that have been scanned on low-cost scanners, which also rely on CCDs.

Figure 2-13. *The weak blue channel degrades the entire image.*

Warming up with tints

Brad Johnson of Second Story has found that the images produced on digital cameras are invariably a bit cold for his taste. Borrowing a technique that he learned from his life as a painter, he applies a glaze or tint to warm up an image. His technique for doing this is similar to the one that he applied to the camera, described earlier in this chapter. Instead of applying a bright violet color, he applies a yellow-orange. To warm up an image, he follows these steps:

Figure 2-14. *The green channel captures the image well.*

1. First, he creates a new layer above the layer containing the digital camera image: from the Layers palette, he selects New Layer.

2. He fills this layer with yellow-orange (Red = 255, Green = 102, Blue = 0).

3. He selects Color Burn from the blending modes. Then he plays with the opacity until he gets it right.

Brad also uses his Gaussian blur technique to clean up shots taken with a digital camera and make them look less electronic. He creates a duplicate layer containing his photograph, applies a Gaussian blur to the duplicate layer, leaves the blending mode at Normal, and adjusts the opacity. When he is finished, he merges the two layers. Figure C-17 shows a photograph to which Brad applied both of these techniques.

Putting your photos on the web

Organizing and keeping track of your images is a never-ending task. Previous versions of Photoshop did little to help manage your images. Photoshop 5, however, introduced a helpful contact sheet feature; Photoshop 5.5 not only improves that feature but also allows you to turn your contact sheet into an interactive web page.

Making a contact sheet with 5

With Photoshop 5, you can create a batch of thumbnail previews on a single sheet from the files in the selected folder. I find this feature especially useful in organizing my digital camera photos, which download as JPEGs without any representative icons.

Photoshop 5.5 comes with Contact Sheet II, an improved version that has the option of including the filename with each thumb, the choice of whether or not to include subdirectories, and the choice of different display fonts (but not font size).

To create a contact sheet:

1. Make sure the image files you want included are closed, then choose File → Automate → Contact Sheet II. You can determine how many images you want to include by changing the size of the sheet. See Figure 2-15.

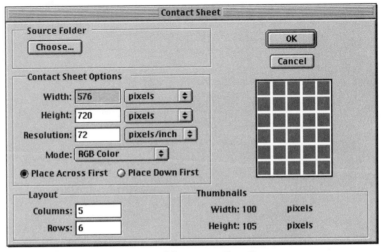

Figure 2-15. *The default settings of the Contact Sheet II.*

You can change the size of the thumbs by changing the number of columns and the number of rows. The default setting is 576 × 720 pixels, with 5 columns and 6 rows, which creates a 100 × 105 pixel thumb.

2. Choose a source folder and click OK. Photoshop does the rest. It goes through the folder, opens each file, resizes it, and places an icon on the sheet.

Making a web photo gallery

With Photoshop 5.5, it's easy to convert a folder of images into an interactive online gallery. 5.5 prepares both thumbnails and full-size images and even creates HTML pages and navigable links!

To create the pages shown in Figure 2-17 and Figure 2-18, I did the following:

1. I placed 12 photos from my collection into a folder I named "Portfolio." Since Photoshop can preserve and publish the filenames of the individual images, I wrote descriptive filenames, i.e., *Japan, Prague Castle, Vice-President Gore*, etc.

2. From 5.5's menu, I chose File → Automate → Web Photo Gallery. See Figure 2-16. In the dialog box, I chose my source (the Portfolio folder containing my images) and named the site "Portfolio." Under Photographer, I typed my name and dated the work. Photoshop gives you a choice of Small, Medium, and Large thumbnails. I chose Small, which produces a thumbnail approximately 50 × 34 pixels.

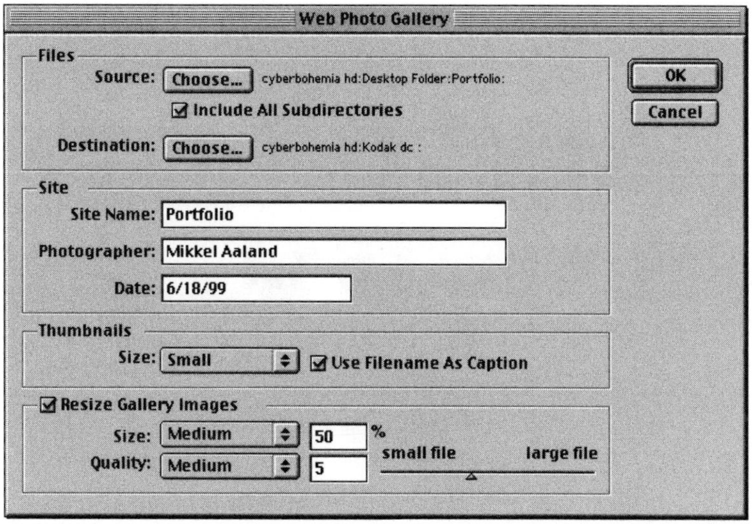

Figure 2-16. *Web Photo Gallery dialog.*

Photoshop also gives you the option of resizing the source images. Since my originals varied greatly in size, for the sake of consistency, I let Photoshop resize the images. By choosing Medium, my horizontal images were resized to approximately 255 × 180 pixels and my vertical images were resized to approximately 185 × 250 pixels. The Quality setting determines how much JPEG compression is applied. I left my setting at the default Medium setting which, with the Medium size setting, produced files ranging from 13K to 30K. (Images that contain few details generally produce smaller JPEG files.)

3. After I set the options and clicked OK, Photoshop did the rest. It opened each image, created both a thumbnail version and Galley version, and regardless of the original file format, saved the file as JPEG. It also created an HTML index page and three folders containing the thumbnail images and navigational GIFs, gallery images, and HTML pages. It also generated a separate file called *UserSelections.txt*, which stores the settings from the Web Gallery dialog box. This way if you only change, delete, or add a single file, and don't change any other options, Web Photo Gallery will process only the files it needs to make the update.

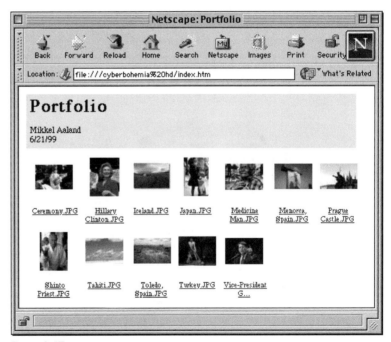

Figure 2-17. *Web page generated by the Gallery Maker.*

Figure 2-18. *Clicking on a thumbnail brings up the full image.*

The amount of time it takes for Photoshop to process the images varies depending on how many images are in the source folder and the speed of the CPU. You can stop the process at any time by typing Command-Period.

Because this is an automated process, there are limitations to creating a Photoshop Web Photo Gallery. The same amount of JPEG compression is applied to each image, regardless of content. Because of this, you won't get optimal file size. Resizing is not done incrementally, which is acceptable if your source images are relatively small and not more than twice the final published size. However, if your original images are larger, you'll get better results by resizing them yourself, following the suggestions in the "Resizing" section earlier in this chapter.

Most likely, you'll also need to tweak the HTML. The default settings create a white background (#FFFFFF), which you might want to change to black (#000000) for optimal viewing. You may also want to go into the HTML pages and change the type style and size as well as edit the filename captions so they don't include the *.JPG* extensions. Before you place the Gallery on a server, you might need to edit the links to reflect a proper directory path.

Photoshop's Web Photo Gallery feature is especially useful when you have a folder full of digital camera shots that you want to present on the Web. In this case, speed may be more important than quality.

CHAPTER THREE

MAKING GREAT GIFS

What's more important—a site that loads fast or a site that looks great? If you simply convert your art to a GIF or JPEG file, accept the default settings, and save the file, chances are you'll wind up with graphics that are neither good enough nor small enough.

Through the next four chapters, you'll learn tons of tricks and techniques to make the most effective web graphics with Photoshop. In this chapter, we'll deal with converting existing images to GIF. Chapter 4, *Creating GIFs from Scratch*, shows you how to create original GIF files. Chapter 5, *Special Effects with Transparent GIFs*, covers transparent GIFs. And Chapter 6, *JPEG: All the Color You Want*, shows you how to make the best JPEG files.

GIF or JPEG?

The primary decision you have to make for any web graphic is file format. Make the wrong choice and you'll wind up with files that are larger than they need to be and images that don't look as good as they could. Make the right choice and you'll be assured that your images load fast, look reasonably good, and work for users of all platforms and screen displays.

Although there are many graphic file formats, GIF and JPEG are the most important ones for the Web, since they are directly supported by web browsers. All versions of Photoshop will read and write the basic GIF and JPEG formats. Photoshop 4 and 5 (and earlier versions, with the help of plug-ins) will read and write later variations of the formats (such as progressive rendering for JPEGs and transparency for GIFs). Photoshop 4, 5.0, 5.02, and 5.5 offer support for PNG, a relatively new file format that is gaining widespread support (and which is discussed in more detail in Appendix A, *The PNG Format*). Photoshop 5.5 offers improved PNG support.

Both the GIF and JPEG formats give you ways to control the file size of your web graphics—a critical feature considering the Web's current limited bandwidth capabilities. JPEG does this by compressing and actually throwing away data it considers unnecessary. GIF controls file size through a combination of compression and color reduction.

So, GIF or JPEG? The answer depends on the image's content and on how it will appear on your web page.

There are a number of crucial differences between the two formats:

- GIF is an 8-bit format. JPEG is a 24-bit format.
- GIF uses lossless compression (with an exception discussed later). JPEG uses lossy compression.
- GIF uses a color index. JPEG uses the full range of 16 million colors.
- GIF supports transparency. JPEG does not.

In general, GIF works better for images with flat colors and JPEG works better with photographic images, but there are many exceptions to the rule. Table 3-1 gives some general rules for when and when not to use GIF and JPEG.

Table 3-1. *When to use and when to avoid GIF and JPEG*

	Use for:	Avoid with:
GIF	Graphics containing limited numbers of colors, or intricate detail that you want to maintain	Large photographic images or illustrations that contain a lot of color, unless you want to create a floating effect
	Floating graphics from the page	
	Creating a simple animation (with the latest GIF file format)	
	Browser-safe colors—colors that won't dither or change when viewed on an 8-bit monitor	
JPEG	Most photographic images and continuous-tone art that contain subtle shifts in color	Text or graphics that contain detailed edges

Those are the rules of thumb. In the real world, things are a little less cut-and-dried. Take a look at Figures C-18 through C-23 in the color insert to see some actual situations and the decisions that web designers made.

Indexing your image

The most important thing to know about GIF files is that they're indexed images. That is, the file contains an index, or a palette, of all the colors in the image. Because GIF is an 8-bit format, the maximum number of colors in a GIF file is 256. This palette is used to assign a color to each pixel in the image. Actually, each pixel is assigned an index number, and RGB color values are associated with the index number. For instance, index number 22 may be assigned a navy blue color, and number 23 may be assigned sky blue. In the GIF file format, one index number can be tagged as transparent. We'll discuss GIF transparency more in Chapter 5.

Figures C-24 and C-25 make the point. Figure C-24 shows a simple illustration created by the artist James Yang and its color index. You can clearly see how the colors in the index are displayed in the image. In Figure C-25, we have the exact same image, but a different color index. The image changes accordingly.

When you realize how the index affects the image, you can see what havoc would be created if you applied the wrong index to an image.

With Photoshop 5.5, there are three ways to index an image in preparation for the GIF file format:

- File → Save for Web

- Image → Mode → Indexed Color

- File → Export → GIF89a Export module

The Save for Web feature is only available in 5.5, which also has a better Indexed Color feature than do Photoshop 4 and 5. The GIF89a Export module, which is primarily used to create GIFs with transparent areas, has remained the same since Photoshop 4.0.

Each method has its pros and cons:

- The Save for Web plug-in is Photoshop's most useful web-friendly feature to date, but it is limited in the way it creates transparent GIFs.

- The Image → Mode → Indexed Color method is very flexible—you can do things such as applying selective dithering and tweaking the color palette through selections—however, it lacks the full interactive capabilities of the Save for Web plug-in.

- The GIF89a Export module, when used with the Image → Mode → Indexed Color method, is great for creating transparent areas, but its RGB-to-Indexed Color capabilities are rudimentary, especially when compared with the other methods.

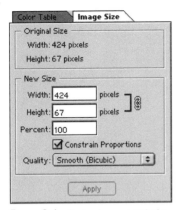

Figure 3-1. *Resize images with the Image Size palette.*

Figure 3-2. *Click on the Original tab to change the optimized settings without applying changes.*

Let's start by indexing an image with the Save to Web plug-in, then move on to using the Image → Mode → Indexed Color method. I'll describe in detail the GIF89a Export module in Chapter 5.

Using Save for Web

When you choose Save for Web, Photoshop 5.5 displays your image in a new window (see Figure C-26). Once you are in this window, you won't have access to any of Photoshop's editing or processing tools. You can, however, resize your image in the Save for Web box. Click on the Image Size tab in the lower-right corner to bring up the Image Size palette shown in Figure 3-1. Regardless of the original image's resolution, the optimized image will always be saved at 72 dpi.

As soon as your image appears in the Save for Web box, Photoshop automatically begins optimizing the image for the web. Photoshop uses your most recently selected optimization settings; if you've never run the plug-in before, the default settings will be used. You don't have to wait for the optimization process to complete in order to customize the settings. After the image loads, press Command-Period (Mac) or Escape (Windows) to stop the optimization process. Make sure you wait for the image to load in, though, as indicated in the progress bar at the bottom of the window; if you abort while the image is still loading, Save for Web will abort, and you'll have to start all over again

Next, click on the Original tab in the upper left of the interface, shown in Figure 3-2. This lets you change the optimized settings without waiting for Photoshop to apply each change. (If you select the adjacent 2-Up or 4-Up tab, you'll get a view of your original graphic displayed side by side with one or three optimized versions of the graphic. You can assign different optimizing settings to each version and compare the effect.)

In order to illustrate what comes next, I'll show two ways to optimize the same image. Both ways will create a good-looking GIF that can be read by all browsers, but that's where the similarity ends. Only the second method will create a graphic that is as small as possible and contains key areas of browser-safe colors.

For my example, I've chosen a graphic created by Valerie Robbins for a *nationalgeographic.com* page. It contains type and a background with solid colors, and will not suffer from being reduced to 256 or less colors. In other words, it is a perfect candidate for GIF.

The easy way

The first way is the easiest: I simply apply Save for Web's default GIF settings. These settings give visually pleasing results for almost every graphic that meets the GIF criteria.

Here are the basic steps:

1. Run the Save for Web plug-in.

2. Wait for the optimizing process to stop, then select the Original tab.

3. If they aren't chosen already, choose the following settings from the drop-down menus in the upper-right corner, as shown in Figure 3-3.

   Format: GIF
   Palette: Selective
   Dither: Diffusion
   Lossy: 0
   Colors: 256
   Dither: 100%
   Web Snap: 0%
   Interlaced box: unchecked

4. Select Optimize from the menu tab.

5. Once the optimizing process is complete, toggle back and forth between the original and the optimized version using the Original and Optimized tabs. Zoom in for a closer look by selecting the zoom tool and clicking on the image. You can also zoom in by selecting the drop-down preview menu found by holding down Control/Shift while clicking anywhere in the Save for Web window.

6. If the optimized graphic looks acceptable, and it should, click OK and save the file. Photoshop automatically adds the *.gif* extension.

Following these steps, I successfully optimized the web graphic shown in Figure C-26, weighing in at 14.31K. The fact is, I can do better. (By the way, the file size circled in red in the lower-left side of the window is accurate, unlike file sizes found in Photoshop's main window, which are approximations.)

The better way

Now, I'll try again, keeping the GIF file format but tweaking the other settings. I've set my window to display 4-Up and zoomed in 300% percent so you can clearly see the effects of the different settings.

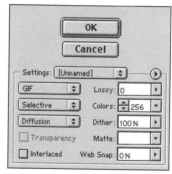

Figure 3-3. *Save for Web's default settings for a GIF file.*

Batch optimization

To apply custom settings to similar graphics, choose Save Settings from the drop-down menu. See Figure 3-4. To embed your settings into the original Photoshop file, hold down the Option/Alt key. The OK button turns into a Remember button. If you select Remember, the next time you open the Photoshop file with the Save for Web plug-in, it will apply the same settings that were applied at the time you choose Remember. (If you don't do this, the next time you open your Photoshop file, it will apply the most current optimized settings.)

Figure 3-4. *You can save settings to apply to similar graphics.*

In Figure C-27, I've applied three different palettes, Perceptual, Adaptive, and Web, keeping my other settings the same as in the first example.

As you can see, the Perceptual palette created a slightly larger file size (14.38K) than the default Selective palette (14.31K). Otherwise, the result is very similar, which isn't surprising because both palettes create a custom color table by prioritizing colors for which the human eye has greater sensitivity. Selective is just slightly better than Perceptual at maintaining broad areas of color and preserving browser-safe colors.

The Adaptive palette (formerly the "best" option in Photoshop 4 and 5), which samples colors from the spectrum appearing most commonly in the image, doesn't do as good a job, at least not in this graphic. Notice the chunky look of the gold around the word "light." The Adaptive palette also produced a slightly bigger graphic (14.59K). Even though the Web palette resulted in a file size of only 11.86K, the graphic looks awful. That's because the Web palette only applies the 216 colors shared by both the Mac and PC platforms.

Based on what I see here, I will stay with the Selective palette. (In general, I find the Selective palette does the best job; however, I use the Adaptive palette when I index a color photograph, and I use the Web palette when a graphic contains a limited number of flat colors.)

In Figure C-28, I've applied three different dither percentages, 0%, 50%, and 100%, leaving the dither type set to Diffusion. The Diffusion option always produces a better result than Pattern. If you are going to slice your image into smaller parts, you might want to try 5.5's new Noise dither pattern, which reduces the seam patterns along sliced edges.

As you can see, as I decreased the amount of dither I've also decreased the file size. However, the difference is so small, I will leave my settings at 100%, which produces a slightly better image.

Figure C-29 shows the effect of Photoshop's Lossy GIF setting. Adobe has come up with a clever technique that actually turns the normally lossless GIF compression process into a lossy one. I'll spare you the technical details of how they do it, but the result is that you can apply greater compression to the GIF file format, albeit with a trade-off in quality. When I set a value of 15, there is little noticeable difference in quality but a nice drop in file size from 14.31K to 12.18K. At a lossy value of 100, the file size is 7.49K, but the quality is unacceptable.

Keep in mind that you cannot use the Lossy option when you've selected the interlace option or when Noise or Pattern dither algorithms are selected. (Interlace, by the way, creates a GIF that loads on a browser window gradually, in successive passes. Interlacing adds file size, so it is best avoided.)

Figure C-30 shows the effect of reducing the number of colors in the graphic. Reducing palette size always yields a substantial reduction in file size. The quality difference between 256 colors and 128 colors is slight and yet there is a drop in file size from 12.18K to 10.84K. Dropping to 8 or 32 colors was unacceptable.

Putting this all together, I now have a graphic with a file size of only 10.84K.

One last thing. How will this graphic look on monitors that can only display 256 colors (8-bit monitors)? Those systems dither any colors not found in the 216-color browser-safe palette. I am not so concerned about the detailed areas of the graphic—they'll still look OK if they dither. It's the solid blocks of color that worry me. If they dither, they will detract from the overall quality of the graphic.

How do you know if a color is browser-safe? How do you change it if it is not? It's easy with the Save for Web plug-in:

1. In the Save for Web box, select the eyedropper tool.

2. Click on a color in your graphic.

3. Turn your attention to the Color Table to the right of your graphic. (See Figure C-31.) The color you selected is represented and highlighted in the Color Table with a white border around it. If the selected colors box contains a black diamond in the center, it's browser-safe. If it doesn't, it's not.

4. To change an unsafe color to a browser-safe color, simply click on the cube icon at the bottom of the Color Table. This will shift the color to the nearest browser-safe color.

5. To prevent the color from being dropped or changed if you alter your color settings, click on the padlock icon at the bottom of the Color Table. A white square with a red center appears in the lower-right corner of each locked color.

In Val's graphic, the dominant red in the background is already browser-safe. But the yellows that make up the gold box are not, as shown in Figure C-31. Using the method outlined above, I'll shift several of the yellows to browser-safe colors to prevent them from dithering. By holding down the Shift key while I use the eyedropper tool, I can make multiple selections and use the cube to shift them all at once, as shown in Figure C-32. I could have also used Save for Web's Web Snap feature. By entering a higher numerical value, it automatically shifts more colors to browser-safe. I prefer, however, to shift colors individually.

Save for Web or ImageReady?

Photoshop's Save for Web has many of the same optimizing controls as ImageReady. So when should you use Save For Web and when should you use ImageReady? Although ImageReady 2.0 ships with Photoshop 5.5, it is still a standalone program. That means it must be launched separately and therefore takes up RAM and hard disk space. Switching back and forth between the two programs is relatively easy, especially between Photoshop 5.5 and ImageReady 2.0, but you still need to leave one work environment for the other, which is inconvenient at best and troublesome at worst. Some web producers have reported data corruption when they've tried to toggle between Photoshop and ImageReady with files containing several type and mask layers. I suggest you stick with Photoshop 5.5 for image optimization and use ImageReady only for such features as slicing, animation and rollovers.

Undocumented feature

In the Save for Web window, clicking Control-Shift (on the Mac) or Control-Shift then right-click (on Windows) brings up a menu combining the Magnify, Platform Preview, and Browser Dither menus.

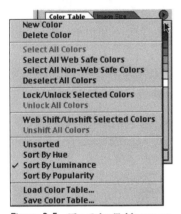

Figure 3-5. *The Color Table pop-up menu lets you change the way colors are sorted.*

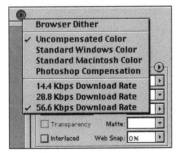

Figure 3-6. *Platform preview menu lets you see how your image will look on a Mac or a PC.*

Here are some other important things you should know about the Color Table:

- You can change the way the colors are sorted in the Color Table panel pop-up menu. See Figure 3-5.

- You can add colors from the Color Table by clicking on the color sample box. Double-clicking brings up the Color Picker. Choose a new color; when you close the Color Picker, the new color will replace the old one in the sample box. Remember, 5.5's Color Picker now has an Only Web Colors option.

- You can delete a color by clicking on it in the sample box and then clicking on the trash icon at the bottom of the Color Table panel. You can delete a number of colors at the same time by holding down the Shift key while selecting and then clicking on the trash icon.

Previewing compression options

In Chapter 1, *Making Photoshop Web-Friendly*, we discussed that differences in monitor gamma will make images that look good on a Mac look dark on a PC and images created on a PC look washed out on a Mac. The Save for Web plug-in includes a feature to preview how your image will look on different platforms. Click on the small arrow in the upper right of the Save for Web window and a drop-down menu appears, shown in Figure 3-6. Choose the platform in which you wish to preview your work. You can also choose Browser Dither, which shows how your graphic will look if it is forced to dither by a browser.

To preview your graphic in an actual browser window, click on the browser icon on the bottom right of the Save for Web window. This brings up a pop-up menu where you can select the browser to use, as shown in Figure 3-7. Photoshop places aliases (or shortcuts, if your prefer) of all browsers found on your hard disk in a folder called Preview In, located in Photoshop's Helpers folder. One of these aliases is surrounded by square brackets. To change the default browser, remove the brackets from the existing browser and add them to the program you want to be your default.

Working backwards

In the previous example, I started with the assumption that quality was the first priority. With the Save for Web plug-in you can also work backwards and prioritize file size. This can be especially useful when you are creating an ad banner that has a specific file size requirement.

To do this, go to the arrow in the upper, far right corner. This Settings pop-up menu includes a command called Optimize to File Size, as shown in Figure 3-8. Selecting this command brings up the dialog box shown in Figure 3-9. Here you can set the desired file size you want to squeeze the graphic into. There are also two radio buttons. Current Settings will keep your file format, changing palette or compression options to fit to the file size. Auto Select GIF/JPEG not only cycles through various palette options until it arrives at the desired file size, but it will also automatically choose whether GIF or JPEG is the better file format.

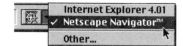

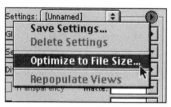

Figure 3-7. *Selecting a browser for previewing the browser.*

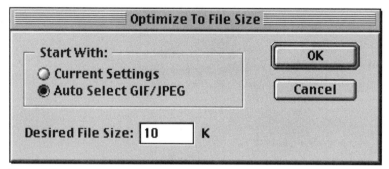

Figure 3-8. *Optimize to File Size guarantees your file will be the right size.*

Figure 3-9. *Auto Select GIF/JPEG not only optimizes to file size but also picks the best format.*

The Indexed Color option

In most versions of Photoshop, choosing Image → Mode → Indexed Color is an effective way to index your image in preparation for saving as a GIF. Using this method you can even do things that can't be done with the Save for Web plug-in, such as tweaking the palette to emphasis certain areas of your image and applying selective dithering; in addition, the GIF89a Export module offers much more control over transparency than does Save for Web.

Photoshop 5.5 has the best Indexed Color capabilities to date. Not only can you preview the effects of your optimizing choices in real-time, but you can apply variable amounts of dither as well. With 5.5's Color Table (Image → Mode → Color Table), there is a certain degree of interactivity which makes selectively adding browser-safe colors easier. There are also more ways to create transparency in 5.5, something I will discuss in more detail in Chapter 5. In Photoshop 5.5, you can go directly from an RGB image to a GIF file via File → Save a Copy; when you choose CompuServe GIF as the file format, the Indexed Color dialog box automatically appears.

Automate/Batch

You can create a folder containing a batch of similar images and use a combination of Photoshop 5's Automate/Batch feature (File → Automate → Batch) and an action to automatically optimize all the images for you. See Figure 3-10. Start by opening an image from the folder and name and record an action that optimizes that image to your liking. You can use either 5.5's Save for Web method or Image → Mode → Indexed Color method.

When you are finished, choose File → Automate, select the recorded action and the folder containing the images you wish to optimize, and Photoshop applies your action to the entire batch of images automatically. If you use Save for Web to optimize your representative image, a Photoshop action will record the various optimizing settings. Unfortunately, however, if you choose Optimize to File Size → Auto Select GIF/JPEG, Photoshop will not automatically analyze each image in your folder but will only apply the optimized settings that were calculated when you optimized your first image and recorded the action.

Figure 3-10. *The Action palette's Batch dialog box.*

To illustrate the Image → Mode → Indexed Color method, I'll index another of Valerie's *nationalgeographic.com* graphics. I'll also note where 5.5's features differ from earlier versions of Photoshop.

Again, I'll try two approaches. One way is easy but won't necessarily produce the optimal graphic. The other way takes a little more time, but the results are better.

Here are the steps to the first method:

1. Working with a RGB image, select Image → Mode → Indexed Color. This brings up the dialog box shown in Figure 3-11.

2. Apply the following settings:

   Palette: Selective
   Colors: 256
   Forced: None
   Dither: Diffusion
   Amount: 100%

3. Save the image, and then Save As to save it as a CompuServe GIF file.

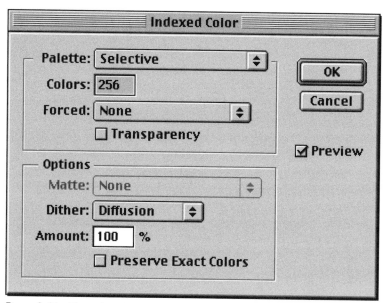

Figure 3-11. *The Indexed Color dialog box.*

In most cases, when a graphic contains more than 256 colors, these settings will produce an acceptable GIF, as illustrated by Val's graphic shown in Figure C-35.

I'll try again. I'll keep my palette set to Selective because I know from experience that it will do a good job on a graphic like this one. (If your graphic contains less than 256 colors, the Exact palette will automatically be selected, which is fine unless you want to use the Web palette. If you apply the Web palette, be sure to follow the instructions outlined in "Special Web palette considerations" later in this chapter.)

I'll try reducing the number of colors and see what that does. At 64 colors the graphic still looks fine, but at 32 colors (see Figure C-36), it doesn't, so I'll stick with 64 colors. (Under the word Preview in the Indexed Color box, a short dash pulses until the optimizing is complete.) Zooming in and out (Control/Command zooms in and Alt/Option zooms out), I can carefully examine the effects of my changes. With Photoshop 5.0 and 5.02, which also have preview capabilities, you can't zoom in and out while your Indexed Color box is open. You must magnify your image before choosing Image → Mode → Indexed Color. With other versions of Photoshop, preview is not an option.

With 5.5, you can fine-tune the amount of dither. After some trial and error, I notice that my graphic still looks good at 80% dither. The less dither, the smaller the file size, so this reduction in dither is good.

With earlier versions of Photoshop, you can only turn dither on or off, and in nearly all cases when you have a complex graphic or a photograph, you'll want to leave it on. Turn dither off for graphics with less than 256 colors.

I'm happy with what I see and now the file size is only 19.8K.

Browser dither

One of the web browser's many jobs is to manage color. This is an issue because web pages typically have numerous images on a single page, so it would be impossible for an 8-bit system to display each image's palette.

That's why browsers have their own palette, generally known as the browser-safe palette, shown in Figure C-33. This is a 216-color palette, the colors of which are common to both Mac and Windows platforms, shown in Figure C-34. Technically, it's called a $6 \times 6 \times 6$ color cube because the 216 colors are generated by combining just six colors.

The use of browser-safe colors is an important concept to understand if you want your images and graphics to look their best on the greatest number of display systems. First of all, if everyone surfing the Web used a display system capable of displaying millions or even thousands of colors, we wouldn't need a discussion about browser-safe colors. There would be plenty of colors to go around. But the fact is the majority of Web surfers use 8-bit display systems.

In general, 8-bit Macs use the 256-color system palette, which contains the 216 browser-safe colors plus 40 more, and Windows computers always use the browser-safe palette. There do seem to be times, however, when Macs use the smaller palette.

As long as your image contains only the 216 colors in the browser-safe palette, there's no problem. What happens when your image contains non-safe colors? The browser either uses dithering to simulate the missing color, or it entirely changes the color to one of the colors in its palette.

Now imagine an image on a blue background. If you pick whatever blue you want and index it, do you get a nice flat color? Not necessarily. If it's a non-browser-safe blue you get dithering, because the browser will try to approximate the color you asked for from the colors in the browser palette. No good.

The solution, of course, is to pick a browser-safe blue for that field. Although you don't have control over what kind of display system your audience is using, nor do you have control over the way in which a browser dithers or changes colors in your image or graphic, you do have control over which colors you choose to use. When you work with the 216 colors that are common to both the Mac and Windows machines, you can be assured that they will not dither or be replaced by a different color. Of course, these colors may not always look the way that you expect because of individual monitor calibration (or lack thereof) and the gamma characteristics of various computer platforms—but the differences are relatively predictable.

The best way to use browser-safe colors is to apply them to areas of large expanses of flat colors, while using dithering on areas of continuous tone, subtle gradation, and anti-aliasing.

Replacing non-browser-safe colors

Let's turn now to the browser-safe color issue. As mentioned earlier, it is not visually pleasing when solid, large expanses of color (such as those found in a background) dither. You could apply the Web palette to the entire graphic, but with a complex graphic, the results generally are not good. Instead, it's better to selectively replace a background or solid color with a browser-safe color and not worry about the other areas.

With 5.5's Save for Web plug-in, selective color replacement is easy. It's a bit more work if you are using the Image → Mode → Indexed Color method, but it can still be done. Here are two methods: the first method requires that you work in RGB mode, replace background colors with browser-safe colors from the swatch or color picker, and *then* index your image; the second method occurs while in Indexed Color mode and uses the Color Lookup Table.

The RGB method:

1. Fill the foreground color box with a browser-safe swatch. (You can select browser-safe colors from your swatch palette or from your color picker.)

2. Use either Photoshop's Magic Wand, magnetic lasso tool, or manual selection tools to select the area of the image that you want to change. You could also use the Color Range tool. (If you use the Magic Wand tool, be sure to experiment with the Grow and Similar commands found under the Select menu. These options are especially useful to isolate large expanses of background or areas of similar color.)

3. Fill the selected area with the color that you chose from a browser-safe palette.

4. To ensure that your browser-safe colors don't shift when you apply the Indexed Color command, check the Preserve Exact Colors checkbox in the Indexed Color dialog box. (This is only an option in Photoshop Versions 5.0, 5.02, and 5.5. With earlier versions of Photoshop, you will need to manually check your colors after you've indexed your graphic to make sure the colors haven't shifted. Sometimes they shift and sometimes they don't. It depends on the image and the palette you apply.)

The Indexed Mode method:

1. Choose Image → Mode → Color Table (see Figure 3-12).

2. Select the eyedropper tool.

3. Click on the area in your image that you wish to alter. The color box in the Color Table will be highlighted and the color you selected will be deleted from the box and from the image.

4. Double-click on the highlighted color box in the Color Table to bring up the Color Picker. Select the browser-safe color of your choice and click OK. That color will now replace your old, non-browser-safe color.

5. Repeat this process on other flat colors that you don't want to browser-dither.

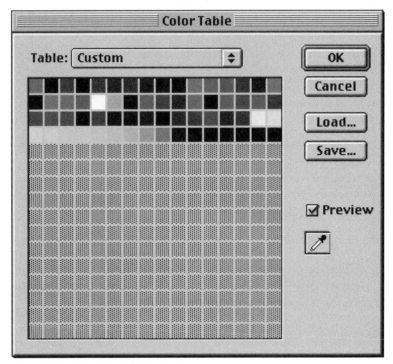

Figure 3-12. *The Color Table dialog box.*

In pre-5.5 Indexed Color Mode, you can use the Color Lookup Table to replace a non-browser-safe color in earlier Photoshop versions. However, this method is a bit awkward because the earlier Color Lookup Tables are not interactive. You can choose a color in the table to edit the image, but you can't click on a color in the image to bring up that color in the table and change it. This makes finding the color you want a hit-and-miss proposition.

To change a color using this method, follow these steps:

1. Open your indexed image.

2. Choose Image → Mode → Color Table.

3. Find the background or dominant color in the Color Table that you want to change to a browser-safe color. (This process is hit-and-miss and requires some guesswork.) Click on the color and the Color Picker appears. Either type in the RGB values that equate to a browser-safe color or simply use the eyedropper tool to click on a browser-safe color in the Swatches palette.

Special Web palette considerations

If you apply the Web palette, you'll end up with an indexed image that contains 216 browser-safe colors. But what if you don't need 216 colors? What if your image contains only 64 colors, or, for that matter, 16? By saving your file with 216 colors you have created an unnecessarily large file. What to do now? You can get rid of the unused colors by following these steps:

1. Switch to RGB mode.

2. Without doing anything else, switch back to Indexed Color mode. If your image has less than 216 colors, the Exact palette should be selected, and the number of colors in the image will be displayed.

3. Click OK, and save the indexed image as a GIF.

The new image will look exactly the same as the original, while the file size will shrink.

Customizing the Adaptive, Selective, and Perceptual palettes

When Photoshop converts an image from the RGB mode to the Indexed Color mode, it treats all parts of the image equally. It doesn't recognize, for example, that you might be more concerned about the foreground of the image than the background. But you're not stuck with this situation—you can create a palette that best represents the important parts of your image.

There are two ways to do this:

• "Tweak" (or influence) the Adaptive, Selective, or Perceptual palettes.

• Create a custom palette.

The first way is easier. To tweak one of the three above mentioned palettes, simply select the area that you want to emphasize with a selection tool. Now when you convert from RGB to Indexed Color

Saving time with Actions

Earlier versions of Photoshop don't have a Indexed Color Preview option, and it is time-consuming to find the happy medium between file size and quality. You have to convert and save many different versions of your image until you find the perfect balance. If you are using Photoshop 4, you can automate the process of applying different color depths and palettes to a single image with Actions.

Take this tip from Sean Parker, the technical wizard at Parker Grove. Sean created an Action that applies the different color depths to the Adaptive palette with diffusion dither, and then applies the Web palette with dither. He has also created an action that applies the different color depths to the adaptive palette with no dither, and then applies the Web palette without dither.

mode, Photoshop will automatically weigh the conversion in favor of the selected area.

In Figure C-37, for example, Rebecca's face is the most important element in the image. However, if the Adaptive palette is applied normally to this photograph, too much emphasis will be placed on the colorful background and not enough of the colors that make up the skin tone will be represented. As Figure C-38 shows, the results are not flattering.

But we can tweak the palette by having Photoshop emphasize the colors in the face and de-emphasize the colors in the background. To do this, simply select the face before indexing, as shown in Figure C-39. The new palette, shown in Figure C-40, contains many more of the subtle tonal variations that make the skin tone more realistic.

In the previous example, we got good results by influencing the Adaptive palette. But we could have gotten even better results if we had created a CLUT (Color Look-Up Table) that put total rather than partial emphasis on the selected area. To do this, you need to create a custom palette. Once you've created this custom palette, you can apply it to your original image or to one comparable in color.

To create a custom palette, follow these steps:

1. Open an RGB image.
2. Make a copy of that image (Image → Duplicate), merging layers if necessary. You'll work on this copy to create the custom palette, then apply the palette to your original.
3. Crop the duplicate image to the most color-critical area. This part of the image will control the color palette.
4. Index this cropped image with the adaptive palette.
5. Save this palette by selecting Image → Mode → Color Table and clicking Save. Give the palette a name and click OK.

Now that we've created a custom palette, we can apply it to the original image. Just index the original and choose Custom palette. This brings up the Color Table dialog. Click on the Load button and select the custom palette you just created. Photoshop will apply the custom palette to your image.

As you can see in Figure C-41, Rebecca's face is nearly color-perfect. However, since our custom palette doesn't include any colors from the background, the background looks terrible. A solution to this problem would have been to include a few background colors in our custom palette, which could have been done by cropping our image looser.

Selective dithering

When you command Photoshop to dither an image, it applies the dither pattern to the entire image, even to areas that you might not want to dither, such as areas containing flat colors. Wouldn't it be great if you could "tell" Photoshop to selectively dither a small part of an image and yet keep the other parts intact?

c|net's Casey Caston has found a way to do just that. To use Caston's method of selective dithering, follow these steps:

1. In RGB mode, copy the part of the image to dither.

2. Index the image.

3. Paste the copied portion back from the Clipboard to the indexed but undithered image. Photoshop automatically dithers the pasted RGB selection, leaving the rest of the image untouched.

Caston regularly uses this technique to give him very specific control over the way his c|net graphics look.

The next three color figures show the results of this approach to indexing a GIF. Figure C-42 shows the graphic indexed to the Web palette. Figure C-43 shows the image with the adaptive palette. And Figure C-44 shows the results of the combination approach: some of the image is dithered, some isn't.

Getting better tiled backgrounds

When an image or graphic is used as the background for a web page, you have to be especially careful to use browser-safe colors. This is because browsers handle background images differently than other images. When it comes to backgrounds, the browser will shift non-browser-safe colors instead of dithering them.

This became quite apparent to designer Gregg Hartling when he tried to use a GIF background tile that he had created using the Adaptive palette. Gregg knew that by using the Adaptive palette he ran the risk of introducing colors that weren't browser-safe. He thought the image might dither when displayed on an 8-bit system, but he didn't see that as a problem because the dither would add a nice effect to the image.

But the background GIF didn't dither. Instead, as you can see in Figure C-45, the browser substituted colors from the Web palette and that's all it did. The result was a clumpy, banding-like effect. Gregg quickly went back to his original image and used the browser-safe palette with diffusion dither selected and got the results he wanted, as shown in Figure C-46.

A little more work

As you've seen in this chapter, using Photoshop to index a graphic in preparation for the GIF file format takes a bit of work, especially if you are trying to get it completely right. Remember, what may seem daunting at first becomes easier and easier as you become familiar with the various Photoshop settings and how they affect different types of images and graphics. In the next chapter, we'll show you ways to maintain even more control over the color in your graphics by using browser-safe colors from the start.

How big is your image file anyway?

As a creator of web content, you need to pay attention to the file size of your image or graphic. Many web designers have decided that the total size for a web page shouldn't be more than 30K, so every kilobyte counts. How can you determine the actual file size of an image you are currently working on?

Photoshop 5.5's Save for Web plug-in displays an accurate file size in the lower-left corner of its window. However, the size that is displayed on the bottom left of Photoshop's main image window has very little to do with actual number of kilobytes that make up the image. If you are working with a JPEG image, it has nothing to do with the actual compressed file size. (Display the size by positioning the pointer over the triangle in the bottom border, holding down the mouse button, and choosing Document Sizes.) These numbers are useful when you want to know the approximate difference in size between a layered and a flattened image. The first value shows the file size of the final file as it would be if its layers were flattened. The second value shows a file size that includes all layers and channels.

When you choose Image → Image Size, the file size number displayed is only a rough approximation of the actual number of bytes of your image.

In versions other than 5.5, you'll need to leave Photoshop and click on your desktop to find the actual file size. In Windows, the file size you see in the file list is accurate. On the Mac, however, this number is usually way off. The Macintosh Finder displays not the size of the file but the amount of hard drive space consumed. To find the actual size of a file, use Command/Control-I (or File → Get Info). The first number shown next to Size is the amount of hard drive space the file occupies. The number next to it in parentheses is the more accurate number.

Ultimately, what really matters is the final size of the image file once it is on a web server. This final file size is often much smaller than you think, because unwanted and unneeded data is stripped in the process of putting an image on a server. This is especially true for Macintosh files because the Mac adds a "resource fork" that is always stripped away by a web server.

CHAPTER FOUR

CREATING GIFS FROM SCRATCH

As discussed in the last chapter, when you use Photoshop to create web graphics and illustrations, it's a good idea to keep the limitations of the Web in mind from the onset. Basically, this means using the browser-safe 216-color palette.

By using these 216 colors and saving your final work in the GIF file format, you can be assured that your work will not dither or otherwise change when viewed on an 8-bit display system. By using just the necessary amount of color, you can also be sure that your file size is as small as possible so that your image will download quickly.

Although 216 colors may not sound like a lot of color, web designers have not only learned to live with this limited palette, but also have found ways to create beautiful and effective work—in spite of the limitations. In this chapter, you'll see how they do it. You'll also learn how to create so-called hybrid browser-safe colors that extend the number of web-safe colors well beyond 216, as well as how to borrow color swatches from other web graphics.

From RGB to indexed color

Corey Hitchcock is an illustrator/designer who works at The Gate, the online service of *The San Francisco Chronicle* and *The San Francisco Examiner.* The web site is updated hourly, and because of the hectic schedule, Corey has quickly learned the ins and outs of the Web. She knows, for example, that by working directly from the browser-safe palette, her graphics will look the way she wants on the largest number of monitors.

She works in Photoshop's RGB mode, which gives her the advantage of all of Photoshop's filters, plug-ins, and layer features; however, in

Locating a swatch

In order to load a
browser-safe swatch,
open the Swatches pal-
ette (Window → Show
Swatches). In the Switch-
es palette, click on the
upper-right pointer and
choose Load Swatches or
Replace Swatches from
the pull-down menu.
Select the Web palette
from the Goodies folder
and click OK. You'll see
the web colors in your
Swatches palette. Select
and choose this file now
or select and load another
browser-safe swatch that
you've acquired.

this mode, there is always a chance that she might introduce non-browser-safe colors into her work. As a result, when she is finished, and when she is ready to convert her work to the Indexed mode so it can be saved as a GIF, she applies Photoshop's Web palette. Figure C-47 shows one of her creations, a colored dragon that was part of a feature on the Chinese new year.

To create the image with browser-safe colors:

1. She loaded a palette of browser-safe colors into her Swatches palette. Corey organizes her palette by hue and value.

2. She opened a scan of the dragon line drawing.

3. She created a new layer.

4. In the new layer, she used the Selection tool to roughly outline the edges of the dragon.

5. She chose a browser-safe red from the Swatches palette as the background color and a browser-safe orange as the foreground color.

6. She used the Linear gradient tool to fill the selection in the new layer, as shown in Figure C-48. (Remember that any of the gradient tools adds additional colors to create the blend between these two colors. The more variations between the two colors, the more non-browser-safe colors will be introduced.)

7. She chose Overlay from the mode pop-up in the Layers menu. This mode nicely blends the graduated colors with the line drawing.

8. She converted her RGB file to Indexed Color mode, using the Web palette. (Because the Linear Gradient tool added a few non-browser-safe colors, there was a slight change between the RGB and the indexed versions.)

In a very short time, Corey created an illustration that not only embellishes a Gate web page, but at 15K also loads fast and looks the same regardless of the monitor it is viewed on.

Controlling anti-aliasing with custom brushes

Like Corey Hitchcock, web designer Brian Frick works in Photoshop's RGB mode and uses browser-safe color swatches. Most often, he uses Photoshop's Paintbrush tool, but he creates and uses custom brushes that reduce the chance of non-browser-safe colors being introduced through anti-aliasing.

The only Photoshop tool that doesn't automatically anti-alias—and therefore add unwanted, non-browser-safe colors—is the Pencil tool. But the Pencil tool creates a very hard, jagged edge that Brian rarely uses. The custom brushes that he makes create a look between the hard edge of the Pencil tool and the normally soft edge of the Paintbrush. Figure 4-1 shows some of the custom brushes he created. The illustrations for Discovery's "The Skinny On..." were created using these custom brushes.

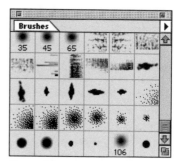

Figure 4-1. *Brian Frick's Brushes palette shows some of his custom brushes.*

The illustrations are also built layer by layer, as shown in Figure C-49. Brian prefers working this way so that he can easily edit any specific part of the illustration at any time.

To create the custom brushes, Brian followed these steps:

1. He created a new 100 × 100 pixel file with a white background that he immediately converted to grayscale mode.

2. He chose one of the non-blurred, medium-sized brush shapes from the Brushes palette and dabbed a gray spot onto the white background. (Upon magnification, a soft edge on this gray dab is noticeable, a result of the paintbrush automatically anti-aliasing.)

3. He increased the contrast of the paint dab by 60% (Image → Adjust → Brightness/Contrast). This made the edge "harder" and reduced the chance of non-browser-safe colors being introduced when Brian used the paintbrush.

4. He selected and copied the paint dab using the rectangular Selection tool. Back in his original file containing the toilet bowl, he opened his Brushes palette and chose Define Brush from the pull-down menu. This loaded the new shape into the palette window, ready to be used in this illustration and others.

Once the brushes were created, he created the toilet bowl illustration:

1. He created a new file with a white background, and then loaded the browser-safe palette into his swatches.

2. He created a new layer and used a custom brush to paint the browser-safe green background.

3. He created a new layer and drew the lime-green vertical lines. Again, he used the custom brush to create the bold vertical lines. To create the dotted lines, he used the same brush but altered it by double-clicking on the brush shape in the Brush palette window, and setting the spacing to 190.

   Whenever Brian finishes with a layer, he selects Preserve Transparency in the Layers palette window. This way he saves the shape of the drawing, but if he wants, he can go back and change the color.

Losing color values

Keep in mind that when you convert from one color mode to another, as Corey Hitchcock did, you've created a permanent change to the color values of the image. When you go from RGB to Indexed Color and then back to RGB, the color values that were lost when indexed are never replaced just by going back to the RGB space. For this reason, it is advisable always to save a copy of the original RGB version.

Also keep in mind that converting to Indexed Color always flattens the layers of an image. If you want to edit the original version with the layers intact, be sure to save a copy of your image before indexing the color.

4. In other layers, Brian made the flowers and the toilet bowl, again using the paintbrush and the brush tip that he created. He almost always uses the Paintbrush tool, although sometimes when he wants to add shades of color, he will use the Airbrush or Dodge/Burn tools—as he did with the toilet bowl itself.

5. He converted his illustration to Indexed Color mode, applying Photoshop's Web palette. In some cases, he applies the Adaptive palette. For example, he did this with the peanut illustration shown in Figure 4-2 because he wanted to preserve the peanut's subtle shades of brown, which were not browser-safe. Since Brian was using Photoshop 4.0, which doesn't feature 5's Preserve Exact Color option in the Indexed Color dialog, the browser-safe green background shifted when he applied the Adaptive palette to the peanut illustration. He then had to go back to the illustration, select the now non-browser-safe green, fill it with browser-safe green, then reconvert his illustration once again to the Indexed mode. This time, the Exact palette was automatically selected.

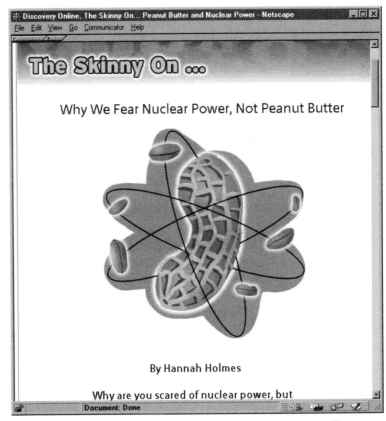

Figure 4-2. *"The Skinny On…" section featuring Brian Frick's peanut illustration.*

When the peanut illustration is seen on an 8-bit monitor, the brown dithers, but the background looks fine. When it is viewed on systems with a greater color capability, everything looks fine.

Working in Indexed Color mode

Designer Valerie Robbins likes a challenge, but that's not the reason she chose Photoshop's Indexed Color mode to create a self-portrait for her web page, as shown in Figure C-50. None of Photoshop's filters, plug-ins, or multilayer capabilities is available in the Indexed mode (drawing tools and some selection tools are available, however), but by working in Indexed Color mode, Valerie is guaranteed that her work contains only browser-safe colors. By controlling the exact number of colors that she used, she also created an image with a very small file size.

This is how she created the self-portrait:

1. She created a new RGB file, 200 × 200 pixels.

2. She changed mode from RGB to Indexed Color. In the Indexed Color dialog box, she chose Web palette and turned off dithering.

3. She loaded the browser-safe palette in the Swatches palette.

4. She filled the background with a blue from the browser-safe swatch.

5. To create the rounded, pea-green box, she made a rectangular selection and feathered the selection 10 pixels (Select → Feather).

6. To paint with the browser-safe colors in the Swatches palette, she clicked on a desired color, making it Photoshop's foreground color and painted with the Pencil and Brush tools. (She compares the process of "dipping" into the color palette and then painting to watercolor painting.) Painting in stages, she first applied the background, then built her drawing up step by step, each stroke applied on top of the previous one.

7. When she was finished, Valerie briefly switched back to the RGB mode. Because she had worked with fewer than 216 colors, the Exact palette was automatically selected when she went back to Indexed Color mode. Photoshop created a color look-up table containing only the colors in the self-portrait, keeping her file size down to a minimum.

Creating an illusion of translucency

Undaunted by the restrictions imposed on her by working in Indexed Color mode, Valerie Robbins figured out a way to create an illusion of translucency, as shown in Figures C-51 and C-52. This is a simple task when you have the benefits of layers, but to do this in Indexed Color mode, you have to rely on visual trickery.

Valerie created a transparent effect in Photoshop 4.0 by following these steps:

1. She created a new 200 × 200-pixel file in Indexed Color mode with a white background.

2. She made and filled a circle with a browser-safe yellow with the Circular Selection tool. (To create a perfect circle, hold down the Shift key while using the Circular Selection tool.)

3. She dragged the still-active circular selection completely to the right of the now-yellow circle.

4. She filled this selection with a browser-safe blue. At this point she had a yellow circle on the left and a blue circle on the right.

5. She dragged the still-active circular selection to the left until it was almost off the blue circle, leaving a crescent area of the blue circle selected. She then deselected the white and yellow areas outside of the selected blue area by Option/Alt-clicking with the Magic Wand. When she was finished, only the crescent area of the blue circle was selected.

6. She then filled this selection with a browser-safe green. She used the Magic Wand to add the rest of the blue circle to the selection, as shown in Figure C-51. With the Move tool, she dragged the now blue and green circle to meet the yellow circle, giving the illusion of a blending of the two colors, as shown in Figure C-52.

Hijacking a color palette

It's difficult to get web designers to admit it, but many of them often "borrow" color palettes from other web sites.

If you want to "hijack" a color palette, and you don't have a moral problem with it, first save the GIF to your system. In most browsers, you can place your cursor over the illustration or graphic you want, and click and hold (Mac) or right-click (Windows) to bring up a pop-up menu that lets you save the file. (There is no point in trying to hijack the colors contained in a JPEG image. JPEG images are not indexed and don't contain a color look-up table.)

Then open the graphic in Photoshop. Because the image is already indexed, you will be able to view its CLUT by selecting Image→ Mode→Color Table. All the colors found in the image will show up in the color palette, as shown in Figure C-53. Save this palette by choosing the Save button. Don't publish the image without getting permission, but the colors are now yours.

You can either apply this custom palette directly to an existing image (index the image, choose the Custom palette, and click the Load button to load your hijacked palette) or open the palette in the Swatches palette and use any of Photoshop's tools to paint, airbrush, fill, or draw with a color selected from the swatch.

Creating your own browser-safe colors

There are 216 colors that have been designated as browser-safe. These are the colors that won't dither or be exchanged when they are viewed on an 8-bit monitor regardless of the computer platform used.

However, you can create your own "hybrid" browser-safe colors and extend the number of safe colors well beyond 216. You can load these hybrid colors in your Swatches palette and paint or draw with them as you would any color. You can also fill selections with them by using the Photoshop's Fill command.

The principle of hybrid colors is similar to that of dithering: by choosing two or more colors and arranging them in a pattern, you can simulate the effect of a new, third color. Because you use only browser-safe colors to start, the third color will also be browser-safe.

Photoshop 5.5 includes DitherBox, a popular, formerly third-party filter that allows you to create custom dither patterns and save those patterns in groups called collections. To run DitherBox, choose Filter→Other →DitherBox. The dialog box is shown in Figure C-54. The filter makes it easy to create patterns based on collections of 4 to 64 web-safe colors.

The 4-pixel method

Here's what Brian Frick did to create a hybrid color, which he used in the background for the Discovery Online page:

1. He started by creating a new file of 2 × 2 pixels (72 dpi).

2. Then he set the Pencil tool to be 1-pixel wide.

3. He loaded a browser-safe swatch and chose a color. He used his 1-pixel pencil tip to place this color in the top-left and bottom-right pixels. He chose another browser-safe color from the swatches and filled the remaining pixels with this color, as shown in Figure C-55.

4. He selected Edit → Define Pattern. To fill a selection with this color, he selected an area, selected Edit → Fill, and chose Pattern in the Fill dialog box. This filled the area with the hybrid color.

Brian has created several hybrid colors this way and saved them in a custom swatch that he can access at any time.

The linear-stripe method

New York designer Tom Walker created his hybrid browser-safe colors a bit differently than Brian Frick, but his results are just as useful. As shown in Figure C-56, Tom created hybrid colors by filling 2-pixel-wide horizontal selections with browser-safe colors.

The random noise method

Tom used Photoshop's Add Noise filter to apply random noise to a selection of browser-safe colors, as shown in Figure C-57. To make sure that he hadn't introduced any non-web-safe colors, he indexed his work using the browser-safe palette.

On to transparency

Now that you've learned to use Photoshop both to convert existing graphics into the GIF file format and to create graphics from scratch using the browser-safe palette, it's time to move on to the next chapter, where you'll learn how to use Photoshop to designate specific areas as transparent and to make them pop dynamically from the electronic page. Onwards!

CHAPTER FIVE

SPECIAL EFFECTS WITH TRANSPARENT GIFs

Photoshop 5.5 offers the following ways to designate parts of your GIF graphic as transparent so your graphic will seem to float on a page, unrestrained by rectilinear edges:

- File → Save for Web
- Image → Mode → Indexed Color
- Image → Mode → Color Table
- File → Export → GIF89a Export

With earlier versions of Photoshop, including 5.0 and 5.02, the GIF89a Export module is your only option except for third party plug-ins, which are discussed in Appendix B, *Third-Party Software*.

Figure C-58 illustrates how awkward graphics can look on a web page without the benefit of transparency. In Figure C-59, the graphics blend seamlessly into the background, creating a clean and professional-looking page.

Save for Web

As we saw in Chapter 3, *Making Great GIFs*, Save for Web is a powerful tool for Indexing RGB images in preparation for the GIF file format. When it comes to transparency, however, it is a bit more limited, especially when compared with the GIF89a Export module. That's because all preparation for transparency must be done in the main Photoshop window before you run Save for Web. Once you are in Save for Web, if you decide to expand or contract your transparent areas you'll need to exit the plug-in and return to the main Photoshop window. There you can use one of the many Photoshop delete methods to get the transparency you want before returning to Save for Web. Once you learn to live with this limitation, you'll find

Figure 5-1. *There are three eraser tools in Photoshop 5.5: the regular eraser (left), the Background Eraser (middle), and the Magic Eraser (right).*

it's actually very easy to use the Save for Web plug-in to create transparent GIFs.

Figure C-60 shows a graphic created by designer Valerie Robbins. If I convert her graphic to the GIF format "as is" with the blue background, and place it on a web page with, say, a lime green background, the telephone and type will float in a rectangular patch of blue. That's not what I want, so I need to remove the blue background, and replace it with transparency. Then the graphic will float against the lime green background. Actually, if I make the blue area transparent, it doesn't matter what color my web page background is, the telephone and type will still appear to float against it.

Photoshop 5.5 includes three new tools to make cutting directly to transparency easy: the Magic Eraser and Background Eraser (see Figure 5-1) and the Extract tool (Image → Extract).

- The *Magic Eraser* erases all similar pixels when you click on an area within your image. You can choose a tolerance that defines a range of colors to be erased. (Normally, if you work on a background layer you cannot cut to transparency. However, when you use the Magic Eraser or the Background Eraser, a background layer is automatically converted into a normal layer that supports transparency.)

- The *Background Eraser* tool erases pixels to transparency by dragging through areas of your image, much like the regular eraser tool but with more erase options and controls.

- The *Extract* command opens your image in a new window where you must manually "paint" the edges of a foreground object. The Extract command then separates the defined edges from the background. In theory, this new tool makes it easy to separate objects that contain wispy, intricate, or undefinable edges from a background.

As it happens, I removed the blue from Val's graphic with the Color Range tool (Select → Color Range), a standard Photoshop technique for selecting areas of similar colors. Once I had a selection, I cut to transparency. (Background layers will not cut to transparency. To change the Background layer into a normal layer, double click on it, and when the dialog box appears, change the name to anything but Background.)

Here's what I did next:

1. I selected the layer that contained the graphic I wanted to index. (You don't have to flatten a multilayered file to apply the Save for Web plug-in. You can select specific layers, but be sure to turn off the eye icons for any layer you don't want to index.)

2. I chose File → Save for Web.

3. In the Save for Web window, I clicked on the Transparency checkbox, as shown in Figure 5-2. (This option is only available if your graphic contains transparent areas. If the box is left unchecked your transparent areas will appear in the optimized view as white, or whatever color you choose in the Matte color box. Once you click on the Transparency box, the transparent areas in your graphic will be designated by the familiar gray and white checkered pattern.)

4. I then choose the appropriate palette, dither, and colors, and optimized the graphic. (Optimizing is described in more detail in Chapter 3.)

5. I previewed my transparent GIF in a browser by clicking on the browser icon in the lower-right corner of the Save for Web box.

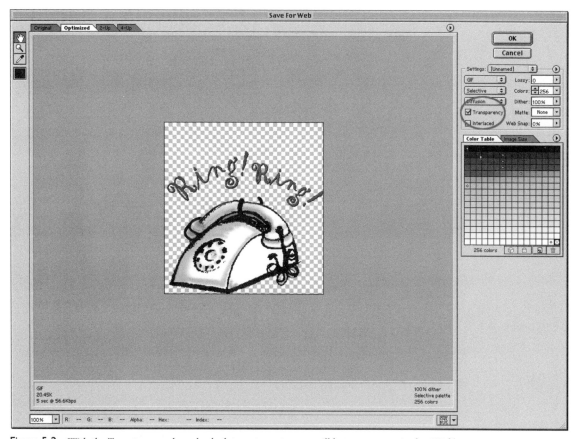

Figure 5-2. *With the Transparency box checked, transparent areas will be transparent in the GIF file.*

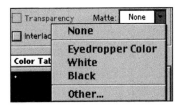

Figure 5-3. *Choose the background color from the Matte drop-down menu.*

At this point, I see a problem in the browser window, magnified in Figure C-61. Placed against a lime-green background, the jagged edges of the type are pronounced and unattractive. This is a problem that can and should be fixed.

Before I get into how to fix this problem, it's helpful to explain a basic fact about the GIF transparency. Variable opacity is not an option in the GIF format. GIF only supports one transparent color, which effectively means a 1-bit mask. Pixels are either transparent or not. A normal Photoshop mask, on the other hand, consists of 8 bits of information and is capable of variable transparency. You can apply a gray or other neutral color and create a semitransparent mask, resulting in just a portion of the background color showing through. By this means, you can achieve smooth, multitonal transitions between visible and invisible areas as in feathering and anti-aliasing. The PNG file format is capable of such 8-bit masks (see Appendix A, *The PNG Format*).

To get around the 1-bit mask limitation, you can have Photoshop create a pseudo-multibit mask. If you know the color of your background, all you need to do is chose that color from the Matte drop-down menu, as shown in Figure 5-3. Photoshop then adds variations of this color to edges of your graphic. If your web background consists of multiple colors, pick a representative color from your background and use that. Creating this pseudo-multibit mask adds some file size to your GIF, but not much. If your background consists of multiple areas of different colors, you'll need to resort to a workaround, detailed in the next section.

Back to my example.

Since I know the graphic will be placed on a page with a lime green background, I choose Other from the Matte drop-down menu, and then in the color picker I choose CCFF33, the hexadecimal value for my color. The selected color is displayed in the Matte box. (If you set the Matte to None, no pseudo-multibit mask is created. Use None if an aliased look is what you want or if you are using the workaround described in the next section.)

A blow up of the edges shows how Photoshop adds variations of the Matte color to the edges of the graphic. See Figure C-62. Now when the graphic is placed against the browser background there is nice anti-aliasing effect, as shown in Figure C-63.

Expanding selections to prevent jaggies and halos

What if I want my graphic to float against a more complex background, such as the one shown in Figure C-64? This background has no single representative color that I can use to create a pseudo-multibit mask with the Save for Web plug-in. I need to approach this problem a bit differently.

This time instead of just cutting to transparency, I'll place the telephone and type against a sample of the background pattern. Then I'll select the graphical elements, expand (or feather) my selection, and then cut to transparency. In this way, I can create my own custom pseudo-multibit mask that takes into account the complex background.

Here's exactly what I did:

1. Placed a sample of the background in a separate layer beneath the telephone and type layer.

2. Held down the Command/Control key, selected the telephone and type layer, and clicked. This automatically selected the elements in the layer.

3. Chose Select → Modify → Expand 1 pixel. See Figure C-65. (Sometimes Select → Feather works better. It depends on the background and the graphic.)

4. Copied the selection by using the Edit → Copy Merged command to include a 1-pixel border of my background colors.

5. Created a new layer and pasted the copied selection into it.

6. Selected the copied layer and turned off the eye icons in the other layers, as shown in Figure 5-4.

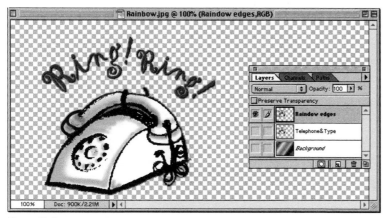

Figure 5-4. *Turning off the icons for undesired layers.*

7. Selected File → Save for Web

8. Turned on Transparency in the Save for Web window and for Matte, chose None, as shown in Figure 5-5.

9. Optimized the graphic and saved my work.

If you use this method, you'll have to be careful when you position the graphic against the actual web page background. The edges must line up for the effect to work.

Indexed Color mode

In Photoshop 5.5, you can also use the Image → Mode → Indexed Color method to designate transparent areas. In earlier versions of Photoshop, you can't use this method to create transparent GIFs. You'll have to use the GIF89a Export module or other third party plug-in.

Figure 5-5. *The image with transparency on and no matte color selected.*

In RGB mode:

1. Cut your background or other areas to transparent.

2. Select Image → Mode → Indexed Color.

3. Select the Transparency checkbox, as shown in Figure 5-6.

   If you know the background color of your web page, and you want to avoid a jagged or halo effect, have Photoshop create a pseudo-multibit mask. In the box next to the word Matte, choose from the presets or enter a color from the color picker. (See the previous section for an explanation of how this matte gets around the 1-bit limitations of the GIF file format.)

4. Select the optimal palette, dither, and color options.

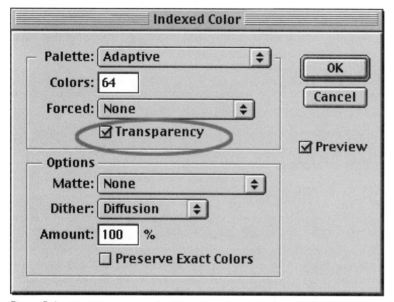

Figure 5-6. *The Transparency checkbox selected in the Indexed Color dialog.*

When you are finished, close the window and do a Save As, choosing the CompuServe GIF format. The areas signified by the gray and white checkers will become transparent.

Selecting Transparency in the Color Table

You can also use 5.5's Color Table to make colors in your indexed graphic transparent. After indexing your image:

1. Open the Color Table (Image → Mode → Color Table).

2. Use the eyedropper tool to select a color from within your graphic. You can also choose a color directly from the Color Table. Any single color you choose will become transparent, and will show up in the color table as a box with a checkered square in it as shown in Figure C-66.

Using the GIF89a Export module

The GIF89a Export module is included with Photoshop 5.5, 5.0, 5.02, 4.0 and with some later versions of Photoshop 3.0. You must have Version 3.01 or later to use the module. If you don't have the module, you can download it for free from Adobe's web site (*http://www.adobe.com/support/downloads/3082.htm*). Once you've downloaded it, place it in the Plug-ins folder within your Photoshop folder.

The module is called the GIF89a Export module rather than the GIF Export module because earlier versions of the GIF format (i.e., GIF87a) don't support transparency.

There are three ways to use the GIF89a Export module. Each method provides an appropriate solution for a variety of situations:

Color-based transparency
In Indexed Color mode, export the image and choose one or several colors to be transparent. This is the fastest and easiest method.

Selection-based transparency
In RGB mode, create a mask, index, and then export the image. The masked parts of the image will be transparent, regardless of the colors they contain. Although this method requires more work, it also offers the most control over how and where the transparency is applied.

Layers-based transparency
In a Photoshop file, export one or more layers as separate transparent GIFs. Any transparent pixels in the layer will be transparent in the exported GIF. This method is particularly useful if you are using Photoshop as a web layout tool.

The color method: quick and easy

Depending on which color mode you're in, you'll get a different GIF89a Export dialog. For this first method, let's assume you're working in Indexed Color mode, as Valerie Robbins and I did for the Sword of Heaven icon for my web site, Cyber-Bohemia. We created this graphic on a one-color background, and didn't use this color in the image itself. Exporting the graphic to GIF89a brings up the Export dialog box shown in Figure C-67.

A preview of the image appears in the top left of the dialog box. At the bottom is a palette of all the colors used in the image. To the right are a number of options and tools, including an eyedropper tool, a move tool (the hand), and a zoom tool. The eyedropper is used to select colors to be transparent, the hand is for positioning the image in the preview window, and the magnifying glass is to zoom into the image. Above these tools is a color swatch labeled Transparency Index Color (we'll get to that shortly).

It's very simple to make the gold background transparent. With the eyedropper tool selected, click anywhere in the gold background area. All the gold in the image turns gray, indicating that it is now transparent, as shown in Figure C-68.

If you want to make additional colors transparent, hold down the Shift key and click on other colors in the image. Alternatively, you can click or Shift-click on the color palette at the bottom to select colors for transparency. You can deselect a color by pressing Command/Control and clicking the color again. Before you click OK, you can restore all the original colors at any time by pressing the Option/Alt key (which changes the Cancel button to a Reset button) and clicking Reset.

Changing the default transparency color

There may be times when you don't want Photoshop to display transparent areas as gray. If your image contains gray, for instance, it may be confusing for gray to be the transparent color. You can select any color you want to indicate transparency; it doesn't really matter. To change the transparent index color to red, for example, just click on the color swatch to bring up Photoshop's color picker and select a different color. You can change the transparency index color only after you've made a transparent color selection.

It's worth going into detail about what this "transparent index" stuff is all about. While Photoshop presents the color palette of an image visually, in the actual GIF file the palette, or index, is a bunch of numbers with colors assigned to them. Rather than thinking about the specific colors in an image, the GIF file thinks in terms of index numbers. Each index number has a color value associated with it. Representing colors as RGB values, the value of 1 might be 60,20,255; the value of 2 might be 125,0,255; and so on.

So a GIF file actually associates index numbers (not absolute color values) with each pixel in the image: this pixel is color 0, this pixel is color 1, and so on. (Actually, GIF compresses images by not repeating data for every single pixel; when contiguous pixels have the same value, the index is just given once.) So how is transparency defined in a GIF file? A transparency flag is assigned to one index number. If the gold color in the previous example were color 0 in the index, then 0 would be flagged as transparent. The important point is that the index, not the actual color, defines transparency.

You can actually see this designated color if you open a GIF89a image and look at its CLUT (Image → Mode → Color Table). The color will usually be in the first or last position of the CLUT. You might also notice elsewhere in the CLUT a color that looks exactly the same. Because GIF is an indexed color format, it's entirely possible to have two index numbers with the exact same color value—but only one will be transparent.

When the color method doesn't work

The color-based method won't work if your background color is found elsewhere in the image. For example, I indexed a navigation bar from the Castle web page, choosing the Adaptive palette and diffusion dither because I wanted to maintain the soft shadows. I then ran the GIF89a Export module and began selecting colors with the eyedropper tool. Because the graphic contained some of the same colors found in the background, I ran into trouble, as shown in Figure C-69. Part of the graphic itself turned red, meaning it had become transparent. Placed on a web page, critical parts of the graphic would disappear. Oops.

So what's the solution for this color-bleeding effect? There are a couple of different approaches for making the background transparent but preserving the image:

- Change the background color.
- Mask off the image.

Preventing unwanted color bleeding

In many cases, there's a simple workaround for the color-bleeding problem we just described: just change the background color to some color not found in the image. That way, when the background color goes transparent, the image will remain intact. This method is insufficient for anti-aliased images and those that contain features like drop shadows. In these images, selecting a single background color as transparent results in a "halo" effect. Solutions for this problem are discussed in "The dreaded halo syndrome" section later in this chapter.

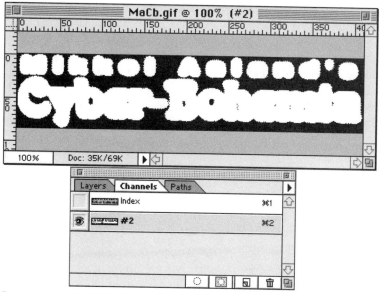

Figure 5-7. *When you open a GIF89a with a transparent color in Photoshop 5.0, 5.02, and 4.0, an editable mask appears in the Channels palette. When it is opened in 5.5, the transparent areas are designated by a checkered pattern which can also be edited.*

Editing transparent areas

Here's one of the coolest things about creating and editing transparent GIFs in Photoshop 5 and 4. When you open a GIF89a file (whether it was created in Photoshop or some other application), check the Channels palette. You'll see that Photoshop creates a channel mask of the transparent areas, as shown in Figure 5-7. This is a very powerful feature because it lets you add to or subtract from the transparent area by using standard painting and drawing tools. (With Photoshop 5.5, you won't see this channel mask. Instead, transparency is designated in the image window by a checkered transparency pattern, which can also be edited.)

You can also use channel masks in conjunction with the GIF89a Export module to define transparency from the get-go. See the later section "Working with masks."

To edit the transparent area, follow these steps:

1. In Photoshop 5.0, 5.02, and 4.0, open your GIF89a file. If it contains a transparent area or color, you will see the "mask" by viewing the Channels palette.

2. Open the channel containing the mask. You can add to the mask and therefore to the transparent areas by painting or airbrushing dark colors and subtract from the mask by adding lighter colors or erasing.

3. When you save, these new transparency settings will be applied.

Luke Knowland used this idea to produce a striking graphic for
HotWired's Web Monkey site, shown in Figure C-70. Because he
created a colored tint not found in other parts of the image, there is
no bleeding of the transparency effect into unwanted parts of the
image. Luke's original image of Wendy Owen was taken with a
Kodak DC-50 digital camera. Keep in mind that Luke's method is
useful only if you work with an image or graphic that lends itself to
tinting.

Here are the steps Luke took to create this graphic:

1. Opening the image in Photoshop, he used the Hue/Saturation
   dialog (Image → Adjust → Hue/Saturation) to desaturate the image
   until it was essentially a monotone image. Since that made the
   image quite flat, he boosted the brightness and contrast (Image
   → Adjust → Brightness/Contrast).

2. He created a new layer and filled it with pure blue (Red=0,
   Green=0, Blue=255). This blue will tint his monotone image and
   provide a color absent from the live image.

3. He made another new layer and pasted in a template with an
   orange background that he'd made, containing an oval shape
   with the letters "webmo," as shown in Figure C-70.

4. To blend the two layers, he selected Difference in the Layers
   palette blending pop-up menu. Using the Opacity slider, he
   chose 100%.

5. He changed modes to Indexed Color (Image → Mode → Indexed
   Color), flattened the layers, and selected the Adaptive palette
   with no dither.

6. In the GIF89a Export module, he clicked the eyedropper tool on
   the orange color he wanted to be transparent, confident that the
   orange color was absent from the blue-tinted photograph of
   Wendy. Figure 5-8 shows the (black) area that would be masked
   out or transparent.

7. He clicked OK and saved the file. Figure C-71 shows the final
   image on the web page.

Working with masks

There are times when applying a mask is the best way to go when
you want to add transparent areas to your graphic. This is my favorite
method to create transparent GIFs, but it requires an understanding
of Photoshop's powerful masking capabilities.

Let's go back to our earlier example of the navigational graphic,
described in "When the color method doesn't work." The image

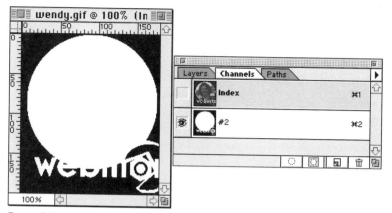

Figure 5-8. *The black defines the area to be transparent.*

contained the same color as the background. Selecting the background color as transparent also made those portions of the image transparent. One way to avoid this would be to select a different color (one not found in the image), but this is insufficient for anti-aliased images.

By creating a Photoshop mask, however, we could have controlled the area of transparency instead of the color. This, in effect, would protect our graphic and keep it intact, but make the areas outside of it go away or become transparent.

To create a mask that protects specific parts of your image, you can:

- Make a selection, either with selection tools or the Color Range dialog (Select → Color Range) and save it as a channel (Select → Save Selection).

- Make a selection and then create a Quick Mask.

Masks appear in the Channels palette where you can edit them at any time.

Applying masks with GIF89a

Once you've created your transparency mask, apply it to your image in the GIF89a Export module by selecting it from the Transparency From pull-down menu, as shown in Figure C-72. In this example, the mask is identified as Quick Mask. The name you'll see will be whatever you've called the channel that contains the mask.

When you choose a channel from the Transparency From menu, the GIF89a Export module automatically applies the mask to your image, making the masked areas transparent. In the preview window, you'll see exactly how the mask is applied.

Saving photos as GIFs

This chapter has several examples of photos saved as GIFs, rather than JPEGs. There are times when you should choose to save a photograph in the GIF format, especially if you want to utilize the handy GIF89a transparency feature.

Just keep in mind that saving a photo in the GIF format means two things: first, you won't be able to achieve the smallest possible file size, and second, you'll have only 256 shades of gray or color to work with.

Although you can still get good results—especially with Photoshop 5's improved color indexing capabilities—you'll need to experiment. Some photos look good only if you use the Adaptive palette and diffusion dither. Sometimes you'll need to tweak the Adaptive palette, and sometimes, especially with monotone photos, you can use a browser-safe palette with no diffusion and get good results.

Selecting transparency via masks instead of colors offers much more control over transparency in GIF images. Once you get the hang of it, you'll be hooked.

Going for speed and control

Photoshop wizard Brian Frick efficiently used the masking technique to create a smart-looking page for a Discovery story on computer hackers, shown in Figure C-73. (Pay particular attention to step 8, where Brian quickly creates a mask from a transparent layer. Learning shortcuts such as this one will improve the ease and productivity with which you create transparent GIFs.)

1. Brian began by drawing the illustrations on paper, as shown in Figure 5-9, and then scanned them as 1-bit graphics.

2. In Photoshop, he selected the white background area with the Magic Wand, and deleted it, leaving only the black outlines of the letters against a now-transparent background.

3. To make his graphics look chunky and fit the spirit of the story, he clicked the Paint Bucket and turned off Anti-alias in the Paint Bucket Options palette.

4. He filled the letters with browser-safe colors.

5. He opened a separate file that contained the background.

6. He selected and copied the "hackers" graphic.

Figure 5-9. *Brian created the text and graphics by hand, then scanned them and filled them with color in Photoshop.*

7. With the two files open, he pasted the graphic file into the background file. This created a new layer in the background file. He
named the graphic layer *screen* and the background layer
Pattern.

By selecting the illustration and placing it against the busy
background, Brian was able to visually inspect the relationship
between the illustration and the background, a valuable step in
ascertaining the overall effectiveness of his work.

8. To quickly create a channel mask, he held down the Command/
Control key and clicked on the screen layer in the Layers palette.
Presto! This instantly selected the graphics on that layer, and he
saved the selection, thus creating a mask. In Figure 5-10, the
mask appears as channel #4 in the Channels palette.

9. Then he merged the two layers and indexed the image with the
Web palette, no dithering.

10. To reduce the number of colors in the file, he converted back to
RGB mode, then indexed the image again, this time selecting the
Exact palette. This reduced the number of colors from 216 to 29,
reducing the file size.

11. He exported the image to GIF89a, selecting channel #4 as his
mask to make the background transparent, shown in
Figure C-74.

Exactly the effect he was looking for! He then went back and
performed the same process on the two remaining parts of the
graphic.

The dreaded halo syndrome

In the previous example, Brian worked with aliased graphics to
achieve a particular, but often unwanted, hard-edged effect. But what
happens when we apply a mask to anti-aliased text, or to a graphic
with a soft drop shadow, such as the navigation bar for the Castle
page we looked at earlier? If you're not careful, you'll end up with
the dreaded halo effect—a colored edge around the image, which
you'll see if you skip ahead to Figure C-75.

The following step-by-step example describes how I created and
edited a Quick Mask and applied the mask to the navigational bar
using the GIF89a Export module. Although I created a graphic that
"floats" on a web page, I lost the smooth look of the drop shadow
because I didn't take into account the halo effect.

Here's what I did:

1. I selected the navigation bar.

Fast merging

For a quick way to merge
layers, in the Layers
palette, hold down
Option/Alt while clicking
on the line between the
two layers.

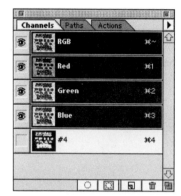

Figure 5-10. *The mask in channel
#4 becomes available as a
transparency mask in the GIF89a
Export module.*

2. I clicked the Quick Mask icon at the bottom of the Toolbox, turning the selection into a Quick Mask, which appears in the Channels palette, as shown in Figure 5-11. I didn't make any changes to the mask, but at this point, one can edit the mask with the Airbrush, Paintbrush, Selection, or Eraser tools. To add to the mask, use colors as dark as or darker than the mask. To subtract from the mask, use colors lighter than the mask.

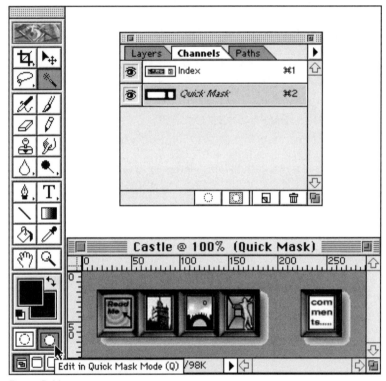

Figure 5-11. *First create a selection.*

3. I switched to Indexed Color mode and then ran the GIF Export module. (You must be in Indexed Color mode to use quick masks with the GIF module.)

4. In the dialog, I selected Quick Mask from the Transparency From pop-up menu and clicked OK (see Figure 5-12). Figure C-75 shows the problematic result.

So how could I have avoided the halo effect and kept the gradual tonal transition of the drop shadow? There are a couple of solutions to the halo problem. First, you can avoid using anti-aliased text or graphics like Brian did. This is fine for certain graphics and small text that you want to appear crisp and readable. But for most graphics

Figure 5-12. *Finally, apply the Quick Mask to the image using the GIF89a Export module.*

and larger text this isn't a practical solution. The jagged edge of aliasing can be distracting unless it is deliberately used for a special effect (as in Brian's case).

The real solution is to produce your graphic against the background color you'll use on your page. When you place the graphic on the page, the anti-aliasing blends with the background, resulting in a halo-free page. If you have a multicolor background, you can use a dominant color from your background. The next two sections explain how to do this.

Using the same color background

A simple and practical solution to these limitations of GIF89a is to create your graphic against the background color of your web page. When you create a mask, don't mask out the soft edges of your text or any shadows that you want to retain. It doesn't matter if you pick up some of the background color because the colors will blend when the graphic is placed against the web page of the same color.

This is what I did to get the effect shown in Figure C-76. I followed the same procedures outlined above to create and apply a Quick Mask to my navigational bar, except this time, I began by placing my navigational bar on the web page background image.

This method works best when your background is a single color. If your background contains many colors, you'll need to use the next method.

Preserving an anti-aliased look with a multicolored background

For a Discovery story on tornadoes, our man Frick has found yet another technique to avoid unwanted halos and keep the soft, anti-aliased look even when the background is multicolored. The key here is Brian's choice of a dominant color from the cascade of colored strips that make up his background:

1. He began by selecting a dominant color from his web page's multicolored, tiled background.

2. He then created a new file and filled a background layer with that color.

3. He placed anti-aliased text on top of the color and indexed the image. After experimenting with different color-depth options, he finally chose the Adaptive palette and 7-bit color depth with diffusion dithering.

4. Finally, he selected the background of the image as a transparent color. This drops out not only the background of the image but also some colors in the type, as shown in Figure C-77. But here's the thing: it doesn't matter. When the graphic is placed on the web page, the missing color is supplied by the page's background.

As shown in Figure C-78, Brian successfully maintained the anti-aliased look that he set out to achieve.

Transparency direct from layers

A third method of creating transparent areas or colors requires that you target one or more specific transparent Photoshop layers and export those layers directly into the GIF89a Export module. When you apply the GIF89a Export module, all the areas that were transparent in your layers will remain transparent when you open your graphic on a web background.

This method is very useful if you are using Photoshop as a web page layout tool, as described in Chapter 11, *Laying Out Pages in Photoshop*. You can keep your file intact and convert individual layers containing specific graphics one at a time into the GIF89a format. It's also convenient for creating GIF animations, since you can create your entire animation in one Photoshop file and export each layer out as a separate GIF file.

Using this layer method, you'll still have to go through several steps to create a graphic that contains a transparent area. And you'll have to rely on the merely sufficient indexing tools in the GIF89a Export module.

To use layers to create transparent GIFs, follow these steps:

1. Organize all the graphics for your web page in layers. (See Figure 5-13.)

2. Target and select the layer or layers containing the image you want to export. Turn off the eye icons for all other layers. If you keep other eye icons on, you'll export more layers than you want.

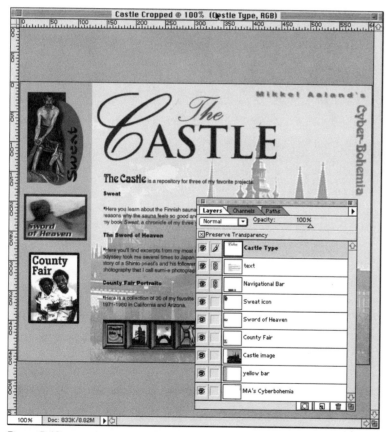

Figure 5-13. *Create transparency from layers by targeting the layer you want to export. Be sure to turn off the eye icons from the layers you don't want to export.*

3. Crop the file to the size you want to export, so the final GIF won't contain large blank areas.

4. Choose the GIF89a Export module; notice how the GIF89a dialog shown in Figure 5-14 differs from the dialogs we've seen earlier. This is because our graphic is still in the RGB mode, and needs to be indexed. With this dialog, you can choose how your RGB graphic is color indexed (with the Palette and Colors settings) and what color will be used as the background color (Transparency Index Color). You can also choose Load for custom color palettes, such as the browser-safe palette. Keep in mind that even with all these options, the GIF89a Export module doesn't give you as much control over the indexing process as you would have if you went directly from RGB to Indexed Color mode in Photoshop. However, if you want to use the layer method described here, you have no choice but to use the GIF89a Export module's indexing options.

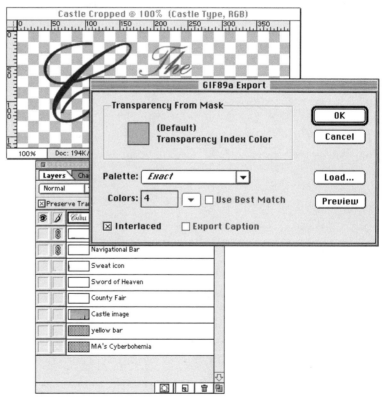

Figure 5-14. *When you export a layer from Photoshop to the GIF89a Export module, you get this dialog box.*

Click Preview after you've chosen your color indexing options. The
Preview dialog appears, as shown in Figure 5-15. The color swatch at
the bottom shows exactly what and how many colors are contained
in the graphic. You cannot edit these colors. You can use the Hand
tool to move the image around the frame and the Zoom tool to zoom
in and out. Click OK to close the dialog.

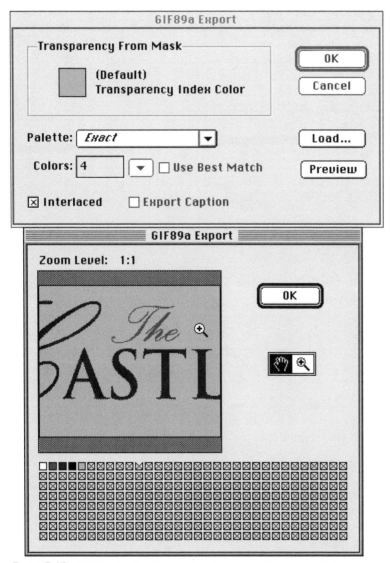

Figure 5-15. *Clicking Preview brings up a separate box that shows what your
indexed image will look like.*

You can reset the image to its original colors by pressing Option/Alt and clicking Reset. Once you're satisfied with the results, click OK, and name and save your GIF file.

When you export a Photoshop layer to the GIF89a Export module, you will achieve a transparent effect only if your layer is transparent.

How can you tell if you are working with a transparent layer? Easy: a checkered pattern is visible (or whatever pattern you've set your transparency settings to in Preferences). If no checks are visible, you've either inadvertently left on additional layers or you are working with a background layer. Be sure all eye icons are off, except the one on the targeted layer.

Creating glow effects with the layer method

Using a transparent layer and the GIF89a Export module, it's easy to create a soft, dreamy effect that will add zing to your web page. To have your graphic actually appear to glow, follow these steps:

1. With any of the selection tools, select the portion of your graphic that you want to glow.

2. Feather the selection (Select → Feather) at least 10 pixels, as shown in Figure C-79.

3. Choose Select → Inverse and delete the selected area, as shown in Figure C-80.

4. If you are working with a single-layer image, double-click the Background layer and rename it, so the layer can contain transparency. If you are working with an image containing multiple layers, be sure to target the layer you are working on and turn off the eye icons of the other layers.

5. Open the GIF89a Export dialog. Notice the Transparency Index Color box—this is the secret to creating that cool look. It is set at default gray, but you can click on it to change it to any other color with the color picker. Use the color picker to choose a color that matches the color of your web page background.

Figure C-81 shows the results of setting the transparency index color to the same color as the web page background. Voila! It now has the soft, dreamy glow.

If you leave the transparency index color at the default gray, you won't like the results, shown in Figure C-82. This is because Photoshop achieves the glow by mixing variations of the transparency index color you chose into the edges of your graphic. If you chose a transparency index color other than the color of your web page background, the wrong colors will be added and the effect will be lost.

A transparent look without transparent colors

You can create a transparent look without using the GIF89a Export module. Simply create your graphic on a sample of the background color or pattern. The background of your graphic will merge with the background of the page when you place it on a web page, making the graphic appear to float in space.

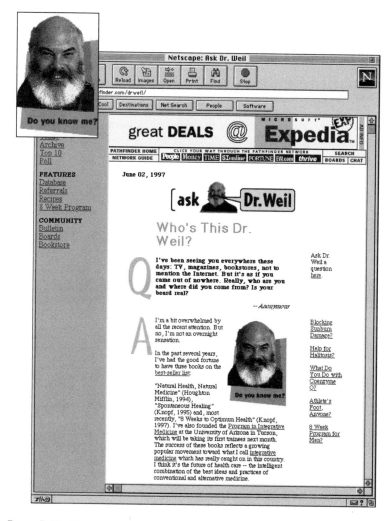

Figure 5-16. *The original GIF was created against a white background with no designated transparency. When placed on a web page with a white background, it appears to float on the page.*

This method has its limitations. (Anything this simple must have a drawback, right?) Background colors often shift from platform to platform and from browser to browser. This means your image may be left high and dry on a viewer's monitor, its rectilinear edges evident against the web page background. And of course it won't work at all on patterned backgrounds.

Designer Judd Vetrone used this technique effectively in Photoshop to simply cut and paste a photo onto a white background, the same color as his web page background (shown in Figure 5-16). He used the GIF file format because the image was small to begin with and he could be assured that there would be no color shift between the background color of the image and the background color of the page.

Familiarity counts

The ability to create transparent areas in your graphic is fundamental to good web design. In this chapter, we've shown you several methods of achieving this look. Clearly, it's not always easy to get the perfect look. However, what seemed difficult at first will become routine with a little time and effort.

CHAPTER SIX

JPEG: ALL THE COLOR YOU WANT

N
ow that you've seen that creating GIFs for the Web can be as tedious as rebuilding a car engine—from selecting a color palette, choosing the optimal color depth, and deciding whether or not to dither—you're in for a pleasant surprise. Creating JPEGs for the Web is the automotive equivalent of changing your engine oil.

This chapter is organized into four main parts. In the first part, "Compression versus quality," you'll learn the effects of compression settings on image quality and file size. In the second part, "Saving JPEG files," you'll learn how to use Photoshop 5.5's Save for Web plug-in and how to work with the limitations of earlier versions of Photoshop. In the third part, "Optimizing for compression," you'll learn tricks for preparing an image before applying JPEG compression. In the fourth part, "Other JPEG issues," you'll learn how to convert from GIF to JPEG and how to use JPEGs for browser backgrounds. There is also a special section on making better grayscale images.

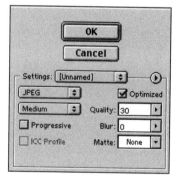

Figure 6-1. *Save for Web's JPEG options.*

Compression versus quality

To get a JPEG just right, you need to strike a fine balance between quality and file size. With Photoshop, you can choose how much compression is applied. If you apply too little compression, you'll have a beautiful image that's way too big for the Web.

With Photoshop 5.5, you can choose compression settings for your image both in the Save for Web plug-in window (Figure 6-1) and when you choose Save, Save As, or Save a Copy and select the JPEG file format (Figure 6-2). In Photoshop 4,0, 5.0, and 5.02, compression settings are available only when you choose Save, Save As, or Save a Copy and select the JPEG file format. See Figure 6-3.

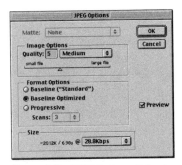

Figure 6-2. *JPEG Options dialog in Photoshop 5.5.*

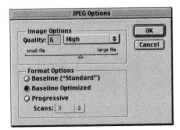

Figure 6-3. *JPEG Options dialog in earlier versions.*

The level of compression is set by a slider that is organized by image quality, with 10 (100 in Save for Web) offering the highest quality and the least compression and 0 the worst quality and the most compression. Photoshop also offers a drop-down menu with four quality settings—Low, Medium, High, and Maximum—which correspond to numeric values on the slider.

Although the maximum JPEG setting in Save for Web is basically the same as the maximum setting in the other versions of Photoshop, its lowest setting produces more compression. This is certainly an improvement, but the JPEG format offers more compression than even Save for Web is capable of. The HVS JPEG and ProJPEG plug-ins, for instance, offer higher possible compression settings. See Appendix B, *Third-Party Software*, for more about these and other Photoshop plug-ins.

Because JPEG images can contain up to 16.8 million colors and still compress to a small file size, JPEG is best used on photographic images and graphics that contain subtle gradations in tone or color. Because it's a "lossy" technology—it literally throws away high-frequency data—JPEG is not good for line drawings, text, or any graphic than contains intricate detail. Unlike with the GIF89a file format, you cannot make part of a JPEG image transparent. Photoshop 5.5 does, however, offer pseudo JPEG transparency via its new matte option.

Compression comparison

Let's look at some examples. I've used 5.5's Save for Web plug-in to apply compression to a photograph of a parrot to give you an idea of how JPEG compression works. The plug-in is especially great for applying JPEG compression not only because it give you a real-time view of the effects of different compression settings, but by choosing 4-Up, you can view the original, uncompressed image, and three versions with different compression settings applied to each.

In the upper-left corner of Figure C-83 you can see my original photo, magnified 152%. The file size is listed below the image, 117K. To the right of that version is another version with a compression setting of 100. It is 51.37K. In the lower left is an image with a compression setting of 40, and it is 8.177K. The last version is in the lower-right corner, and at the lowest compression setting of 0, it is only 3.38K. As you can see, there's not as much image degradation as you might expect, even at the maximum compression setting. (Remember I've magnified the images so the effects are exaggerated.)

While you might suppose that each step reduced the file size by a standard amount, this is not the case, at least for this image. (Every image is different and the effects of JPEG compression will vary depending on the characteristics of your image.)

Notice, for instance, that the image compressed at 100 is just less than half the original (2:1) and the image compressed at 40 is a 14 times less than the original's file size (14:1). But compressing the file at 0 yields a file that is 34 times less the size of the original.

Amazingly, even at 34:1 compression, the parrot image holds up pretty well. But as mentioned above, Photoshop's 0 setting isn't really maximum JPEG compression. Photoshop plug-in HVS JPEG offers much more extreme compression than this. Admittedly, you may not want to push compression much further than Photoshop's maximum compression setting, but it's handy to be able to compress heavily when you want to.

So what does an over-compressed image look like? Figure C-84 is a fair example. This image has been compressed at HVS JPEG's 6 setting, which yields a 1.3K file, for a 90:1 compression rate. Obviously this image is unacceptable. The image has broken down into blocks of color. There are hard lines around each block and very poor color transitions between adjacent blocks.

How JPEG compression works

What's happening here? This image actually provides a good view into the behavior of the JPEG compression algorithm. When you save a file as a JPEG, the algorithm samples the image in 8 × 8 squares— one at a time. It's looking for similarities in tone and contrast. It then transforms each block into mathematical equations that represent the relevant color and brightness values. Saving data this way is much more efficient than saving the RGB values of each pixel, but the process discards RGB data that is deemed less important.

At lower compression rates, we usually don't notice that data is missing, because JPEG takes advantage of the psycho-physics of human perception and throws away the spatial frequencies (mostly the higher ones) that the human eye is least likely to notice. At higher compression rates, more and more data is thrown away, until the image breaks down.

To understand high and low spatial frequency, think of a bearded man's face: the thousands of fine strands of hair that make up the beard are considered high spatial frequency, while the smooth, relatively consistent areas of exposed skin are of low spatial frequency.

If you magnify a highly compressed JPEG image, you can actually see the distinct blocks of pixels that are the artifacts of this sampling process, as shown in Figure C-85. The more compression that has been applied, the more evident these squares are.

As we saw above, the parrot photograph, with its subtle gradations and generally soft characteristics, compressed quite well. Generally, softer or more impressionistic images maintain quality at higher compression rates, while very detailed images do not. Also, images with lower contrast compress more, with less degradation, than images with higher contrast, as shown in Figures C-86 and C-87.

Saving JPEG files

Now that you have a better understanding of what happens in JPEG compression, let's look at the process of saving JPEG files in different versions of Photoshop.

Creating JPEGs in Save for Web

When you choose File → Save for Web, you are faced with several options. Before changing any of the settings, click on the Original tab in the upper-left side of the Save for Web plug-in window.

Now follow these steps:

1. Select the JPEG format from the pop-up window.

2. Deselect the Progressive box, and select the Optimized box. Progressive creates a JPEG that downloads in increments, but isn't read by all browsers. Optimized creates a better and smaller JPEG file. (A detailed explanation of these settings is found in the sidebar, "JPEG formats.")

3. Deselect the ICC Profile box, if it is selected, to prevent Photoshop from adding basically useless information to your file. This will only be an option if your Photoshop color preferences are set to include ICC color profiling, which I recommend against.

4. Choose 4-Up from the tab in the upper-left corner of the Save for Web window. Obtaining the smallest possible file while maintaining acceptable image quality is a matter of trial and error. With four views showing the effects of different settings, it's much easier to compare and decide on the optimal setting.

5. Apply the High setting from the pop-up window to the first image, and then apply Medium for the second, and Low for the third. When you preview the compressed images, use the Save for Web zoom tool and look for loss of detail or for compression artifacts. Keep in mind, however, that viewers will ultimately see your work at 100%, so don't get too hung up on how the magnified image looks.

Sometimes, depending on the image, you can produce very good quality at Photoshop's lowest setting. Even the 0 setting can be used on some images. You can get the 0 setting by using the compression slider or by typing in a numerical value in the Quality box. Most often you'll settle on Photoshop's Medium setting, which is a good compromise between quality and file size.

Another point to remember is that you always lose some data when you compress with JPEG. If you want your image viewed at its best—if you are a visual artist, for example, presenting your portfolio for art directors to view and evaluate—you'll probably settle for only the highest quality settings. Keep in mind that even when you choose Maximum, there is some loss of image quality that can never be replaced.

As discussed earlier, JPEG is not a very good format for text and lines. If you must use JPEG on images with sharp-colored edges, you'll get better results if you choose the Maximum setting. At this setting, Photoshop automatically turns off Chroma downsampling, a process that works well with photographic images but causes fuzziness or jaggedness around the edges of hard lines. Chroma downsampling samples color areas at a rate of 2 × 2 pixels rather than 1 × 1 pixel. This relatively coarse method of throwing away color data results in smaller file sizes but creates 2 pixel jaggies around sharp color boundaries.

JPEG formats

There are three format options for JPEG files:

Baseline (Standard)
> This is the default setting, since it is universally supported.

Baseline (Optimized)
> This option was introduced in Photoshop 4 and represents an evolution in the JPEG standard. When you choose this option, you get an image slightly smaller in file size (a couple hundred bytes) with better color fidelity. Current web browsers support this format. There are, however, other (mostly older) programs that have trouble opening a baseline-optimized JPEG. If you have any doubts about what program will be used to open your image, you should choose the Baseline (Standard) option.

Progressive
> See the "Progressive JPEGs" sidebar later in this chapter.

Faking JPEG transparency in 5.5

The JPEG file format does not support transparency; however, Photoshop 5.5 includes a new feature that creates a pseudo-transparent look. It works like this: if your Photoshop file contains transparent areas, as signified by the gray and white checkered boxes you can select, the Matte option is available in either the Save for Web plug-in or the JPEG option box that comes up when you choose File → Save, Save As, or Save a Copy.

If you turn on the Matte option, you will also need to choose a matte color. This color should be the color of your web page background. Photoshop then fills the transparent areas with this color, blending the edges with variations to make a smooth transition. See Figure C-88. When you view your graphic on a web page, it will seem to float against the background. Of course, it's not really floating, and if you have a complex background, or you change your mind and use another background color, what seemed transparent will now look ridiculous. Another thing to keep in mind is the fact that there is no such thing as browser-safe colors in JPEG files. Colors shift unexpectedly when JPEG compression is applied. Even if you carefully choose a browser-safe matte color for your JPEG, once compressed, the color will never exactly match another browser-safe background color.

Save for Web's global blurring

As we've noted, the JPEG compression works more efficiently on images that contain fewer details. The global blurring found in the Save for Web plug-in window allows you to apply a global Gaussian blur that reduces the high frequency data in your image. The results are an image with a smaller file size. The more blurring, the smaller the file size. Generally small amounts of blur won't effect the quality of the image while larger blurring will. For a more sophisticated approach to optimizing before you apply the JPEG compression refer to the section "Optimizing for compression" later in this chapter.

The File → Save method

With 5.5, you can also create a JPEG by choosing File → Save, Save As, or Save a Copy. When you select the JPEG file format, you get the dialog box shown in Figure 6-2. Just like in Save for Web, you can choose your compression settings, JPEG format, and, if your original Photoshop files includes transparent areas, even add a pseudo-matte. By selecting Preview, you can get a real-time view of the effects of your JPEG settings on your original image. Zoom in and out using the normal Photoshop zoom commands to get a better view of the effects. Disregard the file size estimate; it is not accurate.

In Photoshop Versions 4.0, 5.0, and 5.02, when you're ready to save your file as a JPEG, simply select Save, Save a Copy, or Save As, change the file format to JPEG, give your file a name with the extension *.jpg* or *.jpeg*, and click OK. Note that if you have multiple layers, you'll have to flatten the layer before the Save As dialog will let you save it as anything but a Photoshop file. The Save a Copy dialog, however, automatically flattens the image when you choose the JPEG format.

Next, you'll see the JPEG Options dialog, shown earlier in Figure 6-3, which contains the compression slider as well as a choice of format options, and an option to Save paths. I recommend using Optimized but avoiding Progressive. See the sidebar, "JPEG formats" for more on this topic.

Because there are no preview capabilities with these versions of Photoshop, you'll have to apply your settings, save, and then examine the results. However, the first time you save a JPEG, you may be surprised to see that the compressed JPEG file looks just as good as your original Photoshop file. Actually, it doesn't. Unfortunately, Photoshop doesn't display the effects of JPEG compression upon saving. You'll need to close and then reopen the image file to see what your new file looks like. This is where the capabilities of Save for Web and other JPEG plug-ins really excel.

> ## Exclude Non-Image Data
>
> With Photoshop 5.5, 5.02, and 5.0, if you choose to save an image in the JPEG format by choosing File → Save a Copy, you must remember to select the Exclude Non-Image Data option, as shown in Figure 6-4. If you don't Photoshop will include such data as ICC color profile settings in your JPEG. For the web, this data is not necessary, and it adds file size to your JPEG to boot.

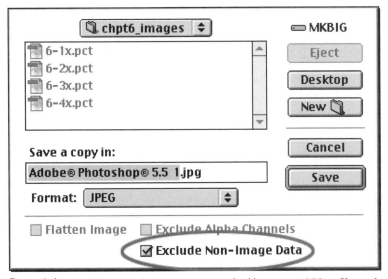

Figure 6-4. *Check the Exclude Non-Image Data checkbox to omit ICC profiles and other unnecessary data.*

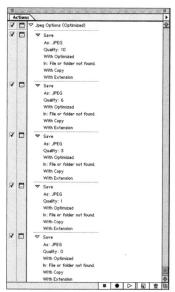

Figure 6-5. *Action for saving several versions of a file at different JPEG settings.*

Automating the process

If you have a lot of images, there's no doubt about it—cycling through all the JPEG settings for every image is a real pain. Why not set up an Action to save your file at different compression settings, so you can easily compare and decide which setting you want? That's what Sean Parker of Parker Grove did. His JPEG comparison action, shown in Figure 6-5, makes it quick and easy to compare effects of different compression settings in Photoshop.

To create such an Action, simply record the process of saving a file in the JPEG format at different compression settings. Save this Action as your JPEG Action, and apply it when needed.

Troubleshooting

If you're having trouble saving your file as a JPEG, make sure you've taken care of the following details:

- When you save an image in Photoshop, JPEG is an option only if your image is in the RGB (or CMYK) mode.

- All layers must be flattened before the JPEG option is available.

- Also note that if you have set your preferences to append the file suffix, Photoshop 4.0 adds *.JPG* to your file name. Many servers don't accept capital letters, so it's a good idea to retype the appended letters in lowercase. Version 5 adds the *.jpg* in lowercase.

- Be sure to turn off the thumbnail options to keep the file size as small as possible.

Optimizing for compression

As we have shown, JPEG works best on images that contain smooth transitions between colors and details. You can use this knowledge to actually optimize an image so it compresses better with less loss of quality.

Selective blurring

Let's start by selectively applying a Gaussian blur before applying JPEG compression. This method can be applied to any image that has large expanses where detail is not critical. It is a method popular with web designers who are willing to spend a little extra time to get both small file size and high quality.

Figure C-89 shows an image with a large expanse of background area (sky and clouds) and details in the foreground (foliage and cityscape). The original Photoshop file is 300 × 440 pixels and 398K. Saved with Photoshop's Low setting, with no optimizing, the file is 50.3K.

By blurring the selected background (with the Gaussian Blur filter set to 0.6) before JPEG compression, the file size is reduced to 47K, a 6% file size savings, with no loss of important details (see Figure C-90).

To push the benefits of blurring a little further, you can apply a Gaussian blur of 0.2 to the entire landscape—in addition to the 0.6 Gaussian blur applied to the sky. This results in a total savings of 14%. The resulting image is shown in Figure C-91.

Global blurring

Making images look good on the Web is a matter not only of aesthetics but also of commerce for photographer, writer, and fine-print master, Ctein. Not represented by any gallery, he uses the Web to sell his work.

Ctein (that's his whole name) tweaks his electronic files to maximize quality, and the results are impressive. Figure C-92 shows a sampling of Ctein's web work. Working with a precisely calibrated monitor and Photoshop, he carefully adjusts the color and tonal balance of his scanned images, comparing the results with the original print. Then he applies a Gaussian blur to the entire image. He uses a blur radius of only 0.2 pixels, which does not produce any visible degradation of the image but results in JPEG files that are about 15% smaller than files of comparable quality. Even slight blurring, it turns out, will suppress some of the higher spatial frequencies enough to significantly reduce the JPEG file.

When Ctein uses Photoshop to convert his files to the JPEG file format, he usually uses a JPEG setting of 5, which results in a compression ratio of approximately 10:1. (This ratio will vary depending on the content of the image.) For some images he applies a setting of 6 or even 7. He is always looking for a compression setting that produces few or no artifacts larger than a single pixel in size.

All his images are placed against a neutral gray background that includes a grayscale swatch, so the viewer can calibrate his or her own monitor to the correct gamma, if desired, for the best viewing of Ctein's work. Ctein also includes a Macbeth color chart on his site as a general calibration tool. The Macbeth color chart is a standardized "test pattern" of colors such as pure red, green, and blue and tones such as white, black, and various shades of neutral gray. It is commonly used by photographers and graphic artists to maintain consistent color and tone throughout a variety of viewing situations.

Checking the code

Although *.jpg* is the universally accepted file suffix for JPEG files, you'll never see the acronyms JPG or JPEG if you view the actual code of a JPEG file. That's because JPEG refers only to a family of compression algorithms, not to a specific file format. Instead, what you'll likely see is the acronym JFIF, which stands for JPEG File Interchange Format.

Ctein has sold many of his prints directly to web viewers. As testimony to his careful work, only one person has returned a print saying it's not what they expected. You can find his site at *http://www.plaidworks.com/ctein*.

Blurring in Lab mode

Photographer (and HyperCard inventor) Bill Atkinson suggests another way to optimize an image before applying JPEG compression. Like Ctein's method described previously, Bill's technique also involves using Gaussian blur to suppress higher spatial frequencies. However, if you convert your image from RGB to Lab color and then apply a Gaussian blur to the a and b channels, you can actually apply much more blur and suppress more of the higher frequencies without noticeable effects. The a and b channels are pure color channels, so because of the nature of human vision, blurring isn't as noticeable.

The actual Gaussian blur setting you use depends on the size of your image. I suggest you start with a setting of 0.5 pixels and keep increasing the amount of blur until you overdo it. Then back off to a lower setting. After you convert back to RGB, apply JPEG compression. The larger your image, the more savings you'll get.

I tried Bill's method on the parrot image, ending up with a Gaussian blur setting of 5.0 with no noticeable degradation in image quality. At that setting, I shaved off 3K using Photoshop's High JPEG setting for a savings of about 10%, and I shaved off 2K from the Low JPEG setting for a 15% file size saving.

Premium JPEGs: A case study

Bill Atkinson is a legend in the computer industry. Not only was he on the Apple computer team that created the Macintosh, he is the programmer who wrote the original QuickDraw program as well as MacPaint and HyperCard. Now he is retired and devotes his time to his passion, photography.

With his wife, graphic designer Sioux Atkinson, and fellow Apple legend Andy Herzfeld, Bill set up a web site to display and sell original prints of his photographic work, *http://www.natureimages.com*, shown in Figure C-93.

Bill achieves a beautiful effect on his web site through careful image processing and the use of a Photoshop plug-in called HVS JPEG, a product available from Digital Frontiers. Bill tried Photoshop's JPEG file converter but found he could get better quality and compression using Digital Frontiers' product.

Here, step-by-step, from resizing to processing to finally applying
HVS JPEG, is how Bill arrives at the quality that is so evident in his
work:

1. Resize in increments.

   Bill starts by resizing his original digital file, which is typically
   100–425 megabytes and saved in the Lab color mode. (His original files are so huge because they are scanned to create high-
   resolution Evercolor prints. These prints are made on a digital
   enlarger and then sold.)

   First, he cuts his original file size in half.

   Then he applies Photoshop's Unsharp Mask filter. His settings for
   the filter are Amount: 150%, Radius: 1.0, and Threshold: 0.

   Then he resizes this file in half and applies Unsharp Mask again
   with the same settings. This goes on until he reaches a file size
   of either 320 pixels tall for horizontal images or 320 wide for vertical images, as shown in Figure C-94.

   By resizing in this manner, he is able to preserve more of the
   detail present in the original high-resolution scan. The process
   sounds tedious, but Bill has created a Photoshop Action that
   does the entire job for him automatically, even applying the
   Unsharp Mask.

2. Convert to RGB.

   He changes the mode from Lab to RGB and saves a copy of the
   file by adding the words "web size" to the filename. This file
   becomes a master file from which he creates both a Macintosh
   version and a PC version as well as thumbnails for both
   platforms.

3. Create custom curves for different platforms.

   He creates these different versions by applying a custom Photoshop curve (Image → Adjust → Curves). He arrived at the settings
   for the curves after visually analyzing the effect different monitors had on his images. One Curve adjusts his image to look
   good at a gamma of 1.8 (Macintosh) and another Curve makes
   his image look good at a gamma of 2.2 (PC). The custom Curves
   affect only the midtones of the image, not the color.

4. Create thumbnails with Unsharp Mask.

   To create the thumbnail version of each photograph, Bill resizes
   the full-size image in one-step increments until he has a horizontal image with a height of 64 pixels or a vertical image with a
   width of 64 pixels. After the first incremental resizing, he applies
   an Unsharp Mask filter with the following settings: Amount:
   150%, Radius: 0.8, and Threshold: 0.

After the second incremental resizing step, he applies an Unsharp Mask once more (Amount: 100%, Radius: 0.6, and Threshold: 0). Again, he uses a Photoshop Action to carry out all these steps. He then increases the canvas size to 116 × 84 pixels (Image → Canvas Size), adds a white border, and then, for the final step, he adds a 1-pixel gray edge to the bottom and right edges to simulate a drop-shadow.

5. Compress with HVS JPEG filter.

   Finally, he manually applies JPEG compression to each image using the HVS JPEG filter, as shown in Figure C-95. First he moves the slider until he sees the image that is displayed in the HVS JPEG window break up or look particularly crusty. Then he pulls the slider back, applying less compression until the photograph appears to look right. HVS JPEG not only previews the effects of compression in real time, but also gives an approximation of the file size and the approximate download time based on a 28.8 modem. Bill also fine-tunes each image by experimenting with different HVS JPEG parameters. Most of the time, he sets his parameter to Textured Images. HVS JPEG actually pre-filters each image and determines what can and cannot be done to optimize an image for JPEG compression.

In Bill's (and Sioux's) web design, the photographs are placed on a gray background, with colorless navigational devices—leaving the color within the photograph to dominate the page. This way the energy is focused on the image, not elsewhere.

By the way, when you try this method, be sure to work on a copy of your original. Going from one color mode to another throws away data and may result in a degradation of quality.

Other JPEG issues

Of course, JPEG images don't exist in a vacuum. When you place JPEGs on web pages, other issues arise. In this section, we'll discuss dithering, converting between GIF and JPEG formats, and creating grayscale JPEGs.

Everything dithers

When you work with JPEG images, set aside what you've learned about browser-safe colors. There's no such thing as a browser-safe JPEG. JPEGs don't contain color lookup tables like GIFs. They save color data as an approximation of the original color. Figure C-96 shows a background created with browser-safe colors, then saved as a JPEG and viewed on an 8-bit display system. The background dithers, as will any JPEG image viewed on an 8-bit display system.

Also forget about matching the background of your image to the background of your web page, the way you can do with GIF files. On some 24-bit systems, you might get a match. But most of the time you will be disappointed at the results. Remember, JPEG and GIF colors rarely match, as shown in Figure C-97. Even what you think is pure white will dither, as shown in Figure C-98.

Always keep in mind that while dithering is very distracting when it appears on solid, flat colors, it can be a godsend on images with smooth color transitions. If how your images look on lower-end systems is important, you should preview the effect of dithering by adjusting your system to 8-bit display or viewing your work on someone else's system before compression.

Converting GIF to JPEG

What do you do if someone hands you an image that has been saved in the GIF format and you decide to incorporate it into another image that is best saved as a JPEG?

Generally it is not a good idea to use JPEG compression on images that have been color-indexed—especially photographic images. In the process of reducing and indexing colors, the image often becomes choppy or coarse. This is because there are fewer colors available to create smooth transitions. Dithering, while fooling the eye into believing that there are more colors, actually introduces even more noise at a subpixel level.

JPEG doesn't handle this high-spatial frequency noise well. The result is often a larger file size than you started with, as well as a lousy-looking image. Figure 6-6, for example, shows a menu bar saved as a GIF and as a JPEG. The GIF (on top) was indexed using the browser palette and is 8.5K. The JPEG (on the bottom) is nearly twice the size, 15.1K. Although we used Photoshop's High JPEG setting, the image quality still isn't as good as the original GIF.

> ### Compression/crunch
>
> Remember that every time you open, manipulate, and save an image in the JPEG format, you lose data. Not only do you lose data, you increase the risk of creating a larger file size. Those distinct blocks of pixels that you saw earlier, the ones that resulted from applying high JPEG compression to an image, actually add high spatial frequency to the image. The more high spatial frequency information in an image, the less efficient the JPEG compression. It's always best to save your original in the Photoshop format (or other 24-bit format) and save subsequent JPEG files from the original.

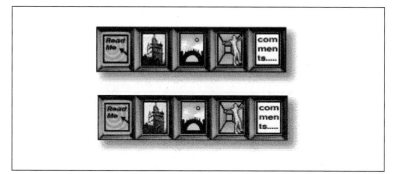

Figure 6-6. *Images starting out as a GIF (top) and then converted to a JPEG (bottom) give less than desirable results.*

If you must turn an indexed file such as a GIF into a JPEG, first convert your file to RGB (or Lab color mode—see the previous section "Blurring in Lab mode"), then apply a Gaussian blur to soften the image as much as possible without noticeable visual degradation. When JPEG compression is applied, there will be less noise to interfere with the compression process.

Making better grayscale images

Black and white images are often used on the Web, not only because they make smaller files, but also because they stand out and grab attention in a gaudy, color-saturated world.

JPEG can compress grayscale images by a factor of about 5:1. This ratio is lower than the ratio for color images because JPEG compresses color data more effectively than brightness or grayscale data. However, because grayscale images are only 8 bits instead of 24 bits, you still end up with a significantly smaller file than if you had used a color image.

In Photoshop, when most users want to convert a color RGB image into grayscale, they simply choose Mode → Grayscale and leave the work up to Photoshop. If you are using Photoshop 5, no problem. Adobe has improved the grayscale conversion algorithm and the results are perfectly acceptable. However, with earlier versions of Photoshop, simply changing modes doesn't produce the best results.

Progressive JPEGs

These JPEGs are useful for large files that take a long time to download. If you choose this option, your image will be displayed in a series of passes; the image improves in quality with each pass.

Baseline JPEGs, whether standard or optimized, are stored as a single top-to-bottom scan of the image. The progressive format contains the same data and is about the same file size, but the data is displayed in a series of scans. The first scan appears quickly because it is equivalent to a low-quality setting, as shown in Figure C-100. With each subsequent scan, more data is provided. Progressive JPEG files are slightly smaller than baseline-standard files.

When you choose Progressive, you can choose the number of scans it takes for the entire image to appear (3, 4, or 5 scans). This is not an option in 5.5's Save for Web plug-in, which only gives you an option of Progressive or not. The actual speed of each scan depends on the transmission speed of the user's system and the computer that receives and decompresses the data. With a very fast computer hooked up to an ISDN line, the image appears nearly instantly, no matter how many scans you choose. Increasing the number of scans increases the file size very slightly—the difference is no more than 200 bytes or so.

While the current browsers support progressive JPEGs, some older browsers don't, so you may not want to want to use the progressive format on your primary pages.

You'll get better looking black and white images if you go through Photoshop's Lab color space because you can isolate the important brightness characteristics of an image rather than its superfluous (in the case of black-and-white images) RGB values.

To convert your color images into grayscale:

1. Convert your RGB image into the Lab color space (Image → Mode → Lab Color). Flatten the layers.

2. Go to the Channels palette and select the Lightness channel. Your image now appears in grayscale.

3. Select channels a and b and delete them. Now you have isolated the grayscale data and discarded the color data.

4. Save your image as a Photoshop file. If you check the mode under Image → Mode, you'll see the image is in multichannel mode.

5. Convert to grayscale mode (Image → Mode → Grayscale).

Now you can edit the image as you wish—by changing the levels, for instance.

Save your file as a JPEG. In order to do this, you will need to convert back to the RGB mode. It will still appear as a grayscale image, but now you can save it as a JPEG at any compression ratio you wish.

Does this really make a difference? Consider a portrait I recently took of Netscape cofounder Marc Andreessen. Figure C-99 shows the original color photo. Figure 6-7 shows the results of simply converting from RGB to grayscale mode. Note the blocking in the shadows and the "chunky" look to the skin. Figure 6-8 shows the results of the Lab process. The midtones are smoother and the shadows are less murky.

Figure 6-7. *Simply changing modes in earlier versions of Photoshop yields an image with blocked shadows.*

Figure 6-8. *Using Lab mode creates a much better grayscale image— notice how smooth his skin looks in comparison to Figure 6-7.*

Pushing the envelope

We started this chapter by saying how easy it is to create a JPEG. However, like so many things in life, if you want to push the envelope and get the most out of the format, you need to work at it. This means familiarizing yourself with the way JPEG works on different types of images, and taking the time to optimize your images before applying JPEG compression. If you do this, not only will the quality of your image improve, but you'll also save anywhere from 5 to 20% of your file size.

CHAPTER SEVEN

CREATING BACKGROUND TILES

You can create an infinite number of custom backgrounds with Photoshop. If you use one of the methods described in this chapter and pay attention to file size, your background will download quickly and give your web site sizzle and pop.

Backgrounds have been a part of the Web for some time and are now considered part of the HTML standard. To add a background to your page, simply add the BACKGROUND extension to your BODY tag. For example, the tag <BODY BACKGROUND="background.gif"> tiles the file *background.gif* across and down the browser window. The text and graphics in your page are displayed on top of the tiled background.

This method of creating a background is not as fast as using hexadecimal code to designate a single color, but if you make your tile small enough and pay attention to its total file size through color indexing and compression, your background will start to appear nearly instantly. To specify a single color, use the following code: <BODY BGCOLOR="#FFFFFF">, where FFFFFF is the hexadecimal code for your color.

You can use either GIF or JPEG files for backgrounds. If you use GIF files, you should use browser-safe colors. If you use JPEGs (something you might do if your background graphic contains subtle gradations or more than 256 colors), you may encounter distracting blotchy effects.

Most web designers use one of three basic techniques for creating backgrounds in Photoshop. One popular method is to create horizontal or vertical strips and selectively fill them with color or graphics. When loaded as a background into a browser, these strips repeatedly tile across and down until the browser window is filled.

This technique is often used to block out a sidebar area of a page, as shown in Figure 7-1. This technique is described in detail in the next section, "Working with tiling strips."

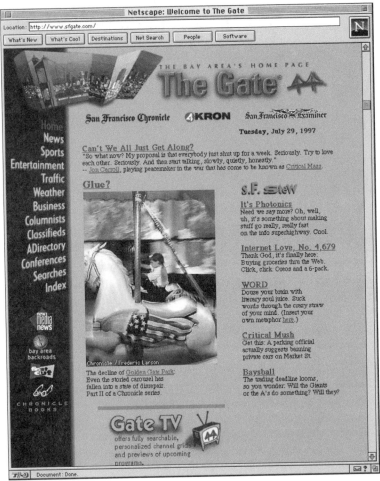

Figure 7-1. *For The Gate's home page, designer Corey Hitchcock created a background that acts as a sidebar, highlighting navigational controls.*

The second method is to create a square tile. If prepared properly, the square will tile and create a seamless background not unlike patterned wallpaper. The image has to be prepared so that the edges will meld seamlessly from tile to tile. Figure 7-2 shows a page that uses this square tile technique. The technique is described in detail in the section "Creating patterns with square tiles."

Figure 7-2. *The Presbyterian Healthcare System home page uses seamless tiles for the background.*

The third method is to load a full-sized image or graphic as a background. Although this method produces unique, picturesque backgrounds, it is practical only if you can reduce the file—through careful color indexing or compression—to a manageable size. Figure 7-3 shows a site that used a single full-size image as a background. This technique is discussed in the section "Compressing backgrounds with JPEG."

Working with tiling strips

If you want to precisely control color and graphic changes in your background, you should use the tiling strip technique. With this technique you can place vibrant graphics in one part of the page, while leaving another part clutter-free for easy reading of text and other content. In this section, we'll go through the following applications for tiling strips:

- Soft-edged sidebars
- Ribbon-shaped sidebars
- Film-strip sidebars
- Color-band effects

Figure 7-3. *The background for Encyclopedia Britannica's Shakespeare and the Globe site is a full-size JPEG image, compressed to 16K.*

Making soft-edged sidebars

To create the background used on The Gate's home page (Figure 7-1), designer Corey Hitchcock used the Linear gradient tool to create the background image shown in Figure 7-4. This image is 1377 pixels wide and 8 pixels high.

Figure 7-4. *This horizontal strip tiles to create the background for The Gate's home page.*

Figure C-1. *Preview your work by changing Photoshop's gray canvas to a color of your choice.*

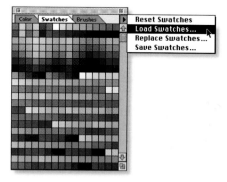

Figure C-2. *With a browser-safe color swatch at your fingertips, you can readily create images that will look great to the most viewers.*

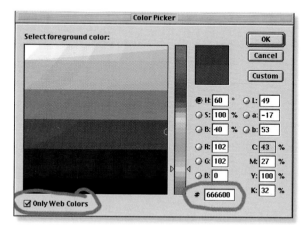

Figure C-3. *Limit Photoshop's Color Picker to web-safe colors by checking the Only Web Colors checkbox.*

Figure C-4. *In this example, improperly prepared photos detract rather than enhance a web page.*

Figure C-5. *In this makeover, the photos have been processed to compensate for flatness, color cast, and overexposure.*

Figure C-6. *A properly processed photo sets a tone of professionalism that permeates an entire site, as does the one shown here in a page that Second Story designed for the National Geographic Society.*

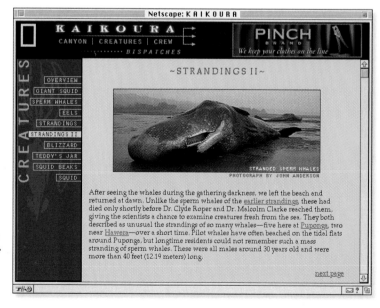

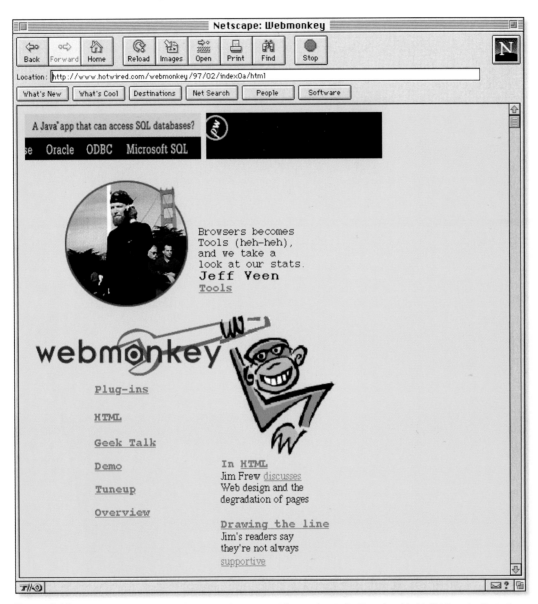

Figure C-18. *Should this photographic image be a JPEG? That's what Luke Knowland initially thought. But when he looked at a JPEG version on an 8-bit display system, he saw dithering that distracted from the image. Converting the image into a transparent GIF gave better results.*

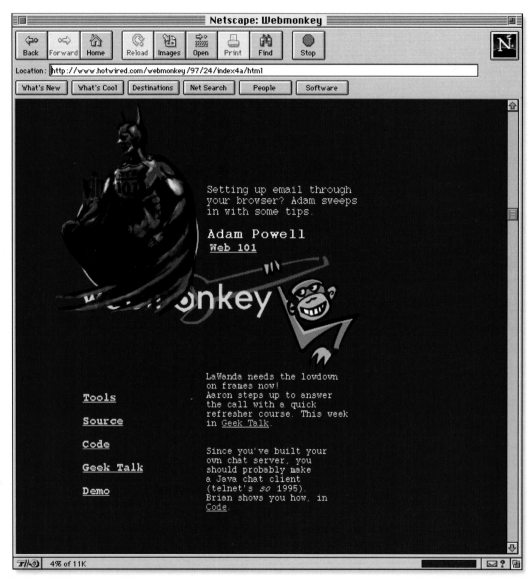

Figure C-19. *Surely this Batman should be a JPEG. The image contains subtle variations in color that would be best represented with thousands of colors. But Knowland tried it as a GIF file (adaptive palette, diffusion dithering). The image dithers, of course, and that's what Knowland liked about it. The dithering actually enhanced the image by giving it a velvety texture.*

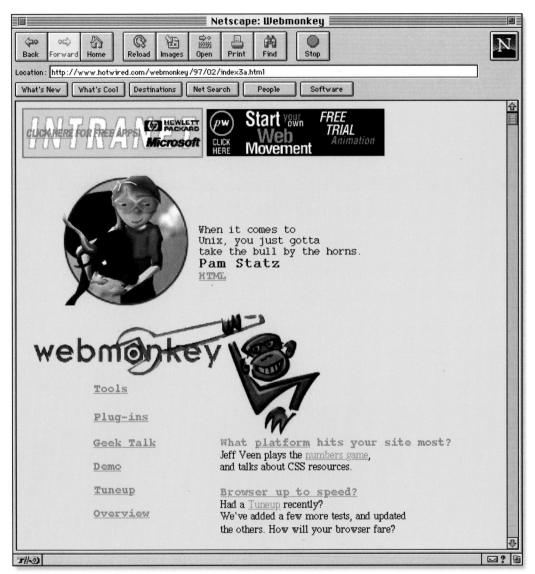

Figure C-20. *For this page, Knowland first saved the graphic as a GIF; however, at points of subtle color transition, the image broke up into distracting bands that looked like the rings of Saturn. Clearly 256 colors weren't enough to represent the graphic adequately. He chose JPEG instead, and it looks fine when it dithers on 8-bit monitors.*

Figure C-21. *Casey Caston is no fan of JPEG: he hates it. Sure, JPEG is great for creating a small file. But poorly applied JPEG compression gives weird color shifts and blocky patterns. He especially doesn't like the way JPEGs dither on an 8-bit monitor. For the image on this c\net page, for example, Caston used a GIF for a photograph in order to maintain precise colors and sharp text.*

Figure C-22. *Sean Parker received several JPEG files with instructions to put them on the page as soon as possible. While converting to GIF would keep the text sharp, it would also mean reducing the colors and possibly changing the overall look and feel of the page. With time at a premium, he stayed with the JPEG format, knowing the result wouldn't be perfect. He managed to reduce the JPEGs to 3.5K each.*

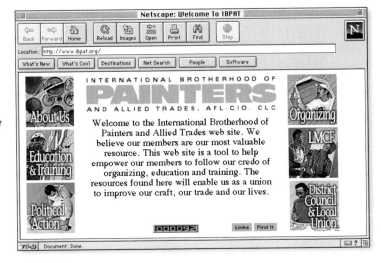

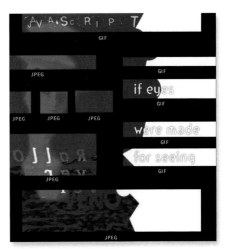

Figure C-23. *As part of an experiment with JavaScript, Gregg Hartling created the page on the left using both JPEG and GIF images. The image on the right shows the individual elements and how they were put together. The woman's face was saved as a JPEG, as was the entire lower part of the page. The text blocks to the right and above her face were saved as GIFs. Breaking the page up like this takes advantage of the best properties of each format.*

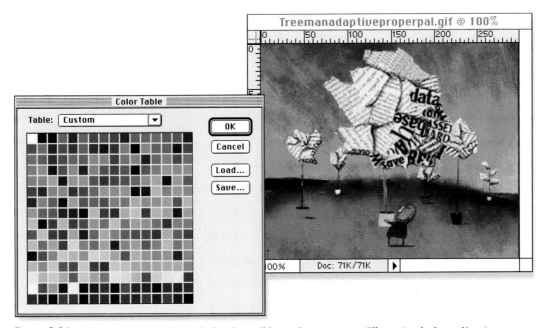

Figure C-24. *The color index defines which colors will be used in an image. (Illustration by James Yang)*

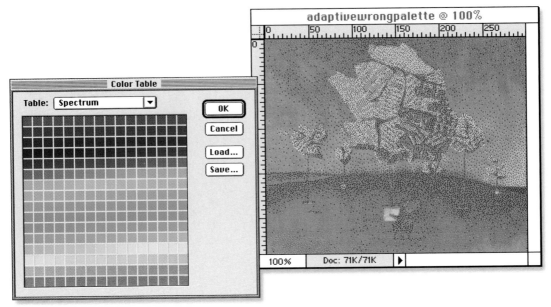

Figure C-25. *Changing the index changes the colors in the image.*

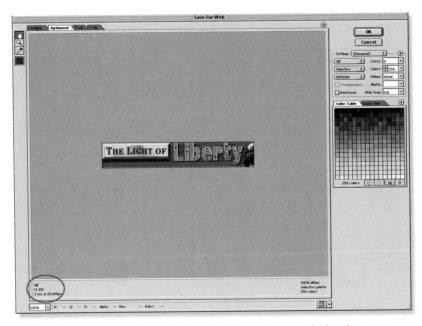

Figure C-26. *When you choose File Save for Web your image is displayed in a new window.*

Figure C-27. *Comparison of three different settings, plus the original, in the Save for Web window.*

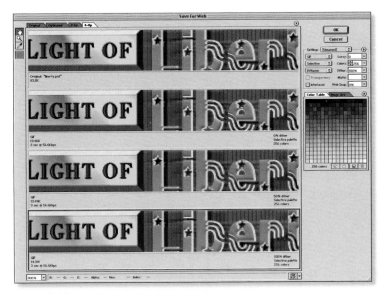

Figure C-28. *Effects of three different dither settings.*

Figure C-29. *Effects of different Lossy GIF settings.*

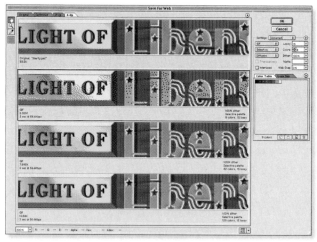

Figure C-30. *Effects of different color settings.*

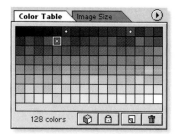

Figure C-31. *If a color box contains a black diamond in the center, it's browser-safe.*

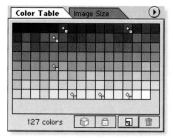

Figure C-32. *By selecting the cube at the bottom of the Color Table, selected colors can be shifted to browser-safe.*

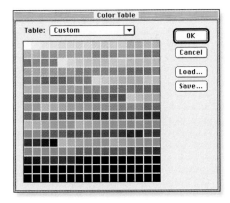

Figure C-33. *The browser-safe palette.*

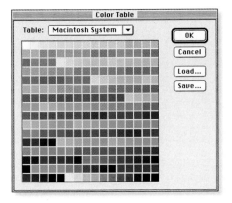

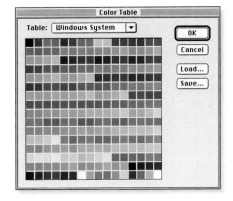

Figure C-34. *Macintosh and Windows system palettes.*

Figure C-35. *Using the default Indexed Color settings, the results are acceptable, but not optimal.*

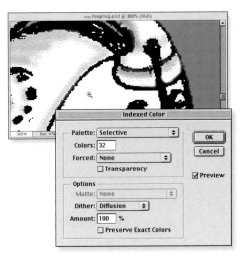

Figure C-36. *At 32 colors, the results are not acceptable.*

Figure C-37. *This image creates problems because it includes flesh tones and a multicolored background.*

Figure C-38. *When the standard adaptive palette is applied, the colored background throws off the flesh tones.*

Figure C-39. *Selecting the face before indexing tweaks the adaptive palette toward the flesh tones and away from the background colors.*

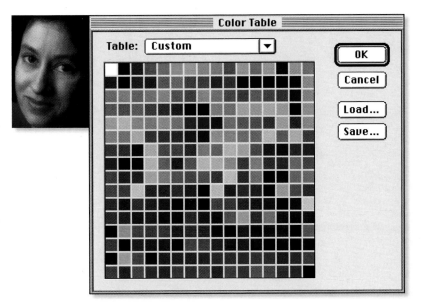

Figure C-40.   *The cropped image and the resulting color table.*

Figure C-41.   *The custom palette applied to the original image.*

Figure C-42. *Web palette, no dither. At 7.7K, the egg looks crunchy, the smoke banded with rings of the wrong grays.*

Figure C-43. *Adaptive palette, diffusion dither. At 9.3K, the image looks fine, but the colors—the yellow background, the green text, and the red logo—have all shifted. Plus, it's the largest file so far.*

Figure C-44. *The combination approach. Coming in at 8.1K, the image was started in RGB mode. The egg and plane were copied to the clipboard. Then the image was indexed using the system palette with no dither. Casey then copied the still-in-RGB-mode egg/plane image from the clipboard into the indexed image. Once placed, the egg and plane automatically dither, while the rest of the image remains the same. This is the image that ran on c\net.*

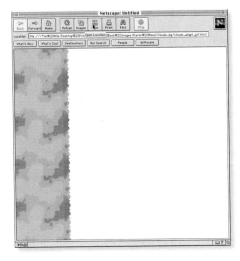

Figure C-45. *Non-browser-safe colors in background tiles don't dither, they shift.*

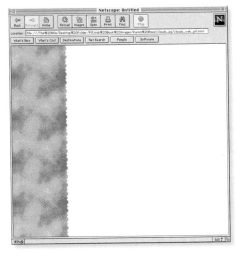

Figure C-46. *The solution is to index with the browser-safe palette.*

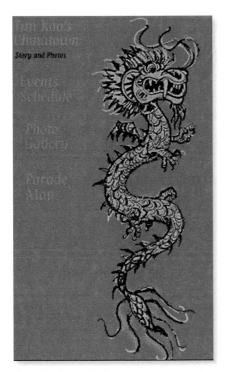

Figure C-47. *The dragon as it appeared on The Gate site.*

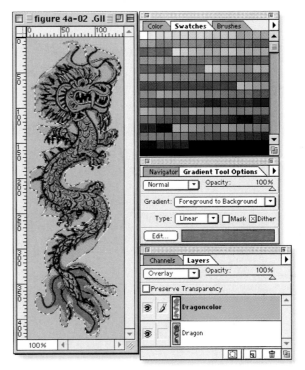

Figure C-48. *Corey Hitchcock used Photoshop's Gradient tool and browser-safe colors to create a dynamic web illustration.*

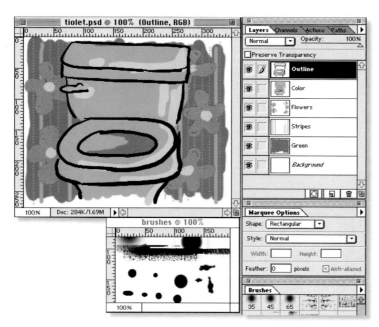

Figure C-49. *Brian Frick uses layers that contain each graphical element— easily accessible for later edits. Also notice the window titled "brushes," which he keeps handy so he can quickly create custom brushes that give him control over the colors used in his web illustrations.*

Figure C-50. *Designer Valerie Robbins created this self-portrait entirely in Photoshop's Indexed Color mode. Although this mode offers fewer options than RGB, it has the advantage of total predictability.*

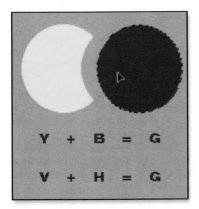

Figure C-51. *When seen this way, it looks as if there are three distinct colors.*

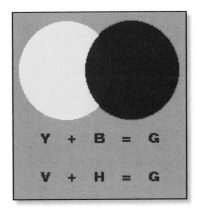

Figure C-52. *When the circles are joined, it now looks as if they are actually overlapping—an effect that is normally impossible in Photoshop's Indexed Color mode.*

Figure C-53. *Selecting Image → Mode → Color Table will display the palette of the image, and clicking on the Save button saves the palette for use with other images.*

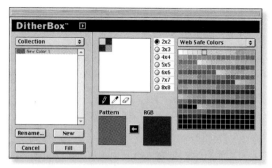

Figure C-54. *Photoshop 5.5's DitherBox plug-in automatically creates browser-safe colors.*

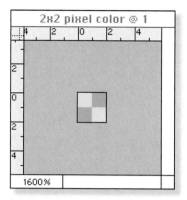

Figure C-55. *Creating a 2 × 2-pixel image and filling alternating pixels with similar browser-safe colors creates a hybrid color.*

Figure C-56. *These hybrid colors were created simply by filling a 2-pixel-wide horizontal selection with browser-safe colors.*

Figure C-57. *Hybrid colors can also be created by applying random noise to a selection and then applying Photoshop's Web palette.*

Figure C-58. *Without transparency, graphics are rectangular and don't blend with page backgrounds.*

Figure C-59. *Transparent graphics allow for clean, sophisticated designs.*

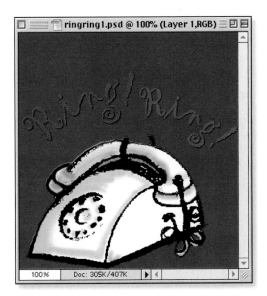

Figure C-60. *We need to turn the background into a transparent color so the phone and type appear to float regardless of the web background color.*

Figure C-61. *Jaggies such as the ones shown here can be avoided by using Photoshop's pseudo-multibit mask capabilities.*

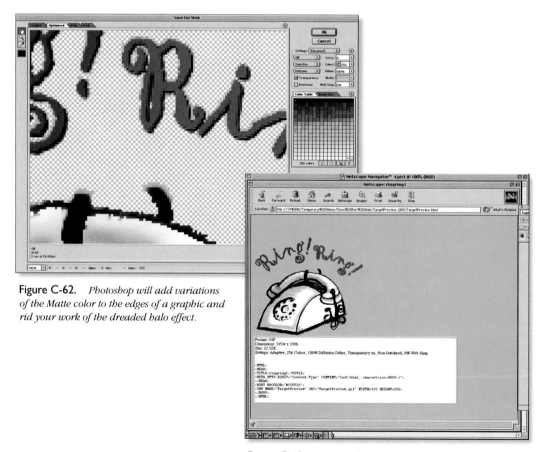

Figure C-62. *Photoshop will add variations of the Matte color to the edges of a graphic and rid your work of the dreaded halo effect.*

Figure C-63. *By matching the Matte color to your web background color, you'll get a nice anti-aliasing effect.*

Figure C-64. *Creating an anti-aliased effect against a complex background such as this one is more difficult.*

Figure C-65. *By expanding a selection a few pixels and picking up traces of a complex background, your transparent GIF will look better.*

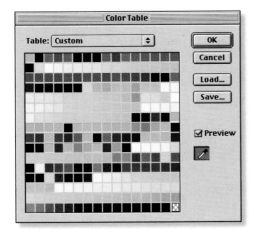

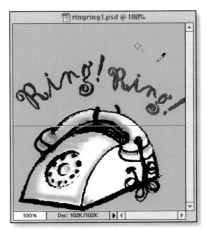

Figure C-66. *With Photoshop 5.5 you can designate transparent colors directly from the Color Table.*

Figure C-67. *The Indexed Color version of the GIF89a Export dialog.*

Figure C-68. *The selected color turns gray, indicating that it is transparent.*

Figure C-69. *Simply selecting the background color didn't work here, since part of the image also turned transparent.*

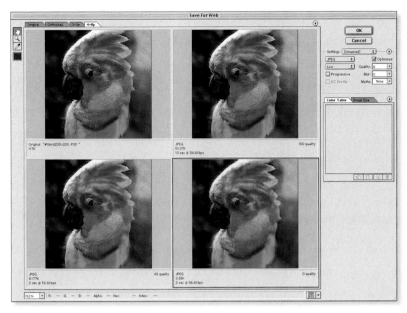

Figure C-83. *Shown here are the effects of three different JPEG quality settings.*

Figure C-84. *Compressed at 90:1, the image falls apart into huge squares of color.*

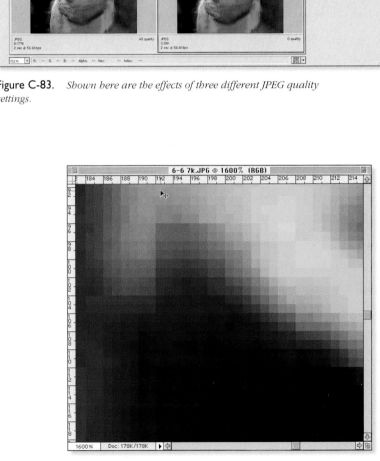

Figure C-85. *Magnification showing compression artifacts.*

Figure C-86. *Saved at Photoshop's JPEG Low setting, this detailed, high-contrast photo falls apart, loses detail, and still takes up 24K.*

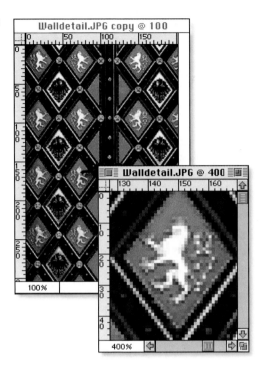

Figure C-87. *Also saved at Photoshop's JPEG Low setting, this impressionistic photograph falls apart from extreme compression, but the effect is not as noticeable because of the nature of the image. It takes up only 7K.*

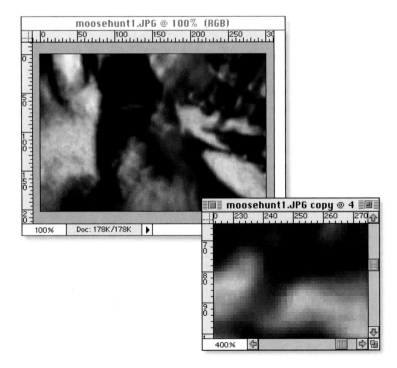

Figure C-88. *If your image contains transparent areas and you turn on the Matte option in the Save for Web palette, you can choose the background color.*

Figure C-89. *With no optimizing, this JPEG image takes up a total of 50.3K.*

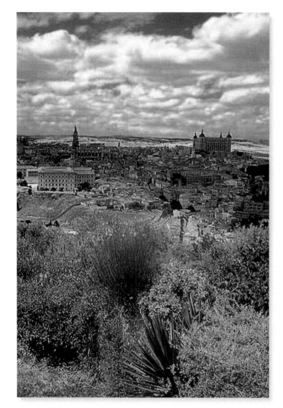

Figure C-90. *With selective blurring to the background sky, the JPEG image takes up 47K.*

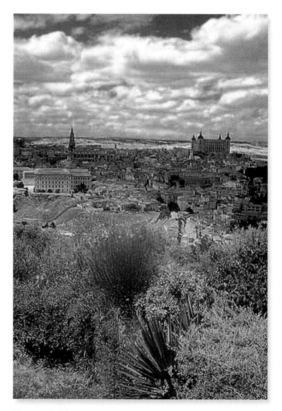

Figure C-91. *With selective blurring to the background sky and global blurring, the JPEG image takes up 43K.*

Figure C-92. *Although this 1020 × 765-pixel file weighs in at 497K, the quality is superlative, thanks to Gaussian blurring and careful image processing. It was converted to JPEG with a Photoshop 2.5 setting of 7.*

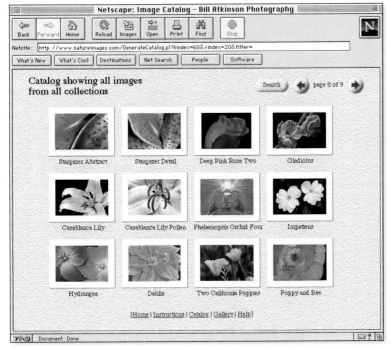

Figure C-93. *Here's a sampling of Bill Atkinson's 117 × 85-pixel thumbnails.*

Figure C-94. *Bill achieves a higher quality version by resizing down, as shown in this 320 × 480-pixel image.*

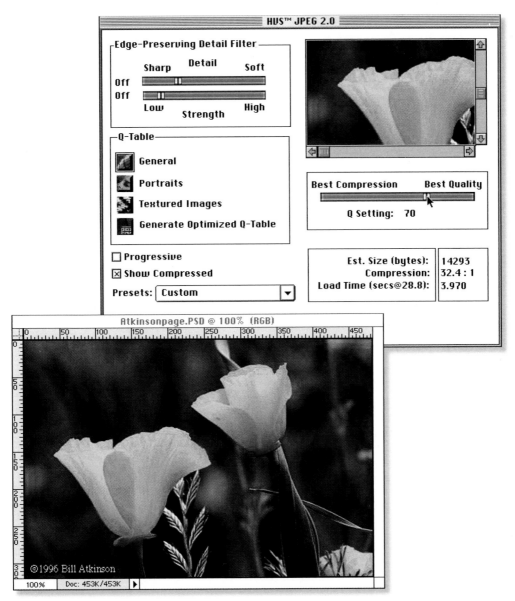

Figure C-95. *With the HVS JPEG plug-in, you get many options to choose from, including real-time viewing of the compression effect.*

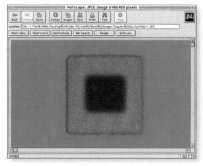

Figure C-96. *JPEGs dither on 8-bit systems. End of story.*

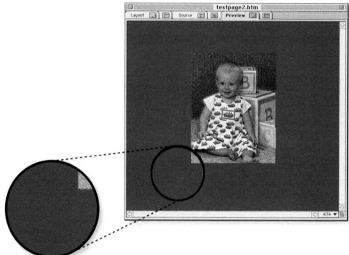

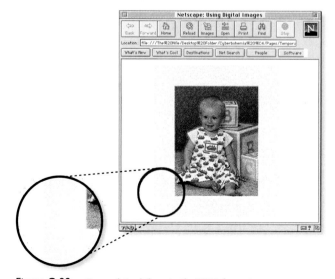

Figure C-97. *A JPEG placed against a GIF background of the "same" color rarely matches on an 8-bit display.*

Figure C-98. *Even white dithers in the JPEG format.*

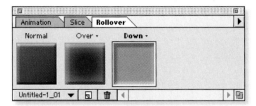

Figure C-153. *Three rollover states, as displayed in ImageReady's Rollover palette.*

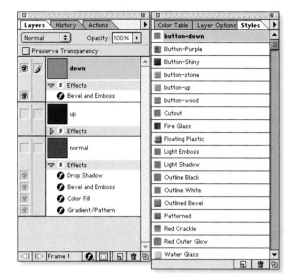

Figure C-154. *The layers and styles palettes.*

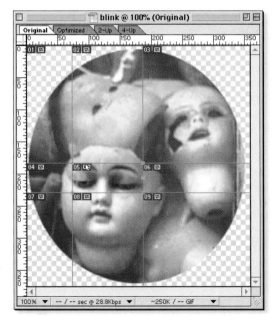

Figure C-155. *Mogensen's image showing slices.*

Figure C-156. *A 64 × 64 tile created using Gradient/Pattern Layer effects and the Tile Maker filter.*

Figure C-157. *A 64 × 64 pixel tile created using Gradient/Pattern Layer effects and the Tile Maker filter set to Kaleidoscope.*

Figure C-158 *Previewing the tile shown in Figure C-156 reveals that it doesn't tile very well.*

Figure C-159. *The tile shown in Figure C-157 tiles much better.*

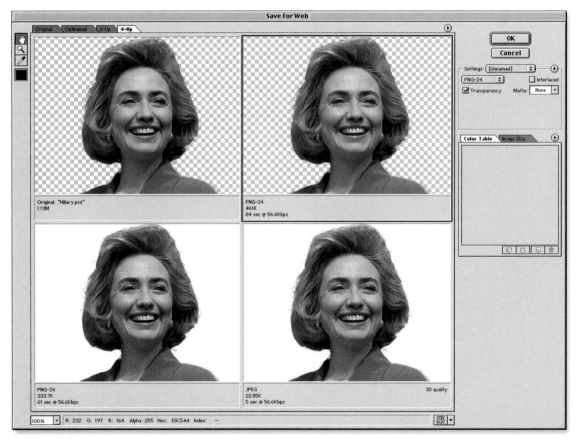

Figure C-160. *The PNG images are much larger than the one with JPEG compression applied.*

To create this background, Corey followed these steps:

1. She created a new file, 1377 × 8 pixels, and filled it with teal (Red = 153, Green = 204, Blue = 204).

2. Working from the left edge of the image, she used the rectangle marquee tool to make a selection 100 pixels wide and filled it with black (Red = 0, Green = 0, Blue = 0).

3. To create a transition from the black to the teal she made a 15-pixel-wide rectangular selection, starting from the right edge of the black area.

4. She selected the Linear Gradient tool and set the foreground color to black and the background color to gray. In the Linear Gradient Tool Options palette, she made the following settings:

   Gradient: Foreground to Background
   Type: Linear
   Opacity: 100%
   Dither: On

5. While holding the Shift key (to constrain the tool to a straight line), she dragged the cursor across the selection from left to right. This created a straight, linear gradation from black on the left to gray on the right.

6. She added another black area to her strip, starting 700 pixels from the left and continuing all the way to the right edge of the graphic, because she didn't want the teal to tile off into infinity. She created a soft-edged look for this right sidebar in the same way as she did for the left sidebar, with the Linear gradient tool. (You don't see the black sidebar on the right in the screenshot because it is offscreen. You can see it in the actual graphic in Figure 7-4.)

Testing the strip

Once you've made your strip, you can simply code up your HTML, check it in a browser, go back to Photoshop to edit the graphic, and then repeat the process until you're satisfied. Ultimately, you'll need to check your work in a browser (more than one, preferably), but while you're working in Photoshop, wouldn't it be nice to get an idea of what the page will look like without having to switch to HTML? Here's how to simulate a tiled background page from within Photoshop:

1. Select all of your background graphic.

2. Define your graphic as a pattern by choosing Edit → Define → Pattern.

3. Create a new file. You can make this screen any size you want, but make it large enough to at least approximate the size of your end users' monitors. Something in the neighborhood of 640 × 480 is appropriate.

4. Select Edit → Fill to bring up the Fill dialog box and choose Pattern from the Use pull-down menu. This option tiles the defined pattern to fill the current window, just as a browser would, as shown in Figure 7-5.

Feathering for gradients

Corey used the Linear gradient tool to create a smooth transition from the sidebar color to the mainbar color. Here's another method for creating the same look by feathering a selection:

1. Create a 1000 × 8 pixel strip, either horizontal or vertical. Fill it with the color you want to use for the main area of the site (teal in The Gate example).

2. Make an *unfeathered* selection about 100 pixels from the edge. Fill the selection with the color for the sidebar area (black in The Gate example).

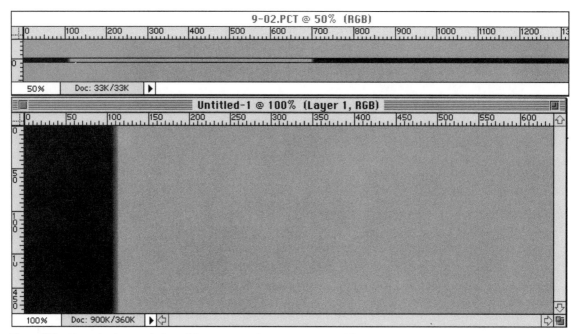

Figure 7-5. *To test background tiling, define your graphic as a pattern and fill a browser-sized file with that pattern. Photoshop will tile the graphic just like a browser.*

3. Open Select → Feather to bring up the Feather dialog box and choose a radius of 15 pixels or so.

4. Fill the feathered selection with the sidebar color you used in step 2. This creates a soft transition between the sidebar color and the main area color.

As shown in Figure 7-6, this makes a solid section of black, then a transitional area from black to teal, and finally the teal section.

Making ribbon-shaped sidebars

Of course, you're not stuck with rectangles for sidebar backgrounds. In Figure C-101, the Home Savings of California's home page, designed by Venu Interactive, uses a ribbon-shaped sidebar, which is notable for the thin, elegant line of black to the right of the ribbon shape. The site uses different colored ribbons on different pages. This description focuses on the blue-green ribbon on the home page.

Designer Gregg Hartling started the process by drawing a ribbon shape in Adobe Illustrator. Then he switched to Photoshop and followed these steps:

1. He created a new Photoshop file, 121 × 1200 pixels, created a new layer called *gray master*, and pasted the ribbon shape onto that layer.

2. He made several copies of this master layer, selected Preserve Transparency in the Layers palette, and filled each layer with a different color.

3. To make the black edge of the ribbon, he copied the master layer again, this time naming the new layer *black under-ribbon*. He selected the new layer and ran the Offset filter (Filters → Other → Offset) to offset the shape slightly up and to the right. Then he filled this version with black.

4. He positioned the colored layer above the *black under-ribbon* layer, turned off the other layers, and saved out the various versions of the ribbon background as GIF files. He ended up with nine "different" backgrounds that he used throughout the Home Savings site. The black under-ribbon and several variations are shown in Figure 7-7.

Figure 7-6. *The feathering technique creates a graduated look yet maintains a definite edge to the sidebar color.*

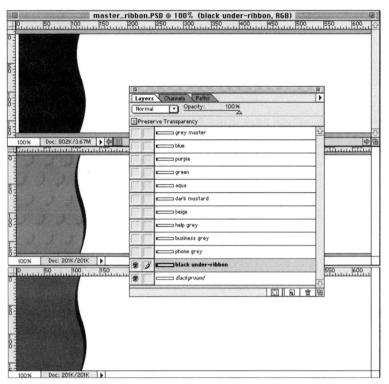

Figure 7-8. *The actual strip used to create the background in Figure C-102.*

Figure 7-7. *The black under-ribbon layer (top) and several of the ribbons created as backgrounds.*

Working with bands of color

Figure C-102 shows the fanciful home page for illustrator John Hersey. He created the background by making a 12-color bar in Illustrator, duplicating it several times, and then dragging and dropping the file into Photoshop. Then he cropped the file to its final size of 2 × 369 and saved it as a JPEG, shown in Figure 7-8. He chose JPEG so he would be able to keep all the vibrant colors. It still looks fine on monitors that display only 256 colors. You can add your own colorful backgrounds by using Photoshop's Linear Gradient Tool Options and Transparent Rainbow fill:

1. Create a vertical or horizontal strip. Select the Linear Gradient tool.

2. From the Linear Gradient Tool Options palette, select Transparent Rainbow from the Gradient pop-up menu, shown in Figure 7-9. (You can edit the colors, transitions, and transparency settings by clicking on the palette's Edit button.)

3. Inside your horizontal or vertical strip, press the Shift key while dragging the cursor the entire length or width of your window to create a straight, even fill of color. When you release the cursor, a rainbow of colors will fill your background strip.

Be sure to test your work by using the fill-with-pattern method explained earlier, in the section "Making soft-edged sidebars." See that your background doesn't overwhelm the rest of your page, unless you want it to!

Figure 7-10 shows another background created as a strip that combines both gradation and a graphical element. Created by Gregg Hartling, the actual tile is 53 × 2600 pixels long, so there isn't any chance that the black, top area will repeat on a viewer's monitor. The total file size is about 10K.

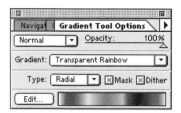

Figure 7-9. *Experiment with the settings in the Linear gradient Tool Options palette to create rainbow and other colored gradients.*

Creating patterns with square tiles

You can create a repeating pattern while keeping your total file size down by tiling squares. This technique is a bit trickier than using tiling strips because all four edges of the square must blend or melt into the adjacent square. If they don't match, you'll get the effect shown in Figure 7-11. Sometimes this may work, but obviously it's not a seamless pattern. The next section shows how to use Photoshop's Offset filter to make all four edges match.

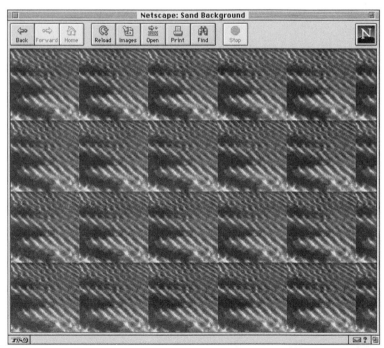

Figure 7-11. *If you just create a square tile and have the browser tile it across your page, you'll often wind up with "seams" between the tiles.*

Figure 7-10. *Gregg Hartling created this tiled background that combines a non-distracting graphic element with a slightly graduated header.*

Figure 7-12. *Offsetting the image by half in each direction positions the top left corner of the image in the exact center of the window.*

Figure 7-13. *Choosing Wrap Around tiles the remaining image around the center but leaves horizontal and vertical creases (increased here for emphasis).*

Figure 7-14. *The background tile with seams removed.*

Creating seamless tiles with the Offset filter

When patterns are used discreetly, they work in harmony with the rest of the page, as in the home page for Presbyterian Healthcare System (shown in Figure 7-2) designed by Bea Garcia of Houston-based Savage Design. She drew the pattern in Illustrator and then brought it into Photoshop, where she created a browser-safe green background, touching up the leaves with a lighter green. To create seamless tiles, she cropped the image to 134 × 134 pixels and used the Offset filter, following these steps:

1. She selected Filter → Other → Offset to bring up the Offset dialog box. In the Horizontal and Vertical boxes she entered values equal to half the dimensions of her image. Since her image was 134 pixels in each direction, she entered 67 in each box. This moves the image 67 pixels to the right and 67 pixels down, as shown in Figure 7-12.

2. Then, in the Undefined Areas section of the Offset dialog box, she chose Wrap Around. This inverts the remaining portion of the image and tiles it in the unused areas (the part that was white in Figure 7-12). The former outer edges now meet in the center of the image (see Figure 7-13).

3. With the Rubber Stamp tool, she removed the seam caused by the outside edges meeting in the center and smoothed out the lines. The result is shown in Figure 7-14.

When she brought this image into the web page, the edges matched and she had a seamless background.

Connecting loose ends with the Offset filter

Here's an interesting problem. How do you get an intricate design—like the one Brian Frick created for a Discovery Online article on hackers, shown in Figure C-103—to work as a tiled background? Surely it would be impossible to make all those little lines match up perfectly.

Once again, it's the Offset filter to the rescue. It's very difficult to give step-by-step instructions on this technique, but essentially, Brian drew the gadgets and wires with the pencil tool and periodically applied the Offset filter to connect the loose ends. He kept repeating the process until he got what he wanted. Figure 7-15 shows the image tile he came up with.

Figure 7-17. *The original cropped image.*

Figure 7-15. *This image creates a seamless background, thanks to the Offset filter.*

Creating textured effects

You can create a texture using just about any graphic, photograph, or illustration. Figure 7-16 shows a background texture that Valerie Robbins created from one of my photos of sand.

Starting with a crop of the photo (Figure 7-17), she lightened the image with the Brightness/Contrast controls, applied the Offset filter as described previously, and smoothed the horizontal and vertical lines that appeared in the center. The resulting background gives a nice texture to the page.

You can also create your own textures from scratch by using any number of Photoshop filters applied to a background or foreground color. Two popular filters are Photoshop's Clouds and Difference Clouds filters found under Filters → Render. If you create your texture using one of these filters and make your tile 128 × 128 or 256 × 256 pixels, it will automatically tile seamlessly. If you use these filters on images set at other dimensions, you'll need to use Photoshop's Offset filter for seamless tiles. The background in Figure 7-18 was created by applying the Clouds filter to a 128-square-pixel image.

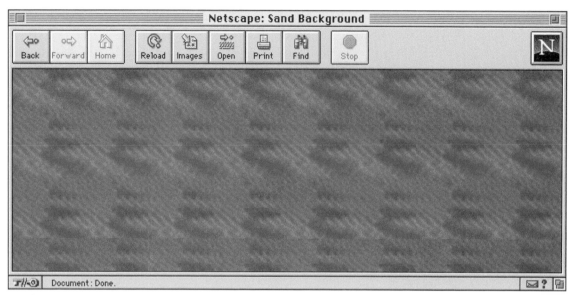

Figure 7-16. *The background for my page is a toned background texture that doesn't interfere with the text.*

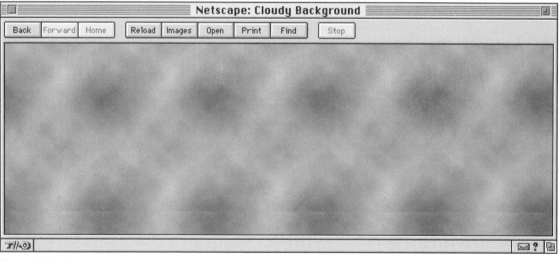

Figure 7-18. *This background tiled seamlessly without the use of the Offset filter.*

Creating a 3D effect

You can easily create simple 3D backgrounds by using the Offset and Emboss filters. To create the background shown in Figure 7-19, Robbins followed these steps:

1. She created a block of 0s and 1s in Illustrator and then copied and pasted them into a 120 × 120 Photoshop file.

2. She then added a yellow background.

3. She applied the Offset filter, with values of 60, 60, Wrap Around.

4. She carefully edited the middle of the tile where the 0s and 1s didn't quite match up.

5. To create the 3D effect, she applied the Emboss filter (Filter → Stylize → Emboss).

Another easy way to give your background a 3D look is to use the Texturizer filter found under Filters → Texture. With this filter, you have several textures to choose from, including canvas, brick, burlap, and sandstone. You can also load your own custom-made texture.

For a more complicated but very effective way to give your background a 3D effect, use the Lighting Effects filter found under Filter → Render. To create a 3D effect using this filter, you need to create a "bump" grayscale image and load it into a separate channel. This bump image can consist of a texture such as paper or sand that bumps light that you control with the Lighting Effects filter from its surface to produce 3D effect. Figure 7-20 shows a burlap texture created with the Texturizer. In Figure 7-21, we're using the burlap texture as a bump map with the Lighting Effects filter.

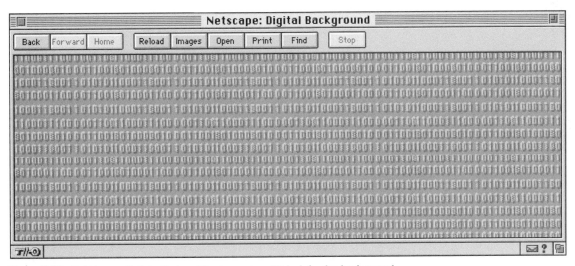

Figure 7-19. *Robbins applied the Emboss filter to create a 3D look for this background.*

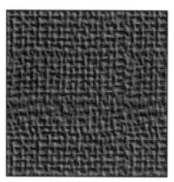

Figure 7-20. *This burlap texture was created with the Texturizer filter.*

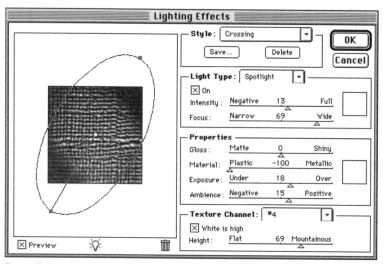

Figure 7-21. *The burlap texture is used as a bump map to create a lighting effect.*

Compressing backgrounds with JPEG

Sometimes a full-size image works great as a background. The secret is to create a small file size, either through compression or careful color indexing. The next two sections present examples of backgrounds created as full-sized images.

Big picture, tiny file

For my web site, Val Robbins turned a color photograph to grayscale as a background. Since she gave me the task of preparing the photograph, I followed these steps:

1. I converted the 580 × 580-pixel color photo to grayscale. (See Chapter 6, *JPEG: All the Color You Want*, for information about the best way to do this.)

2. Selecting the sky and clouds, I applied a Gaussian blur with a radius of 1 pixel in order to minimize the artifacts that occur with extreme JPEG compression.

3. I lightened the entire image using the Brightness/Contrast controls so that overlaying text would be readable. The final image is shown in Figure 7-22.

4. I converted the grayscale image back to RGB so that I could use HVS JPEG, one of my favorite plug-ins.

5. Using HVS JPEG, I was able to apply enough JPEG compression to reduce the file size from about 800K to about 5K! HVS JPEG

allowed me to view the effects of compression in real time, and easily determine optimum file size and quality.

Although the background turns blotchy when viewed on an 8-bit monitor, I am very happy with the results. And at 5K, it certainly downloads quickly enough! (Notice that I use the word "download" and not "appear." This is because the speed in which a highly compressed JPEG image decompresses varies from computer to computer, depending on the processing power of the computer.)

Figure 7-22. *Reduced to grayscale and heavily compressed, this 580 × 580 photograph wound up as a 5K background image.*

Shakespeare as background

Steve Jablonsky of Imaginary Studio feathered the edge of the 560 × 300 Shakespeare collage shown in Figure C-104 and saved it as a JPEG. This is the image used in the Shakespeare web site shown in Figure 7-3. Because it's a background image, the 16K image always loads in the upper-left corner of the browser window, so Jablonsky can precisely position text and graphics to work with the background.

Grabbing backgrounds

Sometimes you might be interested in how custom backgrounds on the Web are created. If you're using Netscape for the Mac or Windows, it's easy to download the actual background tile or image itself. Once you've downloaded it, you can open it in Photoshop, examine it carefully, and through a process of trial and error, approximate the method that was used. Notice that we are not suggesting that you use the actual background itself. Using someone else's creation would be unethical (and illegal!) unless you obtain their permission.

Using Netscape on either a Mac or PC, follow these steps:

1. Once the web page containing the background has fully downloaded, choose View → Document Info. You'll see every item on the page listed. Click on Background, which should be near the top. All the statistics will show up on the bottom, including a small thumbnail version of the background itself.

2. To examine the background more closely, save the file and open it in Photoshop.

On Windows, both Netscape and Internet Explorer bring up a popup menu when you right-click on the background (or any other image). From here, you can view or save the image, or even set it to be your desktop wallpaper.

Another method is to go right to the source code and check the file being called from the BODY tag. Paste this location into your browser and the background file will display.

This can get a little complicated, though. For instance, if the BODY tag reads <BODY BACKGROUND="../graphics/backgd.gif"> and the page is located at *http://www.server.com/magazine/culture/music.html*, you'll need to edit the URL to read *http://www.server.com/magazine/graphics/backgd.gif*.

Alternatively, you can email the site that interests you and ask them to let you know how the page was done. Many designers will be honored that you noticed their work and asked about it and will be happy to share their technique with you.

Remembering the balance

It's easy to make backgrounds with Photoshop. You can create narrow strips that tile or squares that fill the window with a pattern that you've created using any number of Photoshop filters and tools. The real challenge, however, is not technical prowess, but making an effective background that adds to your page visually without distracting from the page's content.

CHAPTER EIGHT

PHOTOSHOP WEB TYPE

There are many ways to use Photoshop to create readable, aesthetically pleasing graphic type for the web. Although you won't have the precise control and flexibility you have with vector-oriented programs like Illustrator, Freehand, and CorelDRAW!, Photoshop's Type tool, especially the one in Photoshop 5, gives you an effective option.

This chapter is organized into three general sections:

*   Working with Photoshop 5's Type tool

*   Working with rendered type

*   Going that extra mile

The first section is only relevant if you are working with Photoshop 5. The other two sections contain tips and techniques relevant to most versions of Photoshop, including 5.0, 5.02, and 5.5.

Working with Photoshop 5's Type tool

Photoshop 5 introduced a new Type tool that creates a special editable type layer. You can now change the font, font style, size, orientation, kerning, spacing, and color of your type at any time. This is radically different than earlier versions of Photoshop, which generated type that was unchangeable once it was placed in a layer. Combined with another Photoshop 5 addition, Layer Effects, it's easier than ever to create type with drop-shadows, neon glows, and special effects that will enhance your web work.

Photoshop 5.5 can set type on a vertical as well as a horizontal axis. Just as with earlier versions of Photoshop, you access the Type tool

Colors and file size

Bear in mind that the need for optimal file size and browser-safe colors apply to type as well as to your other web graphics. Type is likewise ineffective if it takes a long time to download or if the colors unexpectedly shift.

in the toolbar. When you click and hold on the Type tool, however, you'll see four options, not just two. The two new icons are for normal and outline vertical type. A vertical arrow indicates they are for vertical type. Figure 8-1 shows the four type options. With normal type you can always go back and change horizontal type to vertical type and vice versa by choosing Layer → Type, as shown in Figure 8-2. You can't do this with outline type. Just like earlier versions of Photoshop, outline type creates an active selection in the shape of type on the active layer. Once you close the Type dialog option box and fill and deselect the outline type, it becomes just like any other bitmap element in your image. It is no longer controlled by the Type tool or Type tool options.

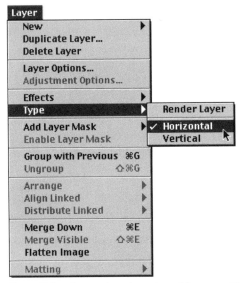

Figure 8-2. *Change the orientation of the normal type at any time via the Layer → Type menu.*

Position the cursor where you want to place type and click. The basic operation of the Type tool is unchanged. A Type tool dialog box appears, as shown in Figure 8-3. Here you can choose a font, font style, size, color, kerning, and other positioning options. If you select Preview, your choices show up in the image and you can move the type in the image by positioning the cursor over it and dragging. After you close the dialog box, a new layer is created. You know it's a type layer and therefore editable when you see a *T* in the layer palette.

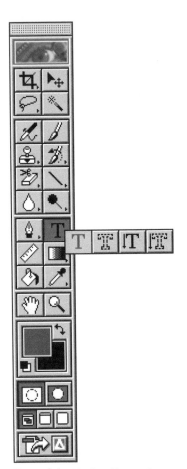

Figure 8-1. *The four Type tools are (left to right) normal horizontal, outline horizontal, normal vertical, and outline vertical.*

Figure 8-3. *The Type Tool dialog box.*

Problems and limitations

Anyone with basic Photoshop skills can quickly master the new Type tool. However, in my experience, and after listening to other web producers, I've identified several areas where further explanation and emphasis is helpful:

- If you use Photoshop 5.0, you need to know that the Type tool in that version is flawed. For example, kerning, which controls the spacing between two characters, barely works. This and other bugs were largely fixed in Version 5.02, which is available on the adobe.com web site as a free upgrade for 5.0 users.

- Pre-5 versions of Photoshop do a good job of rendering bold and italic type, and 5.5's type tool includes the option for simulated bold and italic styles. However, if you are using 5.0 or 5.02 and you don't have the bold and italic versions of your type font installed in your system, creating bold and italic type is problematic. For workarounds to these limitations see the sections "Making italic type" and "Making bold type without bold fonts" later in this chapter.

- Although you can now change the color of your type directly from the Type dialog option box, you can't control the color of individual letters or symbols. Color changes are global and affect all the type in the Type dialog option box. (You can, however, change the size, font, and style of individual letters or symbols.)

For a relatively easy workaround to this limitation, see the "Changing an individual type's color" section.

- If you commonly apply filters to type—and who doesn't?—at first glance you'll be disappointed. Once type is set in a Photoshop 5 Type Layer, filters are not an option. You can apply Layer Effects and Transformation commands under the Edit menu (except for Perspective and Distort), but not filters. This limitation is easily overcome: simply make a copy of your type layer and render the copied layer (Layer → Type → Render Layer). Your type is now uneditable but you can apply any filter effect you want. (It's a good idea to keep a copy of the editable layer in case you want to go back and change your type.)

- As good as the new Type tool is, you still can't create wraparound type without resorting to crude workarounds that produce questionable quality. It's best to use Illustrator or FreeHand for these effects and import your type into Photoshop. (See Chapter 10, *Importing Vectors into Photoshop.*)

Moving and positioning type

In Photoshop 5, you can selectively move characters and words by following these steps:

1. Double-click on the type layer containing the type you wish to move.

2. In the Type option box, place the insertion point between the letters you wish to move. Deselect Auto Kern and enter a kerning value. Positive kerning values move characters apart; negative values move them closer together.

3. To raise or lower type relative to the baseline, select the character you want to move and enter a Baseline value. Positive values move the type up; negative values move type down.

To radically move type up or down, left or right, it is sometimes easier to render the type layer and then follow these steps:

1. Select the layer containing the type you wish to move, then drag with the lasso tool around the desired type or words.

2. Once you are finished selecting, activate the Move tool by pressing the keyboard letter V.

3. Position the pointer inside the selected area (or, if you are moving the contents of the entire layer without a selection, position the pointer anywhere on the screen) and drag to the desired position. To move the selection in 1-pixel increments, press Command/Control and press the arrow keys in the direc-

tion you want to go. To move the selection in 10-pixel increments, press Shift at the same time.

This method works with earlier versions of Photoshop as well.

Layer effects and type

The benefits of using Photoshop's new Type tool in conjunction with Layer Effects are enormous. Since both layer effects and type in Photoshop 5.5 are changeable, you can experiment to your heart's delight, fine-tuning your work until you get it just right. That is what Valerie Robbins did to create the type shown in Figure C-105. She applied a drop shadow (Layer → Effects → Drop Shadow) to a layer containing a dark-brown colored word "Coffee" and to the "decoration" layer, which contained a decorative element. She also applied a drop shadow, an outer glow, and bevel and emboss to a type layer containing a gold-colored word "Coffee."

Distorting 5's type

Although you can't apply filter effects to 5's type layers without first rendering the type—which sets it permanently—you can apply the scale, rotate, skew, and flipping controls found under Edit → Transform. When you apply these commands you can always go back and change the type attributes. However, you can't change the actual transform without using the History palette. If you are not happy with your transform, and the History palette undo is not an option, do the following:

1. Double-click on the layer containing the transformed type you wish to change.

2. Select and copy the type in the Type dialog option box.

3. Close the box.

4. Select the Type tool from the toolbar, and when the Type dialog option box is open, paste your type into it.

5. Close the box, make sure the layer containing the type is selected, and then start over with the transform tools.

Making italic type

If you don't have the italic version of your font loaded, you can create an italic look by slanting the type with a Transform command. This procedure results in "oblique" type and works better on sans serif fonts than serif fonts. When italic type is created by type designers, each character is carefully crafted to imitate a hand-drawn look. You'll never get that sophisticated look with this method, no matter how hard you try.

1. Create your type using the Type tool.

2. Close the Type dialog option box.

3. Select Edit → Transform → Skew and drag the corner boxes that appear around the type to get the italic look you want. (See Figure 8-4.)

Figure 8-4. *Skew sans serif type to create an oblique look.*

Making bold type without bold fonts

If the bold version of your particular type is installed, no problem. You simply select Bold from the Type dialog option box, and Photoshop does the rest. If you don't have the bold version installed, then try the following workaround. Since this method requires rendering your type layer, I suggest you make a copy of your original type layer before starting. Then you'll always have a version you can refer to and change.

To make bold type without a bold font:

1. Render a copy of the type layer containing the type you wish to make bold (Layer → Type → Render).

2. Choose a foreground color and apply the stroke command to the rendered layer (Edit → Stroke). The amount of stroke depends on how much of a bold look you want and the actual typeface you are working with. You'll have to experiment to get it just right. (See Figure 8-5, which was created using a seven-pixel stroke.)

3. Since stroking adds extra pixels to each character it essentially shoves adjacent characters closer. You'll probably want to reposition each letter to make the words more readable. Use the type positioning method outlined in the "Moving and positioning type" section to properly space the characters.

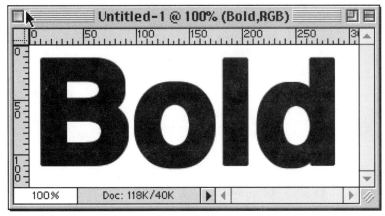

Figure 8-5. *Bold type created with a seven-pixel stroke.*

5.5's anti-aliasing and fractional character width options

New to Photoshop 5.5 is a choice of anti-aliasing options. By selecting different levels of anti-aliasing from the Type Tool dialog box you can create type that is crisp, strong, or smooth. You can also turn anti-aliasing off by choosing None. See Figure 8-6. Remember, the more anti-aliasing you apply, the more new colors are introduced, which increases the file size of your work and potentially adds non-browser-safe colors that might dither. I suggest you stick with the crisp setting and use the strong and smooth settings judiciously, only on larger type. Turning off anti-aliasing completely is only appropriate for very small, sans serif type.

Photoshop 5.5's Type tool displays type using fractional character widths. Unless you are using type smaller than 12 points, keep this option turned on and you'll get more evenly spaced type. However, with smaller type, by leaving the fractional widths setting on, your type may overlap or run together.

Changing an individual type's color

With Photoshop 5, you can choose a color directly from the Type dialog option box and change it at any time. In earlier versions, color was set in the foreground box and couldn't be changed from within the Type dialog box. If you want to change a single letter to another color you are out of luck unless you apply the following workaround:

1. In the Type dialog box choose a color by clicking on the color swatch found in the left side in the box, which brings up the Color Picker. (Remember, from within the Color Picker, you can

select colors from anywhere in Photoshop, including the color swatches palette, by holding the Option/Alt key, which turns the cursor into the eyedropper tool.) Once you've selected the color of choice, close the Color Picker.

2. Close the Type dialog box.

3. From the layer palette, create a new layer that sits above the type layer. Call this layer *color.*

4. Create a clipping path between the *color* layer and the type layer. Do this by positioning the cursor on the line between the color layer and the type layer you wish to colorize, then click. The solid line turns into a dotted one, indicating the two layers are now clipped together.

5. Choose a new foreground color. In the *color* layer, use the paintbrush or airbrush to paint the foreground color into the individual characters. If you want, choose different foreground colors for different characters.

Remember that if you change the size of your type in the Type layer or move the type, the color doesn't change size or location. You'll have to go back and repaint the color from within the clipped *color* layer.

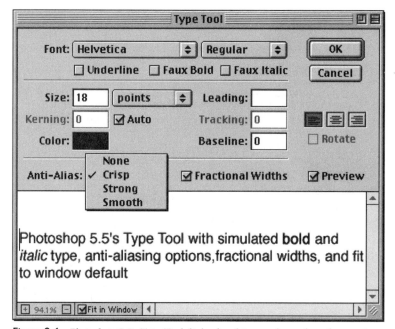

Figure 8-6. *Photoshop 5.5's Type Tool dialog box lets you choose from four anti-alias settings.*

Working with rendered type

There are times when you will want to apply a Photoshop filter to your type. Filters are a good way to create custom-looking type that will help set your web work apart from the pack. To do this using Photoshop 5, you will need to render the type (Layer → Type → Render). This essentially gives it the same characteristics as type found in earlier versions of Photoshop. For this reason, even though some of the examples shown in this section were done using Photoshop 4, the techniques are equally as valuable to users of Photoshop 5.

Using layers to organize rendered type

Once your type is rendered, there is no automatic way to determine which font was used, its size, or its style. So if you want to save time when you update your web pages, it's a good idea to have a systematic plan to organize these details.

Bea Garcia has come up with a clever way to organize this information. When her page contains several typefaces, set at different sizes and styles, such as the page shown in Figure 8-7, she always creates a separate Photoshop layer where she keeps all the information regarding the type used on that particular page.

Figure 8-7. *What do you do when you can't remember what typeface you used? Save the information in a Photoshop layer.*

Figure 8-8 shows the layer containing this information.

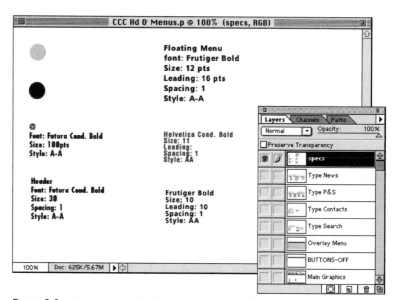

Figure 8-8. *Once you open the layer containing all the type information, it's easy to go back and make the necessary changes.*

A simple way to make a neon effect

Corey Hitchcock at The Gate doesn't have time for fancy methods. If she uses a special effect, it has to be quick and simple. To create the neon effect shown in Figure C-106, she used Photoshop 3.0 as follows:

1. She created the text in Photoshop, placing it as black type, anti-aliased, in its own layer, against a gray background in a separate layer, as shown in Figure C-107.

2. She made a copy of the layer containing the text, turned Preserve Transparency on, and filled the layer with yellow. She positioned this layer under the black text layer.

3. She turned off Preserve Transparency and applied a 4-pixel Gaussian blur to the yellow type layer, as shown in Figure C-108.

4. Then she copied the yellow layer three more times for a total of four yellow type layers. This enhanced the effects of the Gaussian blur and gave the text a neon blur, as shown in Figure C-109.

She then completed the graphic by adding a black background, a circle template she made in Illustrator, and a purple back shadow.

Pumping up your type with graphics

You can easily fill type with an illustration, texture, or even a photo-graph with Photoshop's Type Mask tool. Using the Type Mask tool is essentially the same in both Photoshop 5 and 4. This is an easy way to embellish type and give your web page a personal look and feel. However, be sure to check your final file size. When you fill type with color-intensive photographs or illustrations, it will not only increase your file size, but also introduce colors that dither on some display systems.

Follow these steps to fill type:

1. Open the file containing the image that will fill the type. In this example, we're using a photo of a parrot, shown in Figure C-110. Select and copy all or part of the image.

2. Create a new file for your type. Select the Type Mask tool (click and hold the Type tool to access it, as shown in Figure C-111). Click in the window where you want to place your type.

3. Paste the copied image into your selection (Edit → Paste Into) to create the filled type effect, shown in Figure C-112. This places your image behind your selection, and the selection masks off the entire image except those within the type selection. When you Paste Into like this, you also create another layer, which contains both the pasted image and the image mask (shown in the Layers palette in Figure C-112). You can move the back-ground image by selecting the Move tool (shortcut key → V) and moving the tool within the selection area. When you have what you want, flatten the image and save it as a GIF or JPEG. The color image is shown in Figure C-113.

Graduating colors with clipped overlays

It's one thing to fill type with a single, flat color, and another to create a graduated, multicolored effect that looks good on the Web. Valerie Robbins put in quite a bit of effort to create the type shown in Figure C-114. Her use of clipping groups allowed her to define one layer as a mask for another layer, which gave her precise control over the way the way the type elements in the different layers interacted. "Grouping" layers this way (you'll see how shortly) is simple, and in the case of Valerie's work, it produced an attractive final touch without going through the effort of actually creating a mask.

Valerie used Photoshop 4.0 to create this example. However, if she had used Photoshop 5, she'd do everything the same except, for the final touch, instead of the Gaussian blur filter she'd likely use 5's Layer Effects to create a drop shadow effect.

Here's her process:

1. First she created the type in Adobe Illustrator. She used 56-point Arnold Boecklin.

2. She drag-and-dropped the Illustrator type into Photoshop 4.0, which automatically anti-aliased it and placed it on a new layer, which she named *cyber-bohemia*. (You can control whether Post-Script objects are anti-aliased or not in the File → Preferences → General dialog box. Or copy and paste, instead of drag-and-dropping, to bring up a Paste dialog box, which lets you specify whether your PostScript object will be placed as pixels or paths, and whether the pixels will be anti-aliased.)

3. Next, she created a layer for the background color. She filled this layer with the same yellow color she used for the web page background and moved it to the bottom of the stack, as shown in Figure C-115.

4. She duplicated the *cyber-bohemia* layer, named it *overlay*, and moved it to the top of the stack.

5. She selected the black type. (The easiest way to do this is to press Command/Control and click on the type layer.) Then she removed the color from the type by pressing the Delete key. The result is a transparent layer with a type selection, as shown in Figure C-116.

6. She set her foreground color to rusty red and selected the Gradient tool. Then she opened the Gradient Tool Options palette and selected the Foreground to Transparent gradient. (Since the gradient is Foreground to Transparent, it doesn't matter what your background color is at this point.) With the *overlay* layer selected she applied the gradient across the letters. (Make sure that Preserve Transparency is turned off.) The result is shown in Figure C-117.

7. To this *overlay* layer, she then applied a Gaussian blur with a radius of 0.5 pixels. This removed any jagged edges on the type that occurred during the blending process.

8. In the *overlay* layer, she pressed Option/Alt while clicking the cursor on the solid line separating the *overlay* and *cyber-bohemia* layers. This made a clipping group, and the line became dotted. Essentially, this turned the *cyber-bohemia* layer into a mask. Now the overlay layer's texture and color appeared only in the areas defined by the letters in *cyber-bohemia*. (To unclip layers, press Option/Alt and click the line again.)

After taking care of the letterforms with clipping paths, she applied a few critical finishing touches to this graphic. With the Move tool, she added dimensionality by moving the *overlay* layer up and to the left.

This simple step, combined with the effect of the clipping path, added dimensionality to the type. To see the difference, compare Figures C-118 and C-119.

She now created another duplicate of the first *cyber-bohemia* layer and named it *cyber-bohemia gaussian blur*, moving it below *cyber-bohemia*. Then she deselected the text in the *cyber-bohemia gaussian blur* layer and turned off Preserve Transparency. She applied a Gaussian blur with the radius set between 2 and 3 pixels, giving this attractive lettering a final touch.

Stroking and adding texture to type

Type on the Web that stands out can take both time and advanced Photoshop techniques, but it's worth it. To create the type shown in Figure C-120, for example, Valerie Robbins used a variety of techniques that gave her work a unique look. With Photoshop's Stroke command (Edit → Stroke), which uses a foreground color to paint a border around a selection, she easily created the golden outline around the words "Golden" and "The." She also used one of Photoshop's several texture tools to give the word "Alley" a nice effect.

1. Working in Illustrator, she created the words "The Golden Alley" in the Airstream typeface, at sizes ranging from 50 to 115 points. She also created a geometrical shape to place behind the type as a unifying element. She dragged the type into Photoshop and placed it on its own layer, called *The Golden Alley*, shown in Figure C-121.

2. She brought in the geometrical shape separately, colorized it with a browser-safe gold, and named its layer *Shape*, as shown in Figure C-122. She duplicated each word and placed them in separate layers so she could manipulate each word separately.

3. To create the glow around the word "Golden," she switched to the appropriate layer and selected the type with the Magic Wand.

4. With a web-safe gold color selected as the foreground color, she applied a 4-pixel stroke to the selection, as shown in Figure C-123.

5. To create the dropshadow, she duplicated the *Golden* layer, moved the copy beneath the original layer, and selected the new layer, called *Golden copy*.

   Then she turned on Preserve Transparency and filled the type with a web-safe rust color. With the Move tool, she offset the type down and to the right, as shown in Figure C-124.

6. In the *Alley* layer, she turned on Preserve Transparency, and filled the "Alley" type with a browser-safe pea green.

7. She then duplicated the *Alley* layer and used the Texturizer filter to apply a canvas texture. (In the Texturizer dialog, she set scaling at 120%, relief at 7 pixels, and light direction from the top.)

8. With Preserve Transparency on, she blurred the texture twice, first with a 5-pixel Gaussian blur and then with a 25-pixel motion blur. Then she applied a drop shadow, as with "Golden." Figure C-125 shows the results.

9. As with the other words, she created a drop-shadow for "The."

10. On a new layer, which she placed beneath the *Shape* layer, she created an oval and filled it with an icy blue from the Web palette. Then she gave the oval a 1-pixel black stroke, using a 1-pixel-width black (Edit → Stroke), as shown in Figure C-126.

The final step is simply to turn on all the layers, index the image (using an adaptive palette to retain the texture pattern), and save it as a GIF file.

Again, Valerie used Photoshop 4.0 for this example and again, if she were using Photoshop 5, she'd do everything the same except use 5's Layer Effects to create a drop shadow in step 8 instead of using the Gaussian blur and motion blur filters.

Going that extra mile

Occasionally, you'll get that super-fastidious client who needs perfection in every detail, such as tiny, anti-aliased type. In those instances, you might need to use labor-intensive, tedious techniques that let you go that extra mile.

Making tiny type

Most web designers shy away from type that is smaller than 9 points since it's hard to read on most monitors. There are times, however, when small type is useful, as long as it is customized to be readable on the Web.

Gregg Hartling needed something smaller than 9-point type for a web page that contained several navigational graphics all packed into a small space. Using Photoshop, he painstakingly made his own 6-point type, pixel by pixel. He anti-aliased the type by hand, making the tiny type very readable. These are the steps he followed:

1. With the Type tool, he created an alphabet in 9-point, upper-case, aliased Geneva to use as a model for his tiny type.

2. Zooming in at 500%, he used the Pencil tool set at 1 pixel and carefully duplicated the model at a smaller size. Then he cut and pasted the characters to form words.

Figure 8-9 shows a sample of some of the type he created. The first and third rows are aliased 9-point Geneva; the second and fourth rows are the type he created by hand. The custom anti-aliasing effect shown here also makes the type easier to read.

Anti-aliasing by hand

When you select the Type tool's anti-alias option, Photoshop automatically adds pixels and color to simulate smooth corners instead of jaggies. But you lose control over how and which colors are used. With great effort, Gregg Hartling achieves an effective, anti-aliased look that gives him control. Since he uses only two browser-safe colors—one for the original type and one to create the anti-aliased look—he maintains a smaller file size and prevents unwanted dithering.

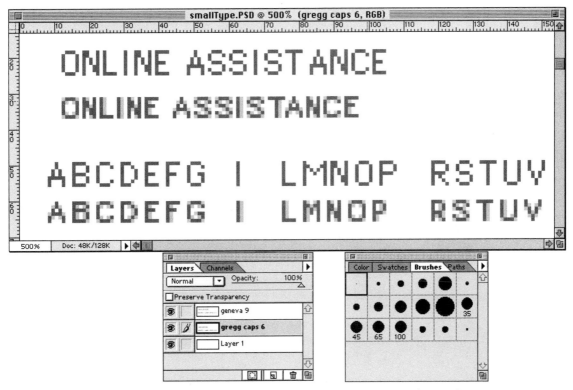

Figure 8-9. *It's quite tedious, but with Photoshop's Pencil tool you can create custom anti-aliasing of type.*

In Figure 8-9, for example, you can see where he added pixels to the letter "A" in the word "ASSISTANCE," making it wider and more readable. Compare this with the Photoshop-generated anti-aliased type shown in Figure C-127, and you'll understand the advantage of this method. The following steps detail his technique:

1. To have both a working and viewing window open, he opens the same file twice. This enables him to have extreme magnification in one window and see the effects of his intricate work in the other window at normal resolution.

2. Magnifying one window to at least 1200%, he picks a browser-safe color that is a darker variation of his background color. Figure C-128 shows the window blown up to 1200%.

3. With the Pencil tool set at 1 pixel, he softens the hard edges and adds weight to an otherwise slender type.

Blur for readability

When Savage Design's Bea Garcia creates graphical type for her web pages, the bottom line is readability. That means no special effects like embossing and no unnecessary colorizing that detracts from the type itself. Garcia consistently sets off her type from the background to ensure visibility. Typically, to do this, she applies a blur effect, either to the type itself or to the background.

She favors the Helvetica Compressed and Gill Sans fonts, especially when she needs to use smaller-sized type, because they display very well on the Web. But she uses other fonts as well. To create the type shown in Figure C-129, she chose Frutiger Bold set at 12 points.

To create a blur effect like the one that Garcia favors you can either apply a blur effect to the type itself with Photoshop 5's Layer Effects. (Layer → Effects → Dropshadow) or, in other versions of Photoshop, use the Gaussian blur filter.

To apply the Gaussian blur filter you should:

1. Duplicate the layer containing your type, and then check the Preserve Transparency box in the Layers palette.

2. Fill the type with a dark gray and then turn off Preserve Transparency. (Note: You can turn Preserve Transparency on and off by pressing the slash key.)

3. Next apply a Gaussian blur with, say, a radius of 1.9 pixels to the duplicate layer containing the filled type. (Make sure that Preserve Transparency is off before you do this or the blur won't have any effect.)

4. Merge the layers.

Applying a blur to type this way produces a subtle effect, but it's just enough to make the letters pop out from the green and make the reading easier for the web viewer. The final image in Figure C-131 may not look much better than the original (Figure C-130) when reproduced in print, but the difference is apparent on screen.

The inherent beauty of type

Virginia designer Chuck Green comes to the Web from the old school of design, where type is an art form into itself. He believes that choosing type carefully and paying attention to how individual letters interact with one another is more effective than spending hours creating some fancy effect.

Figure 8-11. *Green used Photoshop's Free Rotation tool to position his type.*

The type in Figure 8-10 was created with Photoshop 3.0 for Windows. Nothing fancy was done to the type itself—no texture or distortion was applied, only an occasional flat color. Nonetheless, Chuck put a lot of thought into choosing the appropriate typefaces and positioning each letter and each word so that they related to each other in a visually appealing way.

Chuck prefers to move each type element by hand, even though Photoshop's Type tool provides a numerical way to control the amount of letter spacing and leading. Take, for example, the "Try it Free" type shown in Figure 8-11. He used Agenda Bold Ultra Condensed and Fredigor 95 Ultra Black for this graphic. He didn't do anything to the type until after he placed it with the Type tool. Then he used Photoshop 3.0's Free Rotation tool (Image → Rotate → Free) and individually moved the letters until he got them just right. He created a duplicate layer and filled the type with 50% gray, applied a slight Gaussian blur, and offset the whole layer to create a drop shadow. There's nothing fancy here, just a lot of time and patience by a very dedicated man.

What isn't obvious is the amount of time he spends in choosing the correct type to begin with. According to Chuck, the character of a typeface establishes a mood, much like a musical score does for a movie. It is not the primary focus, but it often plays a pivotal role in telling the story. Figure 8-12 shows two of the typeface palettes that he has put together, showing how they each elicit a particular mood or emotion. Note that each example includes a headline, a subhead, text, and a caption.

Making a difference

Even though much of the type you see on the Web is HTML-coded and never touches Photoshop, there will always be a place for graphical type. Custom-made graphical type gives your web page a unique look and feel. It also creates a visual language that helps a viewer navigate through various levels of information. If you've chosen your fonts carefully and vary the size, you can create a visual tension that holds the viewer to your page.

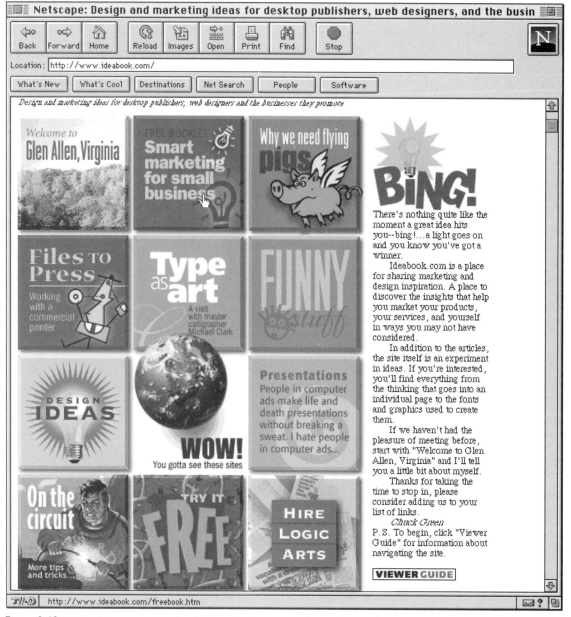

Figure 8-10. *A simple type treatment, but it shows the importance of type selection, kerning, and word spacing.*

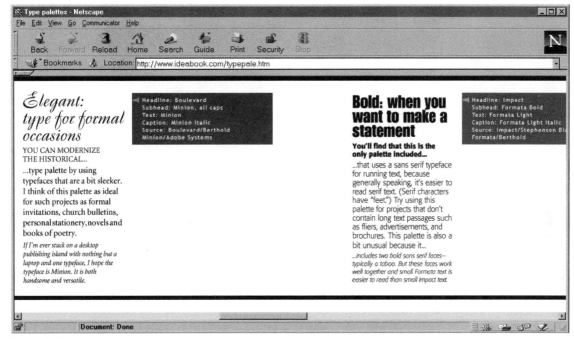

Not only does Photoshop give you the power to create just about any special effect you want, but it also makes it easy to perform subtle tasks such as letter and word spacing that can make all the difference and show your understanding and mastery of type.

Figure 8-12. *Some of Green's type palettes.*

CHAPTER NINE

CREATING NAVIGATIONAL GRAPHICS

W eb designers often use Photoshop to create a variety of navigational graphics, ranging from simple beveled buttons to more complex icons that contain both text and images. By taking the time to create these custom graphics, you can add a unique look and feel to your web pages that is not possible with clipart or, for that matter, simple HTML word links.

This chapter shows you quick and easy ways to spherize photographs into window-like buttons, create square buttons with beveled edges, create up and down buttons, round bullets, and forward and backward arrows, mostly through real-world examples.

It also shows you how to use Photoshop 5's amazing layer effects.

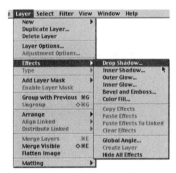

Figure 9-1. *The Layer→ Effects menu.*

Layer effects with Photoshop 5

Many useful effects can now be automatically done using Photoshop 5's layer effects. You can apply a drop shadow, a glow, beveling, embossing, or a color fill (5.5 only) by simply choosing Layer→ Effects and selecting one of the effects options. See Figure 9-1. The layer effects are linked to the selected layer contents, and if you move or edit the contents of the layer, the effects are modified correspondingly. You can also copy and apply layer effects from one layer to another by choosing Copy Effects from the Layer→ Effects menu, selecting a destination layer in the layer palette, and then choosing Layer→ Effects→ Paste Effects.

Layer effects are easily changed or removed by choosing Layer→ Effects or by double-clicking (right-clicking in Windows) on the "f" icon that appears in the layer palette. This brings up the dialog box shown in Figure 9-2. From this dialog box you can fine-tune the effects by choosing such parameters as opacity, angle, blur, intensity, and so on. A Preview option gives you real-time viewing of the effects on the contents of the layer.

You aren't limited to one effect per layer. You can apply several effects to the same layer. To do this, in the Layer → Effects menu simply select the effects you want. A check mark will indicate your choices. If you double-click on the "f" icon in the Layer palette and bring up the Effects dialog box you can scroll and choose from the effects options. When you find the effect you want, click on the Apply button to make the effect active.

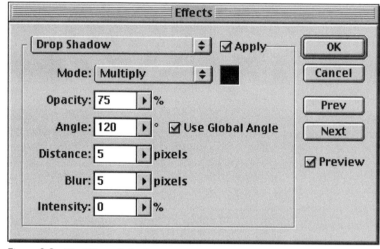

Figure 9-2. *The Effects dialog box.*

In order to alter the effect beyond the options provided in the Effects dialog box—say, for example, apply a noise filter to the effect—you'll need to render the effect as a separate layer. You can do this in the Layer → Effects menu by choosing Create Layer. This removes the effects from the original layer, places them in separate layers and beyond the control of the Effects menu. It also means the effect is no longer linked to the original layer and it will not update as you change the original layer.

Creating photo bubbles

Designer Valerie Robbins created the navigational device for my site, shown in Figure C-132, by using Photoshop's Spherize filter to create bubble-shaped photographs placed in window-like buttons. Here's how she did it.

To create the Castle button on the left, she followed these steps:

1. She began by opening one of my photographs of a castle and scaling it down using Photoshop's Free Transform command (in Photoshop 5, it's Edit → Free Transform; in 4 it's Layer → Free Transform) to the size she wanted. Using the circle selection tool, with the Shift key pressed to constrain the selection to a perfect circle, she copied and pasted the selection into a new document named *Castle Button*, pasting the image onto a white background (see Figure C-133).

   She then selected the blue background and pasted in clouds that she had copied from another photograph.

2. She brightened the background of the photo about 20% (Image → Adjust → Brightness → Contrast) and used the spotlight effect (Filter → Render → Lighting Effects) to bring a little more directional light into the image. To enhance the effect, she selected the lower part of the image and used Brightness/Contrast to lighten it.

3. She then selected the image area and ran the Spherize filter at 25% (normal mode).

4. After she spherized the image, she needed to tweak her lighting. She selected the image, and using the Lighting Effects filter again, she brought just a slight amount of directional light from the top right that darkened the bottom of the bubble.

5. To give the image even more of a bubble effect, she used the Burn tool to darken the bottom-right corner of the circle and the Dodge tool on the top left corner of the circle. Both tools were set at 17% exposure, with Midtones selected.

6. As a final touch, she selected and stroked the bubble with a 7-pixel black border.

She followed similar procedures to create both the Bridge and Golden Alley bubbles. Then she copied and placed all three of these images into a new file called *smaller buttons* and sized them down, as shown in Figure C-134.

To create the Read Me button, Val followed these steps:

1. She set the type in Illustrator using Berthold Akzidenz Grotesk Bold Extended, 14 point on 16 point leading.

2. She then copied and pasted the type into Photoshop.

3. She drew a square with the marquee selection tool, positioned the type in the upper-left corner, and then applied a black 3-pixel stroke to the square selection to make a box around the type (Edit → Stroke).

Custom arrows

A simple way to create a directional arrow in Photoshop is to use the Line tool. Double-click on the Line tool icon to bring up the Line Tool Options palette. Choose Arrowheads and then the shape you want. Once you have made one, you can further customize it with other Photoshop tools. (In Photoshop 5, the line tool is grouped with the pencil tool.)

4. She created a new layer, filled it with a light blue, and used Kai's Power Tools to create the concentric circle behind the Read Me text. To mimic a computer cursor, she chose an arrow from Zapf Dingbats and then played with this shape using Free Transform, sizing and rotating until she got the look of an arrow she liked.

5. She flattened the layers, and for the final browser-safe green border, she selected the square button and stroked it 5 pixels.

When she was finished with Read Me, she aligned the four buttons on the page with the help of Photoshop's Grids feature.

To create the type for the Castle, Bridge, and Golden Alley bubbles she did the following:

1. Set the type (Arnold Boecklin) in Illustrator.

2. Pasted the type over each button, using guides to position them precisely.

3. Created a layer behind the type layer and made three identically sized rectangular selections, which she filled with 30% white so the titles would pop out but the image could still be seen behind.

Creating beveled boxes with the Gradient tool

The photo bubbles that Valerie created worked well on the opening navigational page where size wasn't critical. In order to create a smaller navigational bar for other pages, she created graphical icons and then placed them in beveled boxes that she created using the Gradient tool, as shown in Figure 9-3. (In Photoshop 5, this is done using the Linear Gradient tool.)

Figure 9-3. *On the Castle page, beveled graphics are compact and handy.*

Here is how she made the beveled boxes:

1. With the square marquee, she first drew a rectangular shape in Photoshop, stroking the edge 1 pixel. She then drew another

rectangular shape in the center of the outer rectangle, stroked it with 1 pixel, and filled with it with 20% gray.

2. With the Line tool, she drew from the outer corner of the rectangle to each inside corresponding corner until she had a cut jewel-like shape.

3. Using the Magic Wand tool, she selected the left bevel. Using the Gradient tool she filled this selected shape with a light gray (foreground) to dark gray (background) gradient. In the Gradient Tool Options palette, she set her opacity at 100%, selected Linear and Foreground to Background. She dragged the tool from the outer edge of her frame to the inside, holding down the Shift key to give an even fill.

4. Using the Magic Wand again, she next selected the bottom bevel and did the same as above, dragging the tool from the bottom of the bevel to the inside.

5. For the right and top bevel, she changed her blend, going from dark gray (foreground) to black (background). For the right bevel, she dragged her Gradient tool from the outer edge of her frame to the inside, and for the top bevel she dragged the tool from the top of the bevel to the inside.

She copied and pasted the button for a total of 5 buttons, as shown in Figure 9-4. Using a combination of Illustrator and Photoshop, she created the various icons that would fit inside each box. She added a 1-pixel black frame around each graphic (except for the Read Me icon), which was slightly smaller than the gray fill inside the boxes, to add the appearance of depth. (With the Golden Alley button, she pasted the figure on top of the single-pixel black frame so that it broke out over the frame, giving it more dimension.) See Figure 9-5.

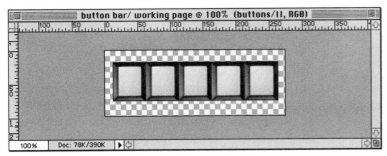

Figure 9-4. *Five beveled buttons.*

To create the drop shadow, she copied the layer containing the icons, named it *blur*, and, with Preserve Transparency turned on, filled the blur copy with 50% gray. Turning off Preserve Transparency, she

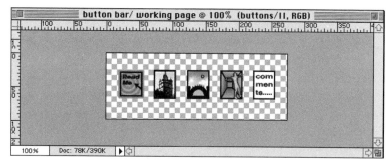

Figure 9-5. *She added a 1-pixel frame, slightly smaller than the gray fill, to add depth to each graphic.*

Gaussian-blurred it to her liking and moved the layer over and to the right, as shown in Figure 9-6. (Making drop shadows with Photoshop 5 is a snap. See the "Layer effects with Photoshop 5" section earlier in this chapter.) Combining these elements creates the effect seen on the web page shown in Figure 9-3.

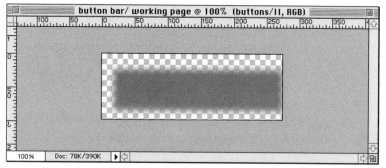

Figure 9-6. *You can make a drop shadow by applying a Gaussian blur to a duplicate layer moved slightly to the right and down.*

Painting beveled buttons

Using the Gradient tool is one way to create a beveled look. Erika Sears, a full-time interactive media designer for Knowledge Adventure Software, suggests another. This method is simple, requires no filters, and relies mostly on the Paint tool.

Erika often makes her buttons "interactive," meaning that she uses Shockwave or JavaScript to make them do something when they are selected. For that reason she often creates both an "up" position and a "down" position, creating the effect of a physical button being pushed.

Here is how she creates a beveled button in the "up" position (as shown in Figure 9-7):

1. She starts with a new layer and calls it *up button.*

2. Using the Marquee selection tool, she draws a rectangle of the desired size. (Remember, you can create a square button by holding down the Shift key while you use the rectangular selection tool.)

3. She fills this selection with a color.

4. Keeping her selection active (or choosing Preserve Transparency from the Layers palette), she sets the Paintbrush to a medium-sized hard edge and "paints" the edges of the rectangle in a specific order, each with different opacities of white and black (described in the next steps). You can easily set your foreground to black and your background to white by pressing Shift and then the D key.

5. She starts at the right side of the top edge with 50% white and her blending mode set at Normal. She holds down the Shift key and drags straight across from right to left.

6. Then for the far-left edge, she changes the opacity to 70%, holds down the Shift key and drags straight down.

7. For the bottom edge, she selects black, sets her Paintbrush opacity to 50% and her blend mode to Multiply, and holding down the Shift key, she drags from left to right across the bottom edge of the rectangle.

8. For the far right edge, she also uses black, sets her opacity to 70% and her blend mode to Multiply, and holding down the Shift key, drags from top to bottom on the right edge of the rectangle.

To create a button in "down" position:

1. She makes a duplicate layer of the *up* button and renames it *down.*

2. She moves this duplicate rectangle to the right of the up button.

3. With the *down* layer active, she flips the button first horizontally and then vertically (Layer → Transform → Flip Horizontal/Vertical), as shown in Figure 9-8.

Embossing and debossing type

Erika also creates embossed or debossed type to represent different positions of a navigational device. To create the embossed type that you see in Figure 9-9, she did the following:

1. She created a new layer and called it *up text.*

2. She chose a black foreground and then typed in the word *button* and clicked OK to place it.

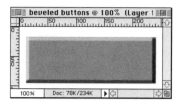

Figure 9-7. *By using the Paintbrush at different opacities, you can make an "up" button with a beveled look...*

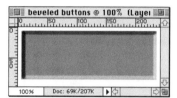

Figure 9-8. *... or a "down" button like this.*

Figure 9-9. *Create embossed type by using a white background set at 30% opacity and moved up and to the right.*

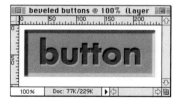

Figure 9-10. *Create debossed type by using a white background set at 30% opacity and moved down to the left.*

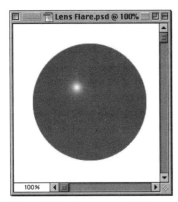

Figure 9-11. *Sears created this bullet ball with the Lens Flare filter.*

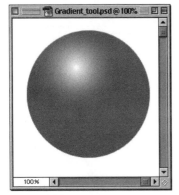

Figure 9-12. *Bullet ball created with the Gradient tool.*

3. Using the Move tool, she positioned it over the beveled *up* button.

4. She then selected a white foreground and typed in the word *button* and clicked OK to place it.

5. She changed the opacity of the layer containing the white text to 30%.

6. She used the arrow keys to position the white text slightly up and to the right of the black button type. This gives it an embossed look.

To give the same type a debossed look, she repeated the same process, but in step 6 she positioned the white text over the black text slightly down and to the left, as shown in Figure 9-10. (Again, Photoshop 5's Layer effects makes creating an embossed look easy. See the "Layer effects with Photoshop 5" section earlier in this chapter.)

Bullet balls with light effects

Bullet balls come in handy as a way to separate large blocks of text and provide an intuitively recognized navigational button. Here are a couple of ways that Erika creates them.

To create the ball of the type shown in Figure 9-11:

1. She draws a circle on a new layer with the circular Marquee, holding down the Shift key to make a perfect circle.

2. She fills this selection with color.

3. She uses the Lens Flare filter (Filter → Render → Lens Flare). Options set → Brightness 85%, Lens Type 105mm Prime.

4. To keep the gradation intact, she converts to Indexed Color mode and selects 8-bit adaptive diffusion.

To create a ball like the one shown in Figure 9-12:

1. She uses the circular Marquee on a new layer to create a circle.

2. She sets the Gradient tool options to Radial, 100% Foreground to Background (with her foreground set to white and her background set to a desired color), dragging a short line from left to right at a 45-degree angle, creating a highlight.

3. To keep the gradation intact, she converts to the Index mode and selects 8-bit adaptive diffusion.

Creating flashy round buttons

Here is another method Erika uses to create round buttons that are a
bit flashier and can be made in an "up" or "down" position.

Figure 9-13. *A button in the up position.*

To create "up" position buttons as the one shown in Figure 9-13,
Erika does the following:

1. Makes a new layer called *base up.*

2. Uses the circle Marquee tool to draw a circle the size of her
   desired button.

3. Selects two colors, a light foreground (preferably white) and a
   dark background.

4. Uses the Gradient tool set at Linear and Foreground to Background with 100% gradation and drags it straight across the
   middle of the circle from the left edge to the right edge.

5. Makes a new layer and calls it *top up.*

6. Draws a smaller circle to fit within the larger one. (The edges of
   the big one should be wide and visible.)

7. Changes the Gradient tool setting to Radial, and keeps 100%
   opacity.

8. Drags the Gradient tool across the middle of the circle from the
   left to right starting in about one-quarter of the total diameter.

9. Positions this circle on top of the larger one on the layer below.

10. Fills the center ball with a color, setting her opacity to 100% and
    her Mode to Soft Light.

Figure 9-14. *A button in the down position.*

To create "down" position buttons such as the one shown in
Figure 9-14:

1. Erika duplicates the layers she called *base up* and *top up* and
   calls them *base down* and *top down.*

2. She then merges *top up* and *base up.*

3. She moves this newly merged button to the right to see the
   objects below.

4. Then she rotates the smaller circle in the *top down* layer 180
   degrees (Layer → Transform → Rotate 180 degrees).

5. Then she merges the *top down* and *base down* layers.

6. As a final step, she fills the center ball called *top down* with a
   color ink, setting the opacity to 100% and mode to Multiply.

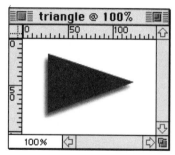

Figure 9-15. *A triangle created using Photoshop's Pen tool.*

Creating navigational triangles

Triangles always make good navigation devices, and they are very easy to create using Photoshop. Here is one way that Erika creates triangles such as the one shown in Figure 9-15:

1. First, she creates a new layer.

2. Then she selects the Pen tool from the Toolbox and uses it to draw a triangle. (To use this tool, position the pointer where you want the first point of the triangle to begin. Click to define an anchor point. Then reposition your pointer to the second point of the triangle, click, and a straight line between the first and second points will appear. Do this again for the third point of the triangle. Create the final line of the triangle by clicking back on the first point that you created.)

3. She saves this as a path by selecting Save Path from the Paths palette menu.

4. She makes a selection from her path by choosing Make Selection from the Paths palette menu, leaving her Feather Radius set to 0, and chooses Anti-aliased. Once she makes her selection, she deletes the path in the Paths palette.

5. She then fills the remaining selection with a color. (If you haven't deleted the original path, an outline of the path will be visible on the parameter of the filled triangle. You can also fill your initial path by choosing Fill → Path from the Paths palette menu, but you won't get a smooth edge.)

6. To make a drop shadow, she duplicates the layer containing the triangle and places this layer underneath the layer containing the original triangle.

7. Then she feathers the selected duplicate triangle 2 pixels and fills the selection with 100% black. She sets her layer opacity to 50% from the Layers palette options pull-down menu. When she is finished, she merges the layers.

Using found objects

With a little help from Photoshop, just about anything can be digitized and turned into a web navigational device.

Mobile buttons

"Terbo" Ted's work, as you can see in Figure C-135, is a visual cacophony. He shies away from using text, using instead pictures and graphics readable in Japan as well as in Russia. His ultimate test is his newborn baby. If the baby responds to the material he puts on his web page, well, it works.

To this end, Terbo photographed his newborn's black and white mobile with a digital camera, and using Photoshop transformed the photos into a series of images that animate and link to other pages.

To create web navigational devices from real-life objects, he followed these steps:

1. He used a digital camera to shoot his child's black-and-white mobile. Figure C-136 shows one of the original camera shots.

2. He removed the background using the Pen tool. He did this by carefully outlining the pertinent parts of the image, making a path from the Paths palette, and then turning the path into a selection and deleting it.

3. He filled the background selections with green, a color he chose to be transparent when he indexed (Image → Mode → Indexed Color) and converted his images to GIFs (see Figure 9-16).

4. Then he scaled the photos down (Image → Image Size).

5. He indexed his images using the Adaptive palette with no dither. Finally, he created a GIF, designating the background as transparent.

Figure 9-16. *After the background was deleted, Terbo filled the background with green, which he would later designate as transparent.*

Scrap buttons

To create the scrap paper button icons shown in Figure C-137, Erika Sears did the following:

1. Scanned a scrap piece of paper at 72-ppi grayscale.

2. She adjusted the brightness and contrast (Image → Brightness/Contrast) to achieve the right highlights.

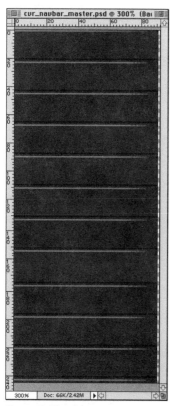

Figure 9-17. *Bobby used the Gradient tool and the Line tool to create these lines.*

3. She placed this scrap on *layer 1* and then created a duplicate image below on *layer 2*.

4. To make a drop shadow, she selected and feathered (Select → Feather) this duplicate image 2 pixels, filled with black, and set the blending opacity at 60%.

5. She gave the scrap paper on *layer 1* a tint by selecting and filling it with yellow, using the Multiply mode at 100%.

6. She then created the type using Photoshop's Type tool, and placed it on *layer 0* positioned over the scrap paper layers. See Figure C-138.

Creating an interactive navigational bar

MSNBC's Bobby Stevens created the complex navigational bar shown in Figure C-139 using 29 layers filled with 11 buttons, drop-shadowed text, and a simulated dithered edge. Because the design called for the navigational bar to change colors when buttons were selected or "rolled over," Bobby created a high-tech navigational bar by following these steps:

1. He created a new file measuring 92 × 244 pixels, a dimension given to him by the programmers at MSNBC.

2. He filled the background layer with a browser-safe gray.

3. Measuring the rectangle into 11 equal parts, he used the Gradient and Line tools to draw two horizontal lines. He created the light line shown in Figure 9-17 (blue in Figure C-139) with the Gradient tool (with two different shades of blue selected as the foreground and background colors and the gradient set to a linear, foreground-to-background blend). Above that line, he created a 1-pixel aliased black line using the Line tool.

4. He then selected the area above and including the lines, and copied and pasted the button so that he had 11 identical buttons, which he included as part of his background.

5. On one layer, he set all the type in Photoshop using Meta Bold type, anti-aliased. He selected and positioned all the type by hand, using guides to set the type 3 pixels in from the left and 2 pixels down from the blue line.

6. He then duplicated the type layer and made a drop shadow. Then he merged the two layers into one layer, as shown in Figure 9-18.

7. He then created a 92 × 19-pixel selection (the size of each button) on a new layer, and filled that selection with a browser-

safe blue. He duplicated that layer eleven times and then dragged each color bar into a position over each button. (The blue shows a web user that the selection is active.)

8. To create the teal color that appears when the user passes the cursor over the button, Bobby simply duplicated his blue button, and with Preserve Transparency on in his Layers palette, he filled the blue area with teal. (The rollover effect was programmed by MSNBC programmers using ActiveX technology. Bobby was able to approximate the final programming effect by turning his Photoshop layers off and on.)

9. Bobby's last step was to create the dither on the right side of the bar. With the Pencil tool, he drew a 2-pixel wide vertical line. Then he went in by hand and used the Pencil tool to add the pixels you see in Figure 9-19, extending them no more than 9 pixels in. It took a lot of experimentation to get an effect that looked right on a variety of platforms and monitors.

Instructions in layers

Figure 9-20 shows yet another example of how a Photoshop layer can be used to provide a very specific set of instructions that always remains with the Photoshop file. In this particular example, MSNBC designer Bobby Stevens included instructions to fellow designers on how to create section banners. Other repeating elements were specified this way as well. This made it simple for Bobby to hand off work and not have to answer endless questions about how repeating elements were created. Notice the click points for aligning type precisely and the color swatch for easy sampling.

The personal touch

In this chapter, we've outlined very specific ways to create navigational graphics. When you follow our step-by-step examples, keep in mind that you can easily add your own personal touch in many ways. For example, when color is called for, most of the time you can add any color. Size too can be altered to fit both the content of the navigational graphic and the needs of your web page.

Figure 9-18. *Text with shadow all on one layer.*

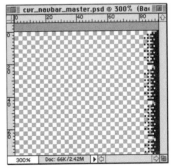

Figure 9-19. *Bobby created this simulated dither look with the Pencil Tool and a lot of hard work.*

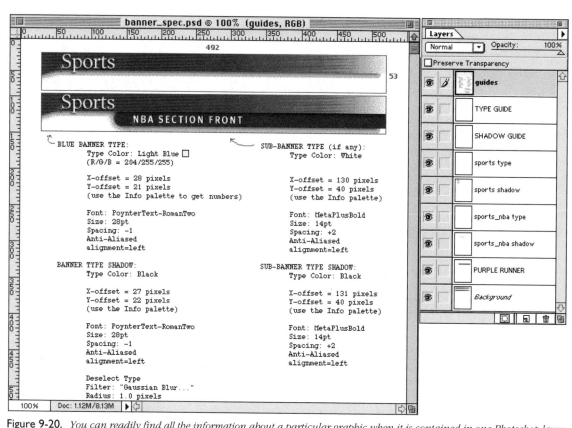

Figure 9-20. *You can readily find all the information about a particular graphic when it is contained in one Photoshop layer.*

CHAPTER TEN

IMPORTING VECTORS INTO PHOTOSHOP

At some point in the web design process, there is a good chance that you'll use a drawing program such as Illustrator, FreeHand, or CorelDRAW! These vector-based programs are quite good for creating text and complex illustrations because they use mathematical equations to define resolution-independent shapes and lines. Photoshop and other bitmap programs, on the other hand, use a limited number of discrete pixels to make up an image.

Since the Web is a bitmap environment, all vector-based graphics must ultimately be "rasterized" or converted to bitmaps. Typically, newer drawing programs provide ways of rasterizing vector graphics into bitmaps. Still, you'll likely find it convenient to import vector images into Photoshop and let Photoshop convert from vectors to bitmaps, as shown in Figure 10-1. Photoshop does an excellent job of converting vector-based graphics into bitmaps, and you can also combine your converted vector graphic with other Photoshop-created elements. By using Photoshop as a web layout tool, you can get an idea of how all pieces interact with each other on the page.

This chapter shows you how web designers bring vector-based drawings into Photoshop, as well as how they work around some of the problems such as color shifts that occur when transferring files between vector-based programs and Photoshop.

Importing vector files

Regardless of which drawing program you use, the process of bringing vector-based graphics into Photoshop is pretty straight forward. The method you use depends on which drawing program you use and the degree of control you seek over how a graphic is placed. For example, if you use File → Place, you can precisely resize

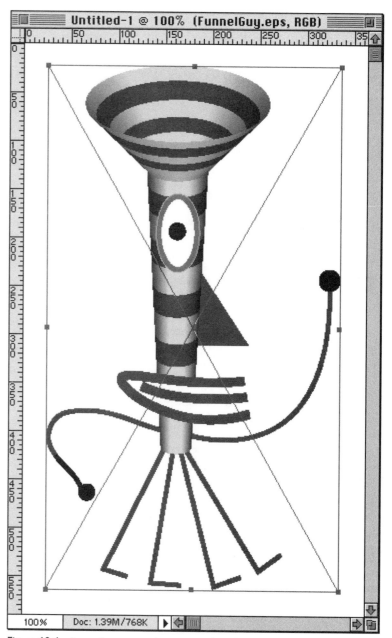

Figure 10-1. *Importing a vector image into Photoshop (illustration by John Hersey).*

any EPS graphic saved in the Illustrator format before it is converted to bitmap. If you copy and paste, you'll get to choose whether to paste vectors as pixels or paths. If you drag and drop from a program that supports this method, you won't be presented with any options at all. Photoshop will automatically rasterize and size the copied item for you.

Working with Illustrator

Illustrator 8.0 and Photoshop 5 work very well together. It is now finally possible to create an illustration in Illustrator, save it as a Photoshop file, and keep the layers and original colors intact. Some color shifting still occurs, but it is nothing like the old days when it was more efficient to bring your illustration *sans* color into Photoshop, one layer at a time.

Although web designer Brian Frick currently uses the latest versions of Illustrator and Photoshop with "good results," his experiences with earlier versions of the two programs are useful for those of us using any other combination of software.

Frick learned to produce the basic shapes of his illustrations in Illustrator, and then bring his work into Photoshop, where he combined it with bitmap figures and added the final colors. Before Illustrator 8.0, there was little reason for Frick to spend time on color in Illustrator— the color shifting between Illustrator and Photoshop was just too extreme.

The secret to this approach was placing each component of his illustration in a separate Photoshop layer. Figure C-140 show how he used each layer to fill or paint colors precisely where he wanted them.

Save in EPS

If you plan to open a graphic that you have created in Illustrator, FreeHand, or CorelDRAW! in Photoshop, it's best to save your graphic in the Illustrator EPS file format and let Photoshop do the actual rasterizing. You can also save your file as a TIFF and open it in Photoshop, but the results won't be as good as if you use the Illustrator format, which is supported by most drawing programs.

With Illustrator 8.0, you can save your file in a Photoshop format that keeps the layers intact. If you use an earlier version of Illustrator or another vector-based program, keep in mind that if the file contains layers, they'll be flattened into one layer when the file is opened in Photoshop. This is downright inconvenient because without layers containing the individual shapes, objects, and lines of your graphic, it is more difficult to colorize and otherwise handle the image. For workarounds to this problem, see the section "Importing Illustrator layers with Painter."

When he worked with an illustration containing only a few objects to colorize, Brian either drag-and-dropped or copy-and-pasted each object into a Photoshop layer. (Either of these two methods can apply to a FreeHand or CorelDRAW! graphic as well, depending on the particular version of the program.) He generally set his preferences so that the objects came in anti-aliased. (If you want to ensure that no new colors are introduced, bring your graphic in aliased.)

These methods were fine as long as there were only a few objects to copy and paste or drag and drop. For complex illustrations, Brian resorted to his own workaround with MetaCreations Painter, a paint program that works with both vector and bitmapped graphics. Using this workaround (described in the next section), he can bring a pre-8.0 Illustrator file into Photoshop with all its layers intact.

Occasionally, Brian opens his pre-8.0 Illustrator EPS files directly into Photoshop. Because this process flattens all the Illustrator layers and makes it harder to colorize the individual objects, he does this only with very simple illustrations where fine-tuning the colors is not necessary.

Importing Illustrator layers with Painter

Although it is now possible to create a layered graphic in Illustrator and bring the layers into Photoshop 5, what do you do if you are using an earlier version of either program?

You might also consider this clever workaround discovered by Brian Frick. If you already have MetaCreations Painter, it won't cost you a thing. If not, the program goes for a street price of around $300. If Painter weren't a great paint program, I wouldn't pass on this relatively expensive workaround.

To convert bitmaps with Painter, Brian follows these steps:

1. He saves his work as an Illustrator file.

2. Importing the file into Painter, he does nothing to it except choose Save As. Painter gives him the option of saving in Photoshop 3.0 format, which he does, as shown Figure 10-2.

3. Now when he opens the file in Photoshop, it opens with all the original Illustrator layers intact and in order, so he can proceed to colorize each object. See Figure 10-3.

The final result of Brian's effort as it appeared on a Discovery site is shown in Figure C-141. Brian used this technique with both Painter 4.0 and Painter 5.0 with good results.

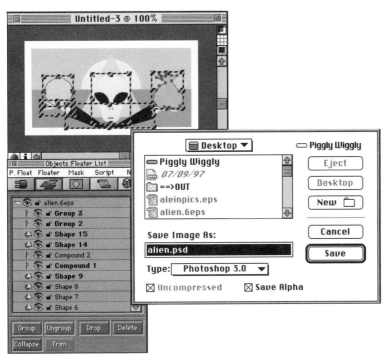

Figure 10-2. *In Painter, Brian saves his Illustrator file with its layers intact as a Photoshop 3.0 document.*

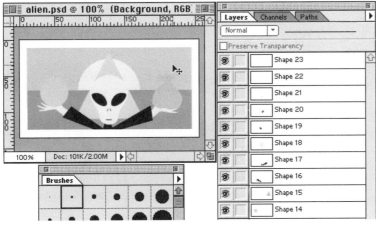

Figure 10-3. *Once Brian opens the file in Photoshop, all the layers are intact and in order, and he proceeds to colorize each of the individual objects.*

Working with FreeHand

At Icon Medialab in San Francisco, Johan Thorngren is a web designer who often creates and converts existing corporate logos for the Web. Starting in FreeHand, he copies and pastes aliased objects into Photoshop for the final rasterizing and colorizing.

His best results occur when he imports the aliased logo at its maximum size and then incrementally resizes it (50%) to the appropriate size.

Here is how he created the logo shown in Figure C-142:

1. In FreeHand, he created the black logo on a white background.

2. He copied and pasted the entire aliased FreeHand drawing into Photoshop and placed it into its own layer.

3. He resized the graphic in Photoshop (Image → Image Size) to reduce the size of the graphic and to simulate an anti-aliased look. By keeping his interpolation setting at Bicubic and incrementally scaling down the logo 50% at a time, he achieved a controlled anti-aliased effect. You can set the interpolation setting in the Image Size dialog box, or in Preferences.

   As covered in Chapter 1, *Making Photoshop Web-Friendly*, the Bicubic setting adds data and color when needed; hence the smooth edges in Thorngren's graphic. If you want to keep the jagged aliased look, you should set your interpolation setting to Nearest Neighbor; you'll need to reset this each resizing.

4. He colored the logo in Photoshop by using the Magic Wand with settings at 0 tolerance and "aliased" to select the white background. He deleted the white to transparent, leaving only the black logo on its own layer. Selecting that layer he chose Preserve Transparency, then selected a browser-safe color, which he applied to the logo by holding down Option/Alt and the Delete key. (This fills the pixels in the layer with the foreground color.)

5. He saved the graphic as a GIF and combined it on a page with the other graphic elements. (The outline and texture for the bubbles were created in a 3D program while the "lens" effect was hand-painted in Photoshop.)

Avoiding color shifts

Whatever method you use to bring a vector graphic into Photoshop, you need to be aware of the inevitable, and for the most part, unpredictable color shifts that occur when moving graphics between these

different programs. You have several choices of what to do about this
problem, including the following:

- Ignore the color shifts, figuring most people use lousy monitors
  and won't appreciate your attention to detail anyway.

- Use the Paint Bucket, Fill, or another Photoshop technique to
  colorize all or part of your illustration and increase contrast or
  boost color saturation.

- Use the workaround suggested by Adobe (described in detail in
  the section "Adobe's solution to color shifting" later in this chapter) to calibrate the way older (pre-8.0) versions of Illustrator and
  Photoshop apply colors.

- Work in your drawing program with the limited, browser-safe
  color palette. This may give you better results than if you added
  color willy-nilly, but even browser-safe colors shift when brought
  into Photoshop. You'll still need to apply Photoshop color carefully to your work.

Bumping up contrast and color saturation

Illustrator John Hersey has an immensely sensible attitude toward
color on the Web. Basically, he doesn't worry too much about it.
That's fine for him because most of his work is personal and styl-
ized. He starts out in either Illustrator or FreeHand and uses any
color he wants. Much of his work is destined for print, so he's often
working in the CMYK color mode. When he brings his illustrations
over to Photoshop using the copy and paste technique, he looks to
see if there were any radical changes in the color. If not, he leaves it
alone.

Often his Illustrator or FreeHand colors seem washed out and dull.
He uses Photoshop's contrast and saturation controls to enhance the
color. It doesn't matter whether it matches the original colors as
long as it looks good to him. Sometimes, he replaces an entire background color with a browser-safe color from his color swatch palette.

Filling shapes with color

In Photoshop, Brian Frick uses two techniques to colorize his Illustrator work. The first technique fills the shape to the parameter,
leaving a black line and creating what he calls a grunge look. The
second technique results in a colored shape with no discernible
border.

Creating a grunge look

To create the grunge look, as shown in Figure C-143, he followed these steps:

1. In Illustrator, Brian created a graphic with black lines and imported it to Photoshop. (He could have just as easily created the simple graphic in Photoshop, but he wouldn't have been able to go back later and adjust or change the lines like he can in Illustrator.)

2. He filled the graphic with the Paint Bucket. As shown in the magnified view in Figure 10-4, the color goes only to the edge of the black line, and because it is anti-aliased, it leaves a slight halo, providing the visual effect he wanted.

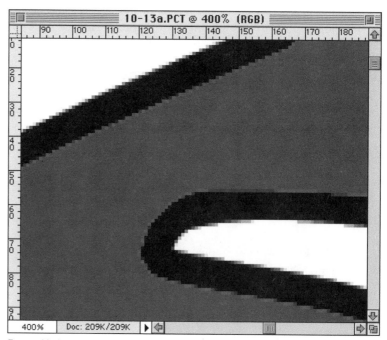

Figure 10-4. *When you fill an anti-aliased shape with the Paint Bucket, a halo effect results.*

Creating a colored shape

Figure C-144 shows the effect of colorizing individual objects placed in their own layers with Preserve Transparency turned on. When Brian uses this method, Photoshop's Fill command and other paint methods colorize the Illustrator-created lines as well, resulting in a shape of color rather than an outline filled with color.

To create a "borderless" colored shape, he followed these steps:

1. In Illustrator, Brian created the basket and its contents and imported it to Photoshop, placing each element in its own layer.

2. Selecting one layer at a time, he chose browser-safe colors, and with Preserve Transparency selected, he filled each layer with color. He then went back and added more colors for texture and odor "fumes" with the paintbrush.

Adobe's solution to color shifting

Adobe suggests a way to minimize the color shift that occurs when you transfer files between earlier versions of Illustrator and Photoshop. Their method actually attempts to calibrate the two programs to a common color specification. It certainly improves the way Photoshop handles Illustrator files, but it is by no means a perfect solution. Colors still shift unexpectedly. However, if you want to avoid the time-consuming hassle of colorizing an Illustrator file in Photoshop, you can at least minimize shifts by creating and loading a color table. To create the table, follow these steps:

1. Create an Illustrator file with seven boxes. Fill the boxes with the color mixes shown in Table 10-1.

Table 10-1. *Values for the color table*

Box	Cyan	Magenta	Yellow
1	100%		
2		100%	
3			100%
4		100%	100%
5	100%		100%
6	100%	100%	
7	100%	100%	100%

2. Leave this window open. Open Photoshop, but don't open any files.

3. Choose File → Color Settings → Printing Inks Setup in Photoshop.

4. Choose Custom from the Ink Colors pop-up menu.

5. To compare colors, align this dialog box as close as possible to the Illustrator window. Then follow these steps:

   a. In the Printing Inks Setup dialog, click the Cyan box. The Color Picker opens.

       b. Adjust the color until it matches the Illustrator window that contains Box 1.

       c. Click OK.

6. Repeat step 5 for each of the seven color boxes. All of them should match the colors you see in the Illustrator window. Click OK to adopt these colors and to return to the Printing Inks Setup dialog.

7. Click Save at the Printing Inks Setup dialog and name your custom ink setup file *Illustrator Colors*. Click OK.

Once you've created this color profile, you can load it in Photoshop by following these steps:

1. Open Photoshop. (Don't open the Illustrator file yet!)

2. Choose File → Color Settings → Printing Inks Setup in Photoshop.

3. Click Load to load the file named *Illustrator Colors*. Click OK.

4. Choose File → Open to select an Illustrator file. Change the mode to RGB. Click OK.

5. The file should now look the same as it did in Illustrator.

Two are better than one

This chapter has shown you some techniques web designers have used to expand the capabilities of Photoshop. When you combine the features of drawing programs with Photoshop, you need a strategy to deal with the likely color shifts. But keep in mind that the resulting dynamic web pages will be well worth the effort.

CHAPTER ELEVEN

LAYING OUT PAGES IN PHOTOSHOP

More and more web designers are using Photoshop as a web design tool—with good reason. With Photoshop, you can comp pages, place text and images, and finesse your design before going to the trouble of saving numerous files and creating the page in HTML.

Unlike most layout applications, Photoshop is a bitmap program, meaning that what you see on your monitor is usually a good approximation of what others will see on theirs. With Photoshop's layers feature, you can quickly turn individual graphical elements on and off to see how they relate to each other. With Photoshop's guides, grids, and snap-to features, you can precisely align type and graphics just as you would in a traditional layout program. If you use animations in your work, you can even create a Photoshop Action that simulates the animated sequence.

Of course, you still need to convert your graphics to an appropriate file format and use HTML code to place them on the Web. Photoshop is good, but not that good! Think of the Photoshop display the same way you think of an Iris print: it's a visual record of what you want your page to look like when all is said and done.

This chapter includes profiles of several web designers who use Photoshop as a layout tool. You'll see how they use guides, grids, and layers to break up complex graphics for optimal downloading and quality.

You'll also learn the basics of creating and using Photoshop's guides and grids, and how to set up a web page template. Since some earlier versions of Photoshop don't offer guides and grids, we'll go through how to create them using layers and drawing tools.

Layers 101

Photoshop's layer capabilities are what makes Photoshop such an effective web layout tool, and a great web production program in general.

Layers allow you to place individual objects on individual transparent layers, and through different opacity and blending modes, control the way they interact. You can work with as many as 100 layers, limited mostly by the memory capabilities of your machine.

Adjustment layers (introduced in Photoshop 4.0) are layers that specifically control color and tonal adjustments to layers below. Since adjustment layers are also masks, it is possible to precisely apply (and remove) tonal and color changes to specific regions of an image.

With layer effects (new in Photoshop 5) you can link automated effects such as drop shadows, glows, beveling, and embossing to a layers contents. These effects can be removed or changed at any time.

Here are some of the more important things you should know about layers that will help you use Photoshop as a web layout tool and as a web production program in general.

Creating and deleting layers

As you build your web page, you'll constantly be adding and deleting layers—whether you mean to or not.

If you want to create a new layer—for example, to store vital production information about your page—you can simply click on the New Layer icon at the bottom of the palette, or choose New Layer from the Layers palette pop-up menu. In Photoshop 5 and 4, you can also choose Layer → New from the menu bar.

Selected layers can be deleted by dragging a layer to the trash can icon on the Layers palette, selecting a layer and clicking on the trash can, or selecting Layer → Delete Layer from the menu bar (Photoshop 4 only).

In Photoshop 5 and 4, every time you paste an object from another file into your active file or use the Type tool, Photoshop automatically creates a new layer.

In 5 and 4, it's easier than ever to create a new layer by converting a selection: simply make your selection, then under the Layers menu choose Layer → New → Layer Via Copy.

Making layers visible and invisible

One of the great advantages of layers is that you can hide parts of the image, so you can work on other parts. To hide layers, just click the eye icon in front of the layer you want to make invisible. To show them, click again. This process can quickly turn tedious if you have 50 layers and you want to show only one. To turn off all layers except the selected layer, hold down Option/Alt and click the eye icon. When you want to turn the other layers back on, simply repeat this process.

→

Making layers active

In order to work on an object, its layer must be active. Only one layer can be active at a time. You can make it active by simply clicking on the desired layer in the Layers palette or, if you are using the Move tool, you can actually select a layer from within the image window itself. To do this, place the Move tool over the object you wish to make active, then hold the Command/Control key while you click. A drop-down menu will appear, giving you the choice of making this the active layer. You can tell that a layer is active when it is highlighted in the Layers palette. This method is particularly useful when you are trying to position lots of type on different layers since it saves you the effort of going back and forth between the Layers palette and the image window.

Preserve Transparency

When you select Preserve Transparency from the Layers palette, you will be able to edit only the areas of the layer that contain pixels. This can be very useful or very annoying, depending on what you are trying to do. For example, if you have a layer that contains a navigational bullet and you select Preserve Transparency, and then you choose Edit → Fill; only the bullet itself will change to your selected color. However, let's say you want to apply a Gaussian blur to the same bullet. You'll quickly see that the filter doesn't have the effect that you wanted. With Preserve Transparency selected, pixels are "contained," and the Gaussian blur won't apply to anything outside the initial boundaries.

Creating special effects using layers

Layers aren't only great for organizing graphics; they can help facilitate special effects as well. Many of the effects mentioned throughout this book rely on the use of the Blending and the Opacity options in the Layers palette—options that determine the way that pixels in adjacent layers interact.

Flattening layers

When you are ready to convert your work to a file format supported by the Web, you will have to flatten the layers, since only the Photoshop format understands layers. From the Layers palette drop-down menu, choose Flatten Image. When you save the file, choose Save As to keep your original Photoshop file with the layers intact for future changes.

Painting design on a web page

Washington, D.C.–based graphic designer Valerie Robbins used Photoshop to create the pages for my personal web site, *http://www.cyberbohemia.com.*

Robbins applies her background as a painter/printmaker to page layout. She often builds her pages in much the same way that she paints on canvas when she is employing the "Old Master" technique. This technique involves sketching out the composition in black and white or a dark color first. Then composition and balance are resolved. Layout in color comes last. Figure 11-1 is a page she designed utilizing this method.

Valerie normally works with Quark for her print projects, but she finds working with Photoshop refreshing. "It's much more like painting," she says, pointing to the ability of Photoshop to turn layers off and on and view the results immediately. She uses grids occasionally, mostly to kern or to align type, but she finds grids a bit distracting. Instead, she usually creates guides as she needs them to align objects.

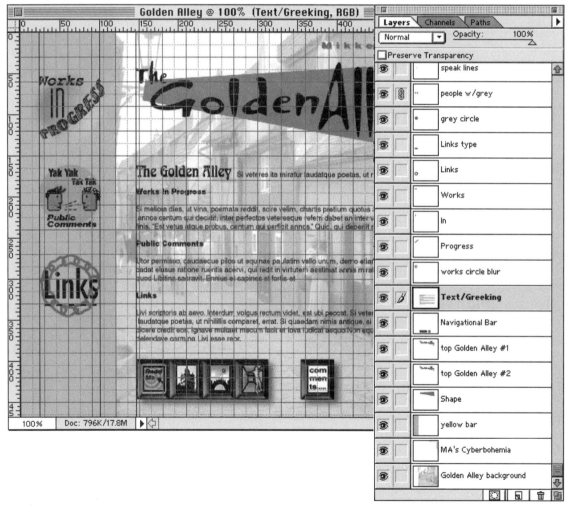

Figure 11-1. *Valerie Robbins works mostly in black and white, adding color later, and aligns graphical elements with Photoshop's guides.*

When Valerie is finished with a page (such as the one in Figure 11-1), she often passes the actual HTML work on to a colleague. She always sends the complete Photoshop file, with layers intact, as a page proof, so there is never any doubt about the way she wants things to look.

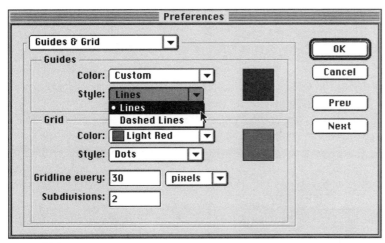

Figure 11-2. *You can customize the appearance of your guides and grids from Preferences with the Photoshop Guides & Grids options.*

Using guides and grids

Guides and grids are accessible from the View menu. To select display options, go to File → Preferences → Guides & Grids, shown in Figure 11-2. Here you will be able to choose the type of line as well as the color of the display line. For grids, you can also set the line spacing, in the Grid-line Every field.

Guides have an advantage over grids in that they can be moved, removed, or locked at any time. They also can be used selectively, reducing the distraction of a full-screen grid.

It's easy to work with guides:

- Drag from the horizontal ruler to create a horizontal guide, and drag from the vertical ruler to create a vertical guide.

- To move a guide, select the Move tool and drag it where you want it.

Guides can be used in conjunction with grids. A guide will also automatically align to a grid if you select View → Snap To Grid. To remove guides, drag the grid outside the image window. To clear all guides, choose View → Clear Guides. While grids will remain visible from file to file as long as Show Grid (View) is selected, guides appear only on the specific image file where they were created. When you save an image or graphic in any file format other than Photoshop, grids (and guides) will not be saved.

Redesigning with layers and grids

HotWired's award-winning redesign is built around rectilinear boxes where each box or series of adjacent boxes contains a color, text, or other graphical element. Anna McMillan, one of several HotWired designers, has done all the design and layout in Photoshop with guides that break the page into squares of 64 × 64 pixels, as shown in Figure C-145.

She actually worked with Photoshop 3.05, creating her grids using a Photoshop plug-in called Grid Creator, available for free at *http://www.edesign.com/filters.* Grid Creator generates grids on any active layer in Photoshop. Shown in Figure 11-3, it's easy to use but doesn't have Photoshop 5 and 4's snap-to features.

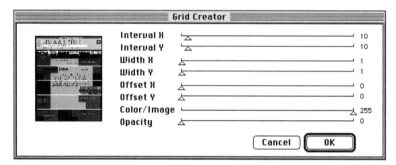

Figure 11-3. *The Grid Creator, a Photoshop plug-in, allows you to create grids in earlier versions of Photoshop.*

Anna created the page shown in Figure C-145 by first opening a 580 × 800-pixel Photoshop file containing a layer with a screenshot of the Netscape browser, and another layer containing the guides. Her first design pass was done mostly without color. She figured if it looked good in gray, it would look even better in color.

To see how the text would look, Anna cut actual HTML text from an HTML editor, clicked Photoshop's Type tool and then her image, and pasted the text. She kept her text options set at their default and chose aliased text. She knew that this would be only an approximation of how the text would ultimately look on a viewer's browser, but it gave her something to work with.

Part of the philosophy behind HotWired's redesign is to create pages that download quickly. This means less use of GIF and JPEG graphics and more emphasis on HTML text and color. Even so, for this page, Anna found herself working with many graphical elements. She placed each one in a separate Photoshop layer. (For other pages, she has used as many as 100 layers.) When she was finished with the page, she printed a color copy that she sent along with the actual Photoshop file that went to a programmer. Then it was back to designing another HotWired page.

Animating your graphics with Actions

If you use animations in your web site—and nowadays, who doesn't?—you'll probably use Photoshop to create and prepare the graphics that make up the individual frames. Wouldn't it be nice if you could use Photoshop to actually see the animation in motion? Sean Parker of Parker Grove nearly always includes an animated object in his web designs. To get a rough approximation of how the animation would look before actually building the animation in a GIF animation package, he used to place the sequence of images he wanted to animate into separate Photoshop layers and turn the eye icons off and on.

With Photoshop 5, he discovered that he could create a Photoshop Action (Window → Show Actions) to simulate the animated look, freeing him of physically turning the eye icons on and off. He finds it easier to design the web page when he knows how the animated object looks in the context of the rest of the static page. He finds his method especially useful when he wants to show a client an approximation of how the page will ultimately look.

This is how Sean does it using Photoshop 5 (as you'll see later, it's a bit more complex with Photoshop 4):

1. He created a document with several layers and turned all of the layers off.

2. He created a new action and started recording.

3. He selected the first layer of his animation and turned the layer on and then he turned it off.

4. He selected the next layer and repeated step 3, repeating this process until he had completed his animation.

5. He then stopped recording.

6. Finally, he created a second action and started recording. He activated the first action several times to create the impression of a looping animation. He then stopped recording.

With Photoshop 4, it is not possible to create an Action that records layer eye icons being turned on and off. Sean recorded instead the addition and subtraction of a layer mask. This results in a similar, layer-on and layer-off effect.

Checking out the browsers

To create a web page template, many web designers set up Netscape or Explorer windows as they might appear on a typical 14-inch monitor and take a screenshot. They open it in Photoshop, cut out the center, then save the file in the Photoshop format. When they want to create a new web page, they either open this file and build their layers on top of the browser cut-out, or drag the browser cut-out to another Photoshop file layer.

Figure C-146 shows a single frame from one of the animations that Sean created for the design firm of Porter/Novelle. This animation was for the web site of the Japanese Automobile Manufacturers Association.

This is how he animated his graphic using a Photoshop 4.0 Action:

1. He created a new Action, named it *Flip Book,* and started recording.

2. Starting with the first animation layer, he selected Layers → Add Layer Mask → Hide All. He repeated this process for each successive animation layer. When a layer mask is applied, an additional thumbnail appears to the right of the layer thumbnail. Black indicates the entire layer is masked, or hidden. White indicates that the entire layer is visible. Layer masks can also control specific areas of a layer (of no value for our purpose here).

3. With the Action still recording, he went back to the first layer of the first frame of animation and selected Remove Layer Mask. (A dialog pops up and gives options to discard layer, apply layer, or cancel. Choose Discard, which then makes the contents of your layer visible.) He repeated this process for each successive layer in the animation. When he was finished, he stopped recording the Action.

Using guides to design and crop

After Gregg Hartling has finished designing and checking his web page in Photoshop, he uses guides and the snap-to feature to crop and save the various components.

Figure C-147 shows the guides in place on one of Gregg's pages. Each component of the graphic is carefully grouped with another component, taking into consideration color palettes and final file size. In this example, each component is saved as a GIF with its own Adaptive palette. By saving each graphic with its own optimized color palette, each component (especially the telephone with all its gradient colors) will display better at 16-bit or higher resolutions and degrade "gracefully" at 256 colors.

To help him design his web pages, Gregg uses other Photoshop features, especially layers. He thinks of the live browser area as a "suitcase" where he needs to fit all the essential information (see Figure 11-4). Photoshop's layers assist him in the shuffling, grouping, and clustering of this information. Often his individual Photoshop files contain 15 to 30 layers.

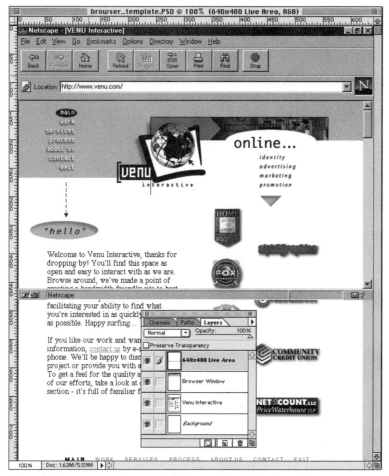

Figure 11-4. *Gregg uses layers to help him get the "fold" in his web pages.*

Gregg always includes a layer containing a screenshot of Netscape 3.0
for Windows displayed on a 14-inch monitor, placing it above all the
other layers. He places his design within the boundaries of this
template, which is always visible. Since this template is 800 pixels
long, he also includes another template in a second layer which
shows him where the "fold" or bottom cut-off will appear, as shown
in Figure 11-4. He clicks this layer off and on so he can see which
part of his page will be visible without scrolling.

Like other designers profiled in this chapter, Gregg works with grayscale graphics, not locking into any specific color palette until the
end. By removing the complexity of color, he finds it easier to
concentrate on shapes and context. When he is ready to add color,

he clicks on Preserve Transparency in the Layers palette so he can selectively add color to each object in each layer.

Gregg has a good trick for getting an idea of how his text will look on a page: he imports the actual text from a browser to his Photoshop file. To do this, he follows these steps:

1. He determines the width of the text area within his Photoshop file.

2. Using an HTML editor, he codes the text into a table of the same width.

3. He opens the table in a browser and takes a screenshot.

4. He opens it in a new Photoshop file and deletes the white background with the Magic Wand set to 0 tolerance and anti-aliasing turned off.

5. Then he runs a Photoshop Action that does the following:

   a. Selects Similar (which takes care of the white inside the letters)

   b. Deletes the selection (which gets rid of the all the white)

   c. Inverts the selection (which selects just the text)

   d. Copies the selection (which gets him ready to paste it into his current document)

Keeping boundaries with templates

Web designer Brian Frick brings the text and graphical elements into a 609 × 1000-pixel template he has created in Photoshop. This width assures that the page fits horizontally on the 640 × 480 pixel monitors typically used by most Discovery viewers. He uses the 1000-pixel length because Discovery has scrolling pages. At 340 pixels down, Brian has set a guideline to remind him that most monitors will cut off at this point. When he designs a page, he tries to keep the most important elements of the page above this line, although sometimes, as a reminder to the viewer that the page actually scrolls, he places a graphic that straddles this line.

The template also contains generic ads, reminding Brian not to design in those areas. As he brings in the design elements, he adds guides as needed to align text and graphics. When he is finished, he adds more guides to help him crop, index, and separately save every element of the page.

In Figure C-148, notice that he has created guides that show where he should crop. With the Crop tool, he cuts one section, then does a Save As. Then he reverts back to the original file (File → Revert), going through each square and repeating this process until he is finished.

Working within the "live" area

After years of working with page layout programs, designer Barry Brooks of Surf Network finds himself thinking about pages differently and now uses Photoshop as his web layout tool of choice.

Since the pages that Barry designs vary from client to client, he doesn't use a standard web template. He places all the most important graphical elements, including navigation devices, the core ingredients, and main message, within a 640 × 480 pixel boundary, an area he refers to as "live." He lets other, nonessential elements bleed off the edge, as shown in Figure C-149.

Most of the time he uses a combination of grids and guides. With his grids at a value of 10 × 10 pixels, he sets the grid line preference to Dots so they are not as obtrusive. For emphasis, he uses guides that are solid lines and a different color than the grids, yet in contrast to the background color. For example, he places a guide to show where a marker or header goes.

While he designs, he turns both the guides and grids off to view his work clean. He uses dummy text and doesn't worry about leading or kerning since most of the text will be placed as HTML text anyway.

With Photoshop's Move tool, he moves graphics around, getting a feel for how they look. He also turns layers off and on. When he is finished, he makes a copy of the entire Photoshop file as "insurance protection" to prevent any loss or damage during the save and revert process. Then on the duplicate, he crops each graphical element out and saves it in either the GIF or JPEG format. He chooses Save a Copy so he can revert back to his original to pick another graphical element to save. Since he is well versed in HTML, he does all the coding himself, using the original Photoshop file as a reference.

Coding layout information in a layer

At MSNBC, the collaborative site of Microsoft and NBC, designers have discovered a way to streamline their web production process. Figure 11-5 shows a Photoshop file created by MSNBC designer

Bobby Stevens, containing a wealth of layout and graphical data. Notice that the *guide* layer is separated from the background image containing the actual page by the *screen* layer, filled with white and set at 70% opacity. This allows parts of the finished page to show through. Because MSNBC programmers, (who actually do the coding and placing of the data on to the site) don't use Photoshop, the layers are merged and saved and printed and given to them either in hardcopy or as a file format they can open.

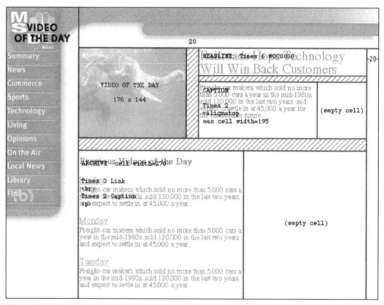

Figure 11-5. *Bobby contains page layout information in a layer to streamline the production process and make it easier to edit later.*

In other large-scale web production environments we've seen, designers design the pages and then "hand off" the components of the page to a programmer who does the actual HTML (or other language) coding. Sometimes designers include an original Photoshop file along with their GIFs and JPEGs so the programmer can see how the elements relate to each other by viewing the layers. Other times a hardcopy composite is given instead of the Photoshop file. In either case, the programmer has to figure out the precise coordinates, color codes, etc. In many cases, this method works fine, but if there is a breakdown in communication between designer and programmer, or if time is limited, design nuances are lost.

Not only does MSNBC's method streamline the production process and make it less error-prone, but it gives the designer a handy reference guide that makes it easy to go back and make changes or update

the page. It also makes it very easy for a designer to pass the work
on to a fellow designer if need be. Granted, it takes work up front to
calculate and enter all this data, but in many situations the payoff
comes later, long after you've forgotten what color or font you used.

Unintended uses

When Photoshop was created so many years ago, surely no one
imagined that one day it would be used like PageMaker or Quark-
XPress as a layout tool. But as you've seen in this chapter, designers
have discovered that when it comes to web work, it is the perfect
layout tool. Not only does it give an accurate representation of how
bitmap creations will look on the Web, but with layers, it is easy to
organize and store every graphical element imaginable. Will we ever
completely mine the depths of this remarkable program?

CHAPTER TWELVE

IMAGEREADY 2.0

Adobe initially released ImageReady as a standalone product to provide web functionality outside of Photoshop. With the release of Photoshop 5.5, Adobe is acknowledging that professional users want web functionality directly in the program. With the addition of Save for Web in Photoshop itself, you might be wondering if there's any reason to start up ImageReady 2.0, which comes in the box with Photoshop 5.5. In fact, there is little point in using ImageReady for the kind of optimization and previewing capabilities offered by the Save for Web plug-in; however, ImageReady 2.0 does offer three core features that are unavailable in Photoshop and are extremely useful for web designers and artists. These features are:

- Slicing

- Animation

- Rollover effects

These three features, two of them new in ImageReady 2.0, are the focus of this chapter. Let's start with some ImageReady basics before looking at specific examples of how to use these three useful features.

From Photoshop to ImageReady and back

ImageReady 2.0 and Photoshop 5.5 were made for each other, literally. When you install Photoshop 5.5, the installer automatically installs ImageReady, and the two programs share many of the same resource files and plug-ins. Although they are two distinct programs, Adobe has made the process of jumping between the two very easy. Jump-to buttons are found in both ImageReady's and Photoshop's

Toolbox, and if you choose File →Jump To in either program, you'll see the other program listed as an option. See Figures 12-1 and 12-2.

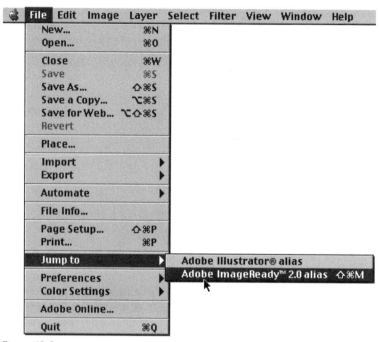

Figure 12-1. *Jump-to commands are found in Photoshop and ImageReady in the tool box...*

Figure 12-2. *...or under the File menu.*

When you install Photoshop 5.5, it searches your hard drive and automatically places aliases of any Adobe editing and graphic applications it finds into a folder called Jump To Graphics Editor. This folder is located in the Photoshop →Helpers folder. You can add to or delete these aliases at any time. To specify which application is launched by the Jump-to button in the Toolbox, or by a keyboard shortcut (Command-Shift-M), place curly brackets ({}) for Photoshop and straight brackets ([]) for ImageReady around the name of the application in the Jump To Graphics Editor folder.

When you jump from Photoshop to ImageReady, you'll first need to save your active Photoshop file. If you don't, when you jump a dialog box appears prompting you to save or not. (Be aware that with Photoshop 5.0/5.02, when you jump to ImageReady 1.0, your file is automatically saved without any warning, whether you want to save it or not.)

In theory, when you jump between programs, all your layers, layer effects, and type layers should transfer intact. Some web producers have reported, however, that type created in a Photoshop type layer shifts when they open it in ImageReady. You might also experience some color shifts when you open a Photoshop file in ImageReady. If you saved your *.psd* file with Photoshop 5's Embed Profiles option turned on, you'll need to choose View → Preview → Photoshop Compensation in ImageReady 2.0 to view your work properly. If you've set your Photoshop color preferences as I suggested in Chapter 1, *Making Photoshop Web-Friendly*, with the new color management features turned off, you can select View → Preview → Uncompensated Color in ImageReady 2.0 to avoid significant color shifts when you jump back and forth between the two programs.

Using ImageReady

If you are familiar with Photoshop, it won't take long to get up to speed with ImageReady. ImageReady's menu bar contains all the same headings as Photoshop's, with the addition of "Slices," as shown in Figure 12-3. Submenus are also similar. To the left of the ImageReady work area is a toolbar, very similar to Photoshop's and containing many of the same tools. ImageReady also uses floating palettes, and as in Photoshop, there is a Layers palette, a History palette, an Actions palette, a Swatches palette, a Color palette, and a Brushes palette.

ImageReady or Photoshop?

ImageReady shares the following features with Photoshop 5.5:

- Interactive color indexing capabilities, which make it possible to easily create GIF images with transparent areas and browser-safe colors
- Real-time viewing of the effects of JPEG compression
- Editable type
- Accurate file size display of both original and optimized images
- Multiple preview windows for comparing quality settings
- Multiple gamma settings for checking appearance on a variety of platforms
- Browser previews and the ability to jump to other Adobe products (Illustrator and GoLive)

All this begs the question, can you make do without Photoshop? The answer is absolutely not. ImageReady lacks many of Photoshop's advanced and powerful image editing and processing tools. In ImageReady, you won't find curves, adjustment layers, the History Brush, the gradation tools, or masking capabilities. You won't find Photoshop's new Extract command. And finally, ImageReady only works in the RGB color space and defaults to 72 dpi, so if you want to create graphics that are useful for both the web and print, you'll have to go home to Photoshop.

However, ImageReady contains several unique palettes:

- An Optimize palette to control color indexing, JPEG and PNG conversion

- An Animation palette to create animated GIFs

- A Slice palette to specify options for image slices

- A Rollover palette to create JavaScript states

ImageReady also has an interactive Color Table palette and a Styles palette, which contain a set of useful layer effects that can be applied to any layer in ImageReady.

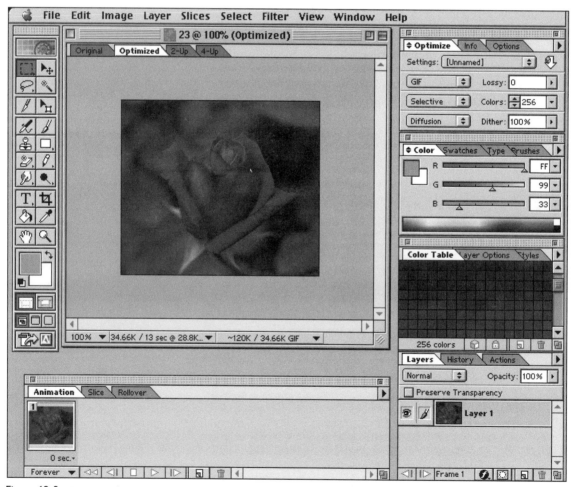

Figure 12-3. *ImageReady 2.0's work area, complete with toolbar, image window, and floating palettes.*

ImageReady's Type tool is also found in the toolbar. However, unlike Photoshop, with ImageReady you place your text directly into the image window. To edit type, you simply select the type tool from the toolbar, select the type directly in the image window and make your changes in the type tool palette, as shown in Figure 12-4.

Type color can be changed by selecting the type and using the Color or Swatch palette to select a new color or by simply selecting a color from either palette and drag-and-dropping it on a type layer. When it comes to anti-aliasing, ImageReady offers four choices—none, crisp, strong, and smooth—just like in Photoshop 5.5. It takes a little getting used to, but many web producers actually prefer editing type in the image window rather than through Photoshop's Type Tool dialog box.

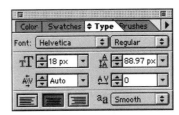

Figure 12-4. *ImageReady's type options are found in a floating type palette. Type is created and edited directly in the image window.*

I've already covered optimizing GIFs, JPEGs, and PNGs with Photoshop 5.5's Save for Web plug-in. This plug-in is essentially a bare-bones ImageReady, with a slightly different interface. If you learn to use the Save for Web plug-in, you'll know how to use ImageReady's Optimize palette. It also works in reverse: if you are familiar with ImageReady's optimizing process, 5.5's Save for Web plug-in will be easy to use.

When it comes to optimizing a GIF, PNG, or JPEG, there are a few differences between the two programs that are worth mentioning:

- In ImageReady, you can stop the optimizing process at any time by clicking on the Stop button at the bottom right of the window area. With the Save for Web plug-in, you can only use keyboard commands (Esc or Command-Period) to stop the processing.

- In ImageReady, monitor and browsers previews are found in the menu bar by choosing View → Preview. Holding Shift while clicking (right-clicking in Windows) anywhere in the image area will also give you a pop-up menu that includes Display and Preview preferences as well as Jump To preferences.

- Photoshop Actions are not compatible with ImageReady, and vice versa.

- The ImageReady 2.0 Optimize palette is deceptive. There is more to it than meets the eye. In order to see all the options, you'll need to expand the palette. To do this, click on the arrows in the Optimize tab, or click on the arrow to the right of the tab and choose Show Options. In the GIF or PNG file format, you'll now see interlace and transparency options. If you are in JPEG, you'll see Progressive, Blur, and Matte options. (The first time I used ImageReady 2.0, I couldn't figure out where these options were.)

Let's move on to the areas where ImageReady really differs from Photoshop: slicing, animating, and creating rollover effects.

Slicing images

In Chapter 11, *Laying Out Pages in Photoshop*, we talked about using guides to slice a graphic into smaller parts. By doing this, you can assign optimal file formats to individual parts of the graphic and thereby decrease the download time. We didn't get into the difficulties of creating HTML tables for each of the slices, which can be a potentially time-consuming task. With ImageReady 2.0, however, it is easy to divide a graphic into separate pieces and optimize each piece and create HTML tables. You can also use ImageReady to create client-side or server-side image maps from each slice.

Here are some basic things you should know about ImageReady's slicing capabilities:

• You can create a slice by selecting the Slice tool (Figure 12-5) and dragging and selecting areas of your graphic, or by converting a guide or a selection into a slice (Slices → Create Slices from Guides or Selection → Slices → Create Slices).

What's new in ImageReady 2.0?

ImageReady 2.0 is a greatly improved version of the original product, first released in 1998. Improvements to the program include:

• Slicing capabilities.

• Rollover effects.

• Improved animation that makes it easier to select frames, to specify delay or duration, and to optimize animation files. With 2.0, you can also import QuickTime-compatible moved formats, including MOV, AVI, and Flic, to view and edit.

• Full Photoshop text support.

• New Layer effects that include a pattern and gradient fill.

• 2-up and 4-up views with linked pans and zooms.

• Stroke tool!

• Clone tool!

• Styles that are automated effects that can be applied to layers.

• New shape tools, including the rectangle, rounded rectangle, and ellipse tools, which let you draw basic shapes on an image.

- Each document contains by default one auto-slice that comprises the full document and one cell in the HTML table that includes the entire image. When you draw a new slice with the slice tool, ImageReady generates additional slices as needed for the HTML table to contain the full document. Slices you draw are called *user-slices*, and slices that ImageReady generates automatically are called *auto-slices*.

- There are important differences between user-slices and auto-slices. With user-slices you can apply different optimization settings to individual slices, or link several user-slices and apply the same optimization settings to all slices in the set. All auto-slices are linked and share the same optimization settings. You can promote an auto-slice to a user-slice in the Slices palette.

- To edit slices, choose the Slice select tool from the toolbar and click on the slice you wish to work with. The thin, translucent film will disappear, and a clear image will appear. A slice must be selected before you can apply optimizations to it or apply other options found the Slices palette.

- In the Slices palette, you can specify slices to be one of two types: Image or No Image. Image slices display image data, which can include rollover states. No Image slices can contain a solid color or HTML text.

- Slices are numbered from left to right and top to bottom, beginning in the upper-left corner of the document. Slice lines, numbers, symbols, and color adjustments in the ImageReady window indicate the location, number, user- or auto-slice status, slice type, link status, and linked group color.

- To hide (or reveal) slice lines and information select Slices → Hide Slices/Show Slices, or in the Toolbox click on one of the two icons found just below the background and foreground color swatches. See Figure 12-6.

Figure 12-5. *ImageReady's Slice (left) and Slice Selection (right) tools.*

Figure 12-6. *Turn slices on and off with the icons below the foreground/background color swatches.*

Using the Slice tool

Bruce Quackenbush used ImageReady 2.0's Slice tool to create the graphic shown in Figure C-150. As you can see by the numbered overlays, the graphic is sliced into 13 parts. While most of the graphic is saved in the JPEG format the middle section, the part with the hand is saved as an animated GIF. The hand moves as if to beckon the viewer for a closer look.

The actual graphic was created using a combination of Illustrator 8.0 and Photoshop 5.02 by Joe Jones. The morphing hand was created in Poser and imported as eight individual layers into Photoshop. The complete Photoshop file containing nine layers was then imported into ImageReady 2.0.

Bruce then went to work to create this eye-catching graphic. Here's what he did:

1. He started by setting four guides that lined up with the edges of the hand. Bruce also set a fifth guide, and I'll explain the logic behind it in the next step. (To create guides, first make sure the rulers are showing View → Show Rulers and then drag and position guides from either the horizontal or vertical ruler areas as needed.)

2. To convert the guides into user-slices, Bruce selected Slices → Create Slices from Guides. He fine-tuned his work by creating yet another slice, this time with the Slice tool located in the Toolbox. In Figure C-150, you can see this slice (it is number 9). Why did he create such a small slice? If you look closely at the content of the slice, you'll see that he starts with vertical patterns and then fades to a solid blue. Bruce wanted this blue to extend to the edge of any browser window, regardless of size. When he was finished creating the graphic in ImageReady, he manually created another table to the right of slice 9. In this image-free table he designated a matching blue background in HTML. This is a clever way to create a larger graphic with no extra file size.

3. Next he created the animated GIF by selecting Make Frames From Layers from the drop-down menu in the Animation palette. He set the delay for each frame at 1.5 seconds and set it to loop forever. See Figure 12-7. (We'll get into more detail about creating animations in the next section.)

4. After he finished creating the animation, Bruce chose the Slice select tool, selected individual slices, and applied an appropriate file format to each. He chose JPEG at a medium setting for everything but the slice that contained the animation, which he optimized as a GIF.

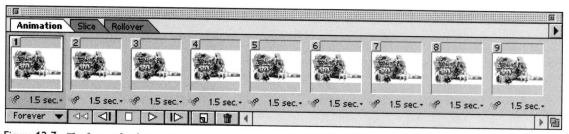

Figure 12-7. *The frames for this animation were made directly from the Photoshop layers.*

To see this animated graphic, go to *http://www.plattcolorado.edu/multimedia.htm* Notice how the blue bar extends to the right regardless of the size of your browser window.

Creating an animated ad with the Slice tool and layer effects

Dave Taylor of Taylor Imaging created the ad shown in Figure C-151 entirely in ImageReady 2.0. Not only did he use the ImageReady's type, slice, and animation features, he used the Bevel and Emboss layer effect to help create an attention-grabbing animation.

He followed these steps:

1. First Dave created a new document 450 × 650 pixels in ImageReady and filled a layer with a gray background.

2. Then he used the Type tool to type the text directly into ImageReady's image window. He applied a Bevel and Emboss layer effect to the "Big & Tall" logo to give it more dimensionality. See Figure 12-8 to see all the layers.

3. He created a set of guides that divided his graphic into 12 parts, as shown in Figure C-151.

4. He turned his guides into slices by choosing Slices → Create Slices from Guides.

5. He created an animation that makes the word "clearance" seem to pulse, like a neon sign. To do this, he first selected the slice and the layer that contained the word "clearance." Next he switched to the Animation palette. The selected layer in the selected slice automatically became the first frame in the animation. Next he created a new frame from the Animation pop-up menu. At this point the two frames were exactly the same—they both contained the word clearance with no special effects. With the second frame selected, Dave applied the Bevel and Emboss layer effect to the selected layer containing the word "clearance." The changes made via the Bevel and Emboss layer effect were now reflected in the second frame of the animation.

   If Dave had stopped at this point, he would have had an animation that went from the hard-edged type of his first frame to the soft, glowing look of the second. But Dave wanted the transition between the two effects to be more gradual, so he used ImageReady's tweening capabilities, which automatically add a number of transitional frames between designated frames.

6. Dave selected Tween in the Animation palette using the pulldown menu and checked the Effects box. He set the amount of tween frames to 4. See Figure 12-9.

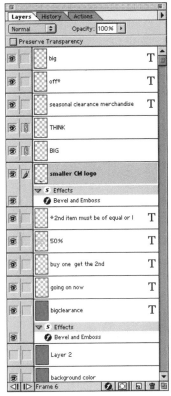

Figure 12-8. *The layers from Taylor's graphic. Note the use of the Bevel and Emboss layer effect.*

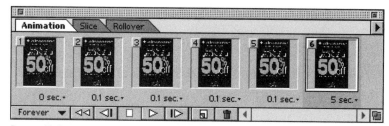

Figure 12-9. *The Animation palette containing Taylor's frames after tweening.*

7. He selected the slice selection tool from the toolbar and selected
   and optimized each slice. All the slices were saved in the GIF file
   format, applying the Selective palette and slight variations in
   color depth.

8. He selected File → Save Optimized As, and he was done. ImageReady created both an HTML document containing all the table
   information and a folder that contained all the sliced images and
   the GIF animation as well.

Dave says the production time for this ad was about 15 minutes. If he
had to cut and optimize the images in Photoshop, then create the
table in GoLive, then create the animation in GifBuilder, it probably
would have taken him about 1 hour. To view the final graphic go to
http://www.thinkbig.com.

Animation

I haven't found a GIF animation program that is easier to use than
ImageReady 2.0. To create an animation, all you need to do is open a
multilayered Photoshop file, choose Create from layers in the Animation palette and ImageReady automatically does the rest. Of course,
to get the animation just right, it takes a bit more work. But with
ImageReady it's easy to edit frames, apply layer changes to single or
multiple frames, and arrange frames in a new sequence. It's also easy
to apply optimization settings to the animation and specify looping
and repeat options for playback.

Before we get to our example, let's discuss some basic things to keep
in mind while creating an animation in ImageReady:

- Make sure that elements to be animated are placed on separate
  layers. Link layers that you want to animate together as a group.

- Preview an animation at any time with play button controls in
  the Animation palette or preview it in a browser (File → Preview
  In → browser of your choice).

- Make changes to layer attributes to create animation effects. Changes you make to an image using Layer palette commands and options (including layer visibility, position, opacity, blending mode, and layer effects) affect selected frames only. These changes can be varied across frames to create animation effects. (This is basically what Dave Taylor did in the previous example, using the Bevel and Emboss layer effect to create an effective animation.)

- Add frames in the Animation palette by clicking the New Frame button in the Animation palette or choosing New Frame from the Animation palette drop-down menu. The content of the frame is determined by the content of the visible layer or layers.

- Add or modify a series of frames between two existing frames automatically by using the Tween command, found in the Animation drop-down menu. Vary the layer attributes (Position, Opacity, or Effect parameters) evenly between the new frames to create the appearance of movement.

- Vary the sequence time between frames in the Animation palette by clicking on the Delay value below the selected frame. If you selected multiple frames, specifying a delay value for one of the selected frames applies the value to all selected frames.

- Specify how many times the animation sequence repeats (once, forever, or a specific number of times) by clicking on the inverted triangle at the left end of the Animation Looping pop-up menu.

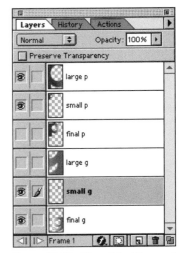

Figure 12-10. *The original layers of Parker's animation.*

Creating an animated GIF

Sean Parker of ParkerGrove created the animation shown in Figure C-152. You can't get the full effect by looking at the static frames, but the two letters P and G do a beautiful dance with various sizes of the letters seeming to morph back and forth into each other.

Here, step by step, is what Sean did to create the animation:

1. He created the text in Illustrator 8 and then converted the text to outline type and filled it with gradients.

2. He exported the file into ImageReady as a Photoshop 5.0 file.

3. He threw away the background layer and created multiple copies of the layers containing the P and the G. Because ImageReady doesn't do a good job tweening between type sizes, he created multiple sizes of each letter for different phases of the animation. See Figure 12-10.

4. Next he turned all the layers off and went to the Animation palette and created a second frame. (The first frame is automatically created when you open the Animation palette.)

5. He selected the layer labeled *small p* and used the move tool to position the small P in the position that he wanted it to start.

6. He created a third frame using the New Frame button located on the bottom of the Animation palette. He turned off the *small p* layer and turned on the layer labeled *bigger.*

7. He created a fourth frame and turned off the *bigger* layer and turned on the *middle p* layer (this will also be the size of the final P in the animation).

8. He created another frame and turned on the layer labeled *even bigger* and turned off the *middle p* layer. He repeated these steps of turning on and off layers and creating new frames until he had all of the keyframes that he wanted. Once he had all keyframes in place, he started the tweening process.

9. He selected frame 1 in the animation palette, and chose Tween from the palette drop-down menu. From the Tween dialog box, he set the Tween With option to Next Frame and added three frames. He left the Position, Opacity, and Effects options selected and left the All Layers option selected as well, as shown in Figure 12-11. He then chose frame 5, which was his original frame 2, and repeated the tween process but this time only adding two frames.

10. He repeated this process for each of the original frames until he got to the last frame. On the last frame, he choose Tween with First Frame, added three frames, and kept the other options as they were so that the animation would loop.

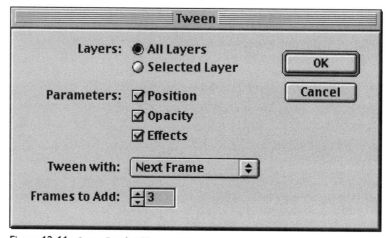

Figure 12-11. *ImageReady's Tween options.*

11. He then selected the frame that had both the P and the G visible and using the frame delay arrow located in the bottom right corner of the frame, set the delay to 0.5 seconds. From the submenu, he then chose Set Replace for all frames.

12. He set his optimization palette to GIF, with a Selective palette, and then from the File menu, he chose Preview in → Netscape.

13. At first he was unhappy with the timing of the animation, so he went back and tweaked a few of the frame's time settings until he came up with an animation he was happy with.

The entire animation takes up 46 frames and, with a 56K modem, takes five seconds to download.

Rollovers

Rollovers are another way to give your viewers a sense of control and interactivity with your work. ImageReady will generate the necessary JavaScript language to create a variety of rollover effects ranging from simple color changes to a more complex display of animation. These states are triggered when a viewer rolls or clicks a mouse over a designated area of your graphic. Using rollover effects and ImageReady's slicing capabilities, you can also create secondary rollovers, in which moving a mouse over one slice causes an image change in another slice.

Rollover states are created in ImageReady's Rollover palette. The actual process of creating these states is very similar to creating GIF animation using the Animation palette.

Before we get to some examples, keep these few things in mind:

• As when working with frames in an animation, use the Layers palette to modify an image for different rollover states. You can make layer-based changes to affect a single rollover state or all states in a rollover. You can also make layer-based changes to affect all states in all rollovers associated with an image.

• Changes you make to a layer in a rollover state that change the layer's pixel values (using painting and editing tools, color and tone adjustment commands, filters, type, and other image-editing commands) affect every rollover state in which the layer is included.

• Changes you make to a layer in a rollover state using Layers palette commands and options affect only the current state in which the changes are made (except for layer masks, which affect all rollover states in which the layer is present). Layers palette commands and options include a layer's opacity, blending mode, visibility, position, stacking order, and layer effects.

- When you save an optimized document with rollover states, each rollover state is saved as a separate file. By default, rollover states are named using the corresponding slice name plus the mouse action that triggers the rollover state. When you change the name of a slice, rollover states in the slice are renamed. You can change the default naming pattern for slices and rollover states in the Slices Preferences.

Creating a basic rollover

Here is how to create one of the most basic of all Rollover effects. In this example, I've created three states: Normal, Up, and Down. The Normal state, is well, normal. Nothing happens until a viewer passes the mouse over this button; then the Up state occurs, saying in effect, "Hey, look at me! Now that you see me, do something!" When the viewer clicks on the button, it activates the third state, which, in effect says, "Hey, thanks. You did something." By attaching a link or hot spot to the third state, you can lead the viewer to another site, another page in your site, or another place on the page.

This is what I did to create the three rollover states shown in Figure C-153:

1. First I created three layers each with a colored rectangular shape. I named these layers: *normal, up,* and *down.*

2. Then, from the Styles palette, I dragged and dropped the style called Button-Shiny onto the *normal* layer. I dragged and dropped the style called button-up to the *up* layer, and dragged and dropped the style called button-down, to the *down* layer. See Figure C-154.

3. I selected the layer called *normal* and turned off the other layers. In the Rollover palette, I noted that ImageReady had automatically created the first state and called it Normal.

4. In the Rollover palette drop-down options, I chose New State. By default, the second state is called "Over" which gives me the effect I want. When the mouse rolls over my button, it will change to a new state. At this point, however, the Normal and Over states are the same. This will change when I select the layer called *up* and turn off the other layers. The *up* layer is now shown in the Rollover palette as the second state.

5. For my third and final state, I repeat the last step, choosing New State from the drop-down menu. By default, the third state is Down which means when a viewer clicks on the state, it will change. In order to make my third button appear in this state, I turn off all the layers except for the layer called *down.*

That's it. I can test my rollovers by clicking from one state to the other in the Rollover palette and viewing the changes in the image window, or I can go to the File menu and select Preview In →
Browser and test it there. In the Browser window, I can also see the JavaScript that ImageReady has generated. See Figure 12-12.

Making dolls come alive

Artist Tom Mogensen wanted to add life to his image of dolls. In the first example, he used ImageReady to create three JavaScript states. When the cursor is placed over the eyes in one of the dolls, the eyes close. When the mouse is clicked on the eyes, they close halfway. In the second example, Tom added a GIF animation to the second state. When the cursor passes over the eyes, they blink rapidly until the mouse is clicked over them.

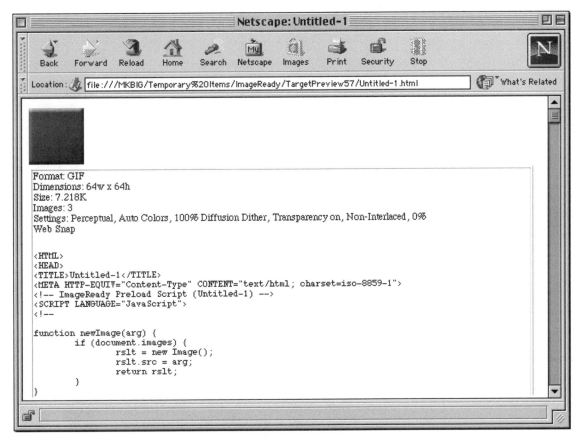

Figure 12-12. *You can preview your rollovers in a browser window and view the JavaScript code at the same time.*

Figure 12-13. *These layers will be used to create three states: eyes open, eyes closed, and eyes half closed.*

Here is what he did for the first example:

1. In Photoshop, Tom created two sets of eyes: one closed, the other half-shut. Now he had three layers, one containing the image of the dolls, the other two containing only the eyes of one of the dolls in different positions. He saved his work and "jumped" to ImageReady 2.0, bringing his layers with him. See Figure 12-13.

2. In ImageReady, with the *image* layer selected and the other two layers turned off, he used four guides to isolate the set of eyes he wished to make interactive. He converted the guides to slices (Slices→Create Slices from Guides) and then selected slice # 5, using the Slice select tool from the Toolbox. See Figure C-155.

3. In the Rollover palette, ImageReady automatically created the Normal state from the selected layer, *image*. Now Tom added another state by choosing New State from the Rollover pop-up menu. This state by default is called "Over." (You can change this to another state by clicking on the arrow next to the word that describes the state in the Rollover palette. A drop-down menu then gives you the following choices: Over, Down, Click, Out, Up, Custom, and None.) At this point, the Normal state and the Over state contain the same image. With the Over state selected, Tom clicked on the layer called *eyes closed*. The image in this layer now becomes the "Over" state.

4. For his third and final state, Tom repeated his last step. He selected New State, which becomes by default "Down." He then turned off the *eyes closed* layer and turned on the *half closed* layer. Now when the mouse is clicked on the eyes, the eyes will look sleepily at the viewer before launching to a new URL. Figure 12-14 shows the three states as they appear in the Rollover palette.

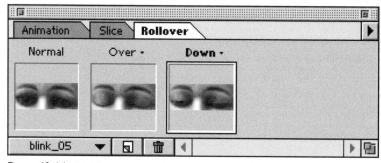

Figure 12-14. *The three states as shown in ImageReady's Rollover palette window.*

5. Tom tested his work by clicking on the Rollover palette from one state to the next and observing the changes in the image window.

When he was satisfied that the eyes were opening and closing as he wanted, he further tested the work by previewing it in a browser.

Adding animation

Tom was happy with the effect he created in the first example, but he wanted the eyes to do more than just open and close when the mouse was passed over them. He wanted the eyes to blink repeatedly. With ImageReady, it is easy to add a GIF animation to a state, and that is what he did.

The work he did in the first example wasn't wasted. To add the animation, all Tom had to do was select the state called "Over" in the Rollover palette. With this state selected, he switched over to the Animation palette. Here he created a very simple animation directly from the three layers:

1. For the first frame, he selected the *image* layer.

2. Then he created a new frame and selected the *half closed* layer.

3. For the third frame he selected the *eyes closed* layer.

4. He set the interframe delay to 0.5 seconds and selected Forever from the looping drop-down menu located at the bottom of the Animation palette.

5. He tested his work by clicking on the play button icon at the bottom of the Animation palette. See Figure 12-15.

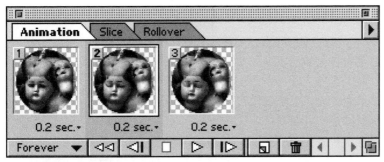

Figure 12-15. *The frames from Mogensen's GIF animation. A rollover effect launches the animation.*

That's it. Tom optimized each slice and then chose File → Save Optimized. ImageReady did the rest. It wrote the JavaScript that launches the GIF animation when the mouse is rolled over the eyes in the image. The animation stops when the mouse is clicked on top of the eyes. Because the animation is built from the slice that contains only the eyes, the whole graphic is reasonably sized and loads very fast.

Tom could create the animation from another doll's eyes as well. To do this, he would select the "Over" state in the rollover palette as he did before; however, in the Animation palette, he would select a slice containing the eyes from another doll and build the animation from that doll with a new set of eyes. Of course, he also would have to create a new set of eyes in various positions that match that doll and put each version in a different layer. If he did this, when the cursor was rolled over the first set of eyes, the animation in the second set would be launched for an even more dramatic effect.

Creating and previewing a tiling background

Using ImageReady's Tile Maker filter and HTML background capabilities, it's relatively easy to both create an effective background pattern and preview it in a browser.

Here's how I created the tiles shown in Figure C-156 and Figure C-157:

1. I used the Gradient/Pattern Layer effects to create the 64 × 64 pixel tile shown in Figure 12-16. (In order for a layer effect to work, your layer cannot be completely transparent; there must be some pixels present.)

2. In the Gradient/Pattern layer palette, I chose Linear and Spectrum from the pop-up menus and angled the gradient 148 degrees.

3. Next, I selected and converted the layer containing the layer effect into a normal layer (Layer → Layer Effect → Create Layer). You must create a normal layer before you can apply filters or other paint commands.

4. I selected the new layer titled *Layer 1* and applied the Tile Maker filer (Filters → Other → Tile Maker). I created two tiles using this filter: the one shown in Figure C-156 was created with Blend Edges set at 10% width; the tile shown in Figure C-157 was created using the Kaleidoscope Tile setting.

5. I then optimized and saved both my tiles.

To preview my work, I did the following:

1. With my tile image open, under the File menu I choose HTML background. Then I selected Image and chose the file I wanted to test, and clicked on OK.

2. Back in the File menu, I chose Preview in → Netscape.

In Figures C-158 and C-159, you can see how my images tiled. You can also see ImageReady data displayed in the browser window. Unfortunately, there is no way of getting rid of this data to get a perfectly clear view of the tiling effect. You can see that the tile shown in Figure C-159 works much better as a background image than the one in Figure C-158.

ImageReady also includes an Offset filter (Filters → Other → Offset), which is similar to the one in Photoshop. For more information on this filter and on creating background images in general, see Chapter 7, *Creating Background Tiles*.

Creating an image map with layers

When you create a slice, you can use the Slice palette to link a slice
to a URL. You can also turn a layer into a link in ImageReady by
choosing Layer Options from the layer pop-up menu, as shown in
Figure 12-16. Image maps offer the advantage of enabling you to link
circular, polygonal, or rectangular areas in an image, while slices
enable you to link only rectangular areas.

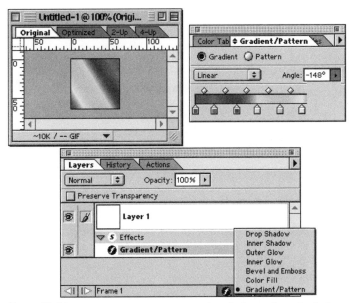

Figure 12-16. *You can create image maps directly from a layer in the Layer
Options dialog box.*

Conclusion

ImageReady 2.0 extends Photoshop's scope way beyond the world of
traditional graphics. You'll still need HTML editors such as Dream-
weaver or Adobe GoLive to create complex web pages and sites.
However, with ImageReady's HTML and JavaScript capabilities
combined with the new web features in Photoshop 5.5, the two
programs will satisfy many of your web production needs.

THE PNG FORMAT

T he Portable Network Graphic (PNG) format is a new file format, which was developed as an alternative to GIF and JPEG. Support for PNG in the web community continues to grow. Microsoft Explorer 4.0 and 5.0 and Netscape Navigator 4.0.4 all partially support PNG. Check Greg Roelofs's PNG-Supporting Applications page at *http://www.cdrom.com/pub/png/* for the most up-to-date information on the PNG file format. There are many advantages to using the PNG (pronounced "ping") format, including:

- 24-bit color support and lossless compression

- The ability to create and use up to 8-bit masks, thereby creating variable transparency

- Gamma controls, which give cross-platform consistency of image brightness

- A more sophisticated interlacing method that displays a preview of an image after only 1/64 of the image has loaded, compared with GIF's preview after 1/8 of an image has been loaded

A PNG plug-in

You'll need Photoshop 4.0 or higher to create PNG files. However, Photoshop PNG plug-ins that support earlier versions of Photoshop for both the Mac and Windows are offered by InfinOp.

Creating PNG files in Photoshop 5.5

With Photoshop 5.5's Save for Web plug-in, you can create either a transparent 8-bit PNG file, which is comparable to a GIF file, or a transparent 24-bit PNG file, comparable to a JPEG file but with full 8-bit masking capabilities.

An 8-bit PNG created with the Save for Web plug-in can generate a color palette that includes browser-safe colors. You can also create a simple, 1-bit transparent effect similar to the one possible with the GIF file format. Figure A-1 shows a comparison of the same image saved in both PNG (with and without interlace) and GIF. You can see that the PNG file with no interlace is slightly smaller than the equivalent GIF (7.984K versus 8.77K).

To create a transparent 8-bit PNG:

1. In Photoshop 5.5's main window, select and delete the areas you wish to make transparent. You'll need to work in the RGB mode to have all the select and delete tools available. (Transparency is signified by the white and gray checkered boxes.)

2. Select File → Save for Web.

3. In the Save for Web plug-in window, choose PNG 8-bit from the pop-up window. Choose the appropriate palette, dither, and other optimization settings from the Optimize panel of the Save for Web dialog box. (For more on these options, see Chapter 3, *Making Great GIFs.*)

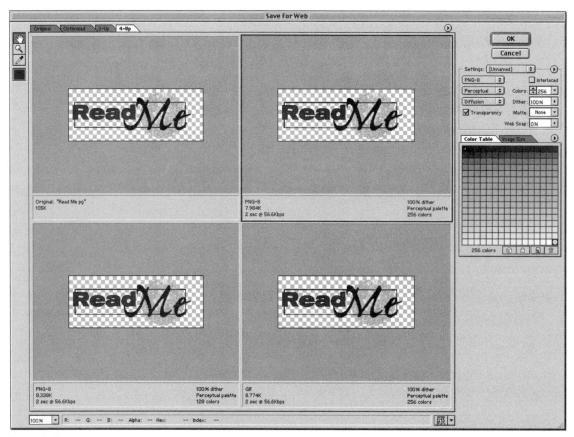

Figure A-1. *Previews of a transparent image saved as PNG with interlacing (top right), PNG without interlacing (bottom left), and GIF (bottom right).*

4. Select the Transparency box. Photoshop will make the designated transparent areas transparent and apply what is essentially a 1-bit mask. (The PNG file format supports variable bit masks—between 1-bit and 8-bit—but this is not a feature supported by Photoshop, or most browsers, at this time.) If you deselect the Transparent option, you can choose from the different matte colors to fill the transparent areas. You can create a pseudo-multibit mask by choosing a matte color that equals or approximates a dominant color in your web page background. Variations of your matte choice will fill the edges between the opaque and transparent areas, simulating the look of a multibit mask.

5. If you choose Interlace, your PNG image will appear progressively on a web page, similar to the way an interlaced GIF appears, taking seven passes before the entire image appears instead of just a couple. This adds to the file size.

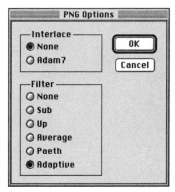

Figure A-2. *The PNG Options dialog box is available through the Save or Save As options.*

24-bit PNGs are an attractive alternative to the JPEG file format, especially since you can define an 8-bit alpha channel as transparent. However, PNG is a lossless file format and 24-bit PNG files are quite large. You'll never get the file size reduction you'll get with a JPEG, as shown in Figure C-159. The PNG with transparency is 461K, while the JPEG created with a medium setting is only 22.85K. (JPEGs are also universally supported while PNGs are not.)

To create a transparent 24-bit PNG:

1. In Photoshop 5.5's main window, in RGB mode, select and delete the areas you wish to make transparent. (Transparency is signified by the white and gray checkered boxes.)

2. Select File → Save for Web.

3. In the Save for Web plug-in window, choose PNG 24-bit from the pop-up window. If you deselect the Transparent option, you can choose from the different matte colors to fill the transparent areas. Keep in mind that an 8-bit mask increases your file size by at least 30%, as shown in Figure C-160. The file with transparency is 461K, while the one without transparency is 333.7K.

You can also create a transparent PNG in Photoshop 5.5 using File → Save a Copy. If you do this, it will bring up the dialog box shown in Figure A-2. (The options are described in detail in the next section.) When you save a RGB image that contains an alpha channel as a PNG, the alpha channel is used to create an 8-bit mask that designates transparent areas. (For more on creating alpha channel masks, see Chapter 3.) If you save an indexed image with transparent areas, 5.5 creates what is essentially a 1-bit mask. The Transparency box in the Indexed Color dialog box must be selected for this method to

The alpha penalty

Since PNG compresses less than JPEG and since the alpha channel adds another 20% to the total file size, you'll want to work only with small images or graphics such as those associated with buttons and other graphical interface elements. You can use bigger images, of course, but you'll be losing out in the battle for smaller file sizes.

Archive with PNG

If you are not ready to include PNG with your web site, at least consider using the PNG format for archiving images. Unlike standard JPEG (even at its highest quality settings), saving, restoring, and re-saving a PNG image will not degrade its quality.

work. If you choose a Matte color from the Indexed Color dialog box, Photoshop will generate a pseudo-multibit mask from the color you chose.

Creating PNG files in other versions of Photoshop

To create a PNG in Photoshop 5.0 or 4.0, simply choose Save, Save As, or Save a Copy and choose the PNG format. PNG is available as a file format option when you save a flattened RGB, grayscale, or indexed image. Figure A-2 shows the PNG dialog box you'll see when you choose the PNG file format.

Adam7 refers to the way PNG displays an image on a browser. If you choose this option, your PNG image will appear progressively on a web page.

The other options allow you to choose the way that PNG applies its special zlib compression filters ("zlib" is the name of PNG's compression scheme). These five filters transform the image data losslessly so that it will compress better. If you choose None, all filtering is turned off, which usually results in a larger file size.

In theory, each of the five options will create a different file size, depending on the nature of your image. You'll have to experiment with your images to find the best setting, but keep in mind that there are only a few kilobytes difference between the settings.

Creating a 24-bit PNG with 8-bit transparency is straightforward. In RGB mode, you simply create a channel layer mask and choose File → Save a Copy → PNG. (See Chapter 3 for more on creating channel layer masks). The channel layer mask will be used to define the transparent areas of your PNG file. You cannot create an indexed or 8-bit PNG with transparency in Photoshop 5.0 or 4.0. This is a limitation in Photoshop's implementation of PNG, not a problem with the file format itself. To create an 8-bit PNG with transparency, you'll need to use Photoshop 5.5's Save for Web plug-in, or File → Save a Copy → PNG method.

You can open a PNG image in Photoshop 5.0 and 4.0, but you won't see the alpha channel or know what areas are designated as transparent. You'll have to inspect your work on a browser that supports transparent PNGs or open your file in Photoshop 5.5.

Making PNG graphics look the same on all systems

The PNG file format allows gamma values specific to an image and a system to be saved. In theory, when a PNG image appears on another system, it self-corrects by comparing the gamma settings of the creator's system with the user's system. Photoshop Versions 5.5, 5.0, and 4.0 set a very simplistic gamma value into PNG files, essentially the platform default. This value is not based on the *.psd* file gamma, nor is it based on user-set preferences. For this reason, it is extremely limited in its usefulness. We can only hope that future versions of Photoshop will provide better support for PNG's gamma embedding feature.

THIRD-PARTY SOFTWARE

F or the typical user, Photoshop out of the box is good enough. You don't need anything else to create JPEGs and indexed GIFs, or to work with web-friendly colors and otherwise create web graphics. However, for web producers who want more control over what they do, the third-party products featured here will be quite useful.

GIF creation software

In general, I like the way Photoshop indexes color images in preparation for the GIF file format. I especially like the Save

for Web plug-in that comes with Photoshop 5.5 and the GIF89a Export module included with all versions of Photoshop for creating transparent GIFs. However, there are a couple of plug-ins that will give you more control over the indexing and dithering process.

HVS ColorGIF (Mac and Windows)

HVS ColorGIF from Digital Frontiers uses a patented "psycho-visual processing technique," which produces smaller GIF files than conventional dithering techniques such as those used by Photoshop. HVS Color also offers a high degree of user control over the color reduction process, including parameters that are not controllable in standard color reduction software, such as gamma basic, thresholding and controlled weighting of color allocation, partition size, and set point.

As opposed to simple statistical methods, HVS tools are able to synthesize and allocate colors in a way that minimizes visible banding without having to resort to diffusion dithering. HVS Color images are comprised of regions of pure color. Because the resulting color structure is less complex, HVS Color images usually compress better than corresponding dithered images.

HVS Color also offers a preview mode so that you can see the effects of your choices before applying them, as shown in Figure B-1.

Digital Frontiers
1206 Sherman Ave.
Evanston, IL 60202
800-328-7789
847-328-0880
http://www.digfrontiers.com

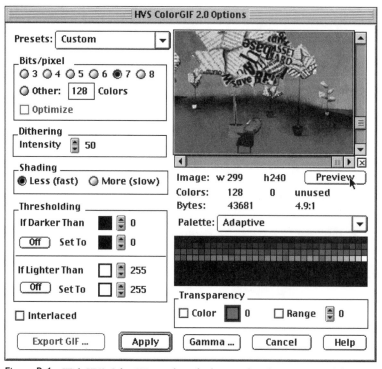

Figure B-1. *With HVS ColorGIF, you have both control and preview capabilities.*

ImageVice (Mac and Windows)

ImageVice is a color reduction filter for Photoshop that helps you create highly optimized, web-ready GIF and PNG graphics. Like HVS ColorGIF, ImageVice offers more control and options than Photoshop and a preview mode so you can see the effects of your choices before you apply them.

Boxtop Software
P.O. Box 2347
Starkville, MS 39760
800-656-5443
http://www.boxtopsoft.com

JPEG plug-ins

I have no gripe with the quality of the JPEGs that Photoshop creates;
however, if you use an earlier version of Photoshop (pre-5.5), there is
no real-time viewing of the effects of JPEG compression. You have to
apply the compression, close the file, and then reopen it to see the
effects. These two plug-ins can help.

HVS JPEG (Mac and Windows)

In Chapter 6, *JPEG: All the Color You Want*, we discussed ways to
optimize an image before applying JPEG compression. Essentially,
this Photoshop plug-in does that for you automatically. You choose
from a variety of optimizing algorithms (depending on the content of
your image) and HVS JPEG does the rest. You can also see the effects
in a preview window before actually applying the JPEG compression
to your image.

Digital Frontiers
1206 Sherman Ave.
Evanston, IL 60202
800-328-7789
847-328-0880
http://www.digfrontiers.com

ProJPEG (Mac and Windows)

ProJPEG 3.1 is another Photoshop plug-in that provides capability for
creating highly optimized, web-ready JPEG and progressive JPEG
images. It also features a live-image quality and file size preview that
allows you to find the right file size to image quality ratio, as shown
in Figure B-2.

Boxtop Software
P.O. Box 2347
Starkville, MS 39760
800-656-5443
http://www.boxtopsoft.com

Browser-safe color palettes

Browser-safe palettes are included in later versions of Photoshop.
However, if your version of Photoshop doesn't include one, you can

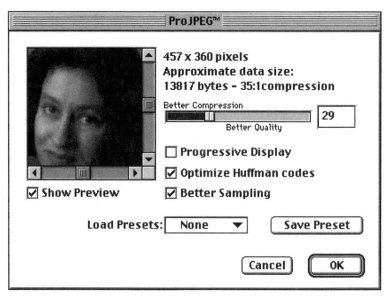

Figure B-2. *With the ProJPEG plug-in, you can see the effects of your compression in real-time and get an approximate idea of the file size.*

either buy a commercial product that will give you access to all the 216 browser-safe colors or download one for free at *http:// www.adobe.com/supportservice/custsupport/LIBRARY/2a7a.htm.*

Pantone ColorWeb (Mac only) and ColorWeb Pro (Mac and Windows)

ColorWeb is a Pantone product that consists of a web-friendly, Macintosh system-level color picker and a chromatically arranged and printed source book (the Pantone Internet Color System Guide), which is in the familiar Pantone fan guide format.

Once loaded onto your system, the color picker is easily accessible from within Photoshop (or any other graphic program). The colors are arranged chromatically with Pantone-assigned numbers that can be cross-referenced with the source book. (The source book contains the Pantone reference numbers as well as the RGB and corresponding hexadecimal values.) ColorWeb suggests an alternative web-safe color, but you can choose any color you wish.

At first glance one wonders, why pay money for a web-safe palette? After all, web-safe palettes are widely available on the Net for free. Furthermore, with Apple's System 8.0, a web-safe palette is part of the Apple Color Picker. The real value of this product is the cross-reference with the source book. Anyone familiar with the Pantone fan format will find it easy to locate the color they are looking for, access it by number in the color picker, and choose it. The guide is printed using Pantone's patented Hexachrome printing technology, so it is more accurate than traditionally printed swatches. ColorWeb costs $29.95.

ColorWeb Pro, which is available for both the Mac and PC platforms, is similar to ColorWeb but offers an extended color guide. It costs $69.95.

> Pantone, Inc.
> 590 Commerce Blvd.
> Carlstadt, NJ 07072
> 201-935-5500
> *http://www.pantone.com*

Web-friendly Actions

Actions are easy to create on your own, but if someone else has gone to all the work to create a useful one, why not use it? You have a choice: shareware or a commercial product.

Photoshop Action Xchange

This is a free site for trading Actions.

> *http://jmc.mit.edu/photoshop/*

KPT Actions

If you own Kai's Power Tools (listed next), spend a few more dollars ($49.95 retail) and get KPT Actions, a collection of 100 actions that will automatically create navigational devices, text effects, and picture frames. If you take a moment and watch each step of a particular Action, you'll also learn some valuable Photoshop techniques that you can apply to your own work.

> MetaCreations
> 6303 Carpinteria Ave.
> Carpinteria, CA 93013
> 805-566-6200
> *http://www.metacreations.com*

Kai's Power Tools (KPT5)

Photoshop wouldn't be complete without the latest version of Kai's Power Tools, KPT5. With these filters, you can create textures for backgrounds, apply sophisticated blurring effects, spherize, and much, much more.

MetaCreations
6303 Carpinteria Ave.
Carpinteria, CA 93013
805-566-6200
http://www.metacreations.com

Hybrid color makers

In Chapter 4, *Creating GIFs from Scratch*, we showed you how to
create your own browser-safe colors. In Chapter 12, *ImageReady 2.0*,
we showed you DitherBox, a plug-in that now ships free with ImageReady and Photoshop 5.5 and automatically converts any RGB color
into a web-safe pattern. Here is another product that will take the
work out of creating web-safe colors.

ColorSafe (Mac and Windows)

ColorSafe extends the 216-color web-safe palette to an almost infinite number of non-dithering hybrid colors and patterns. Download
and try a functional demo at the Boxtop web site.

Boxtop Software
P.O. Box 2347
Starkville, MS 39760
800-656-5443
http://www.boxtopsoft.com

Kodak Photo CD acquire module

Many web producers rely on Kodak's Photo CD process to both
archive and digitize images. In Chapter 2, *Improving Photos for the
Web*, we showed you a way to use the Photoshop Photo CD Acquire
module to do more than simply import your Photo CD images
directly into Photoshop. If you download the proper module (Version
2.2 for the Macintosh, 1.0 for Windows) and open different gammas
of the same image, you can actually improve tonal qualities of the
image.

Photo CD digitizing services, by the way, are commonly available
through local photo finishers and service bureaus. Kodak's web site
has a list of service providers.

To download the Photo CD module:

> *http://www.kodak.com/productInfo/technicalInfo/
>   pcdAcquireModule.shtml*

To find a Photo CD service near you:

> *http://www.kodak.com/digitalImaging/piwSites/piwSites.shtml*

Vector to bitmap

If you want all the advantages of changeable type and vector drawing
without the cost of buying Illustrator or Freehand, consider Human
Software's Ottopaths, a Photoshop plug-in for both PC and Mac.
Retail price is $99. With Ottopaths, you can create a path and wrap
your text to that path without leaving Photoshop (see Figure B-3).

HumanSoftware Inc.
19925 Stevens Creek Blvd.
Cupertino, CA 95014
408-399-0057
http://www.humansoftware.com

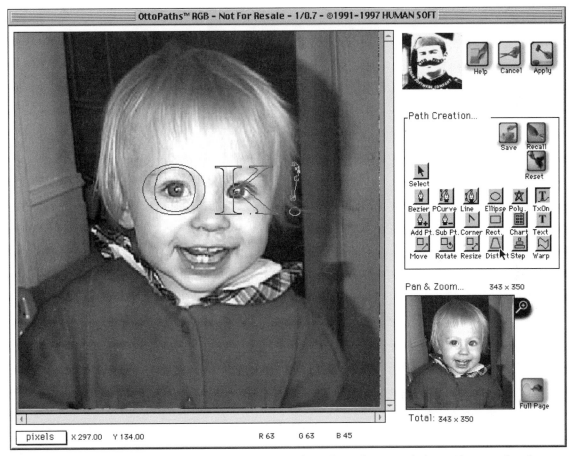

Figure B-3. *With Ottopaths, you can wrap text to a path and perform other tasks commonly done with a vector-based
program such as Illustrator.*

Debabelizer (Mac and Windows)

Debabelizer is still considered an important complement to Photoshop, even though with the release of Photoshop 5.5, this is less true than before. The program recognizes more file formats than Photoshop does, and its color reduction, scaling, and palette manipulating tools are arguably better than Photoshop's. Debabelizer is also very good at creating a "super" palette—a palette that contains colors optimized for series of similar images.

> Equilibrium
> 3 Harbor Drive, Ste.111
> Sausalito, CA 94965
> 415-332-4343
> *http://www.equilibrium.com*

Resource fork stripper

In Chapter 3, *Making Great GIFs*, we pointed out the difficulties in getting an accurate accounting of the true file size of your work. Using Boxtop Software's GIF Prep, a drag-and-drop utility, data from Macintosh graphics resource forks from GIF and JPEG files are eliminated to ensure that the file size you see in the Finder's Get Info dialog is accurate. You could always put your image on a server and get an accurate number that way, but using GIF Prep is much easier.

> Boxtop Software
> P.O. Box 2347
> Starkville, MS 39760
> 800-656-5443
> *http://www.boxtopsoft.com*

CONTRIBUTOR NOTES

Bill Atkinson designed software tools to empower creative people to express themselves. Now the marvelous software tools for digital photography on the Macintosh are empowering Bill to make beautiful color prints of his nature photographs. Whether making computers more humane and fun for people or nourishing people's hearts with images of nature, Bill continues to share his life passions with all of us. He can be reached at *bill@natureimages.com* and *http://www.natureimages.com.*

Casey Caston is a web designer at cnet.com (*http://www.cnet.com*), specializing in GIF animations and web-based advertising. He is also editor of the webzine *Fear Not Drowning* (*http://www.drowning.com*).

Ctein is a photographer, print maker, and author of *Post Exposure: Advanced Techniques for Photographic Printers* (Focal Press). He can be reached at *71246.216@compuserve.com* and *http://www.plaidworks.com/ctein/.*

Brian Frick worked for two years at Discovery Online before taking a job as a web designer at MSNBC in Seattle. His personal web site is located at *http://www.site2site.com/mogul/main.html.*

Bea Garcia is an art director at Savage Design Group, a leading graphic design firm in Houston, Texas. Before joining Savage, she was a designer in Dallas with Tom Hair Marketing Design. Bea designs print material, multimedia programs, and web sites for a myriad of clients and projects. The Savage Design Group web site can be viewed at *http://www.savagedesign.com.*

Chuck Green is an author and designer who heads Logic Arts, a design firm that specializes in creating templates for popular software programs. Chuck is the author of *The Desktop Publisher's Idea*

Book, 2nd Edition (Random House) and *Clip Art Crazy* (Peachpit Press), and is a regular contributor to numerous publications. You can reach him through his web site at *http://www.ideabook.com* or *chuckgreen@ideabook.com*.

Gregg Hartling is a former designer at Venu Interactive, a Los Angeles–based creative agency specializing in interactive media. Gregg now works at Earthlink and continues to crank out amazing work.

John Hersey, based in Marin County, California, has created designs and illustrations for Swatch, Wired, Absolut, IBM, Apple, Adobe Systems, Microsoft, The New York Times, The Los Angeles Times, The Washington Post, and several national news magazines. In addition, he illustrated the covers of *GIF Animation Studio*, *Shockwave Studio*, and *Designing with JavaScript* (all from O'Reilly). A digital portfolio is available on his constantly changing web site at *http://www.hersey.com*. Contact him at *ultraduc@hersey.com*.

Corey Hitchcock, project web designer for The Gate (*http://www.sfgate.com*), in San Francisco, has an extensive background in design and illustration for print and multimedia and is now happily designing, animating, and slinging HTML on the Web for the Chronicle Publishing Company's web site.

Stephen Jablonsky is creative director and founder of Imaginary Studio, a digital design studio in New York City. He can be reached at *steve@imaginarystudio.com* and *http://www.imaginarystudio.com*.

Brad Johnson and **Julie Beeler** are partners in Second Story, a Portland, Oregon–based design studio specializing in entertainment-oriented interactive projects for clients including National Geographic, DreamWorks, NASA, Contax, and Yashica. They can be reached at *info@secondstory.com* and *http://www.secondstory.com*.

Luke Knowland is the former producer for HotWired's WebMonkey (*http://www.webmonkey.com*), and a founding member of the Humboldt Institute for Technological Studies (*http://www.hits.org*). He is presently living in San Francisco. He can be contacted at *luke@arctic.org* or *http://www.arctic.org/~luke/*.

Steve Kruschwitz is a project webmaster at SF Gate. He can be reached at *stevek@sfgate.com* or *http://www.sfgate.com*.

Anna McMillan is currently a designer at Wired Digital, where she works on web page design, animations, and illustration. She is also a partner in UndoAnimations, an animation studio specializing in creating animation for the Internet. UndoAnimations clients include Lucas Film, WebMonkey, and Macromedia's Shockwave. She can be reached at *anna@undoanimations.com*.

Tom Mogensen is an artist in San Francisco whose clients include Oracle, Crown Plaza Hotels, Macy's, and the S.F. Giants. He has been using a computer as a design tool and medium in art for five years. His work can be viewed at *http://www.fotom.com*, and Tom can be contacted at *atom@the-city.net*.

Sean Parker is a principal in the multimedia company ParkerGrove in Washington, D.C. He can be reached at *spike@parkergrove.com* or *http://www.parkergrove.com*.

Bruce Quackenbush has been developing web pages since the very early days of the web. A self-taught computer programmer, in 1996 he quit his job as a manual laborer to team up with artist/designer friend, Joe Jones at Art Works Studio. Visit Art Works Studio on the web at *http://www.artworksstudio.com* or contact Bruce via email at *bruceq@artworksstudio.com*.

Valerie Robbins is a designer based in Washington, D.C. She designed the author's site *http://www.cyberbohemia.com*. She can be reached at *clayval@aol.com*.

Erika Sears is currently a senior web designer at XOR/Redshift Interactive, a Boulder, CO–based company where she helps architect and design large-scale web sites. Erika can be reached at *erika@xor.com*.

Bobby Stevens has been a Photoshop user for six years. He started in print and moved to interactive CD-ROM, and the Web two years ago. He has worked as a freelance graphic designer for clients like Seafirst, Adobe, and now MSNBC. He says his current passion is informational design: "striving to find ways to help viewers navigate in this new and often confusing medium." He can be found on the web at *http://bobbystevens.com*.

Dave Taylor is creative director for his award-winning, interactive media design firm, Taylor Imaging, based in Boston. He has also worked for companies such as Interactive Solutions (now Agency.com), where he served as associate creative director and lead designer. He has managed and created interactive projects for such companies as Sony, Ameritrade, Sheraton Hotels, Casual Male Big & Tall, and Putnam Investments. For more information, email him at *info@taylorimaging.com*.

Terbo Ted is a multimedia artist living in San Francisco. His web work with both *atlasmagazine.com* and *theremediproject.com* is included in the Permanent Collection of the San Francisco Museum of Modern Art, and his interactive pieces have appeared in digital art shows and performance venues internationally. Terbo has been documented in numerous books, magazines and web sites, as well as appearing on PBS, NBC Europe, NHK Japan, and the BBC World Service. He is also a regular contributor to *Zavtone Magazine*, Tokyo and runs the entertainment site at *http://www.speedbass.com*. He can be reached at *shag@sirius.com* and *http://www.terbolizard.com*.

Johan Thorngren is art director at Icon Medialab San Francisco. He can be reached at *johan.thorngren@iconmedialab.com* or through his personal home page at *http://www.portfolj.com/*.

Judd Vetrone, formerly of HotWired, is currently a freelance illustrator, concentrating on illustration and animation for the Web. He also works at Process39, a company specializing in multimedia design. He can be reached at *judd@netjet.com*.

Tom Walker is a New York designer and web producer. He can be reached at *tkwalker@interport.net*.

James Yang is New York–based illustrator with such clients as The New Yorker, The New York Times, and Forbes. He can be reached at *JamesY2200@aol.com*.

INDEX

225

About the Author

Mikkel Aaland is a photographer, writer, web producer, and author of six books, including *Sweat* (1978), *County Fair Portraits* (1981), *Digital Photography* (1992), *Still Images in Multimedia* (1996), and *The Sword of Heaven* (not yet published). He has contributed both text and/or photography to *Wired*, *Digital Creativity*, *Pre*, *American Photo*, *Newsweek*, *Graphis*, *Publish*, and *MacWeek*, as well as several European publications. His photography has been exhibited in major institutions around the world, including the Bibliotheque Nationale in Paris and the former Lenin Museum in Prague. He is the recipient of the National Art Directors award for photography. Aaland is also the co-founder of Tor Productions, a multimedia company founded in 1989 and based in San Francisco, specializing in the use of the still image in new media. He has lectured and taught on that subject at Stanford University, Drexel University, and the University of California at Berkeley, as well as at computer graphics conferences around the country.

Colophon

Our look is the result of reader comments, our own experimentation, and feedback from distribution channels. Distinctive covers complement our distinctive approach to technical topics, breathing personality and life into potentially dry subjects.

The animal on the cover of *Photoshop for the Web, Second Edition* is an Amazon parrot, also known as a blunt-tailed parrot. There are over 320 species of parrots, all of them easily distinguishable from other species of birds because of their large, hooked bills and their feet, on which the first and fourth toes are reversed, creating a pincer that aids in climbing trees. Most parrots also use their beaks to help in climbing.

There are 26 species and 52 subspecies of blunt-tailed parrots. These birds are mostly green, with bright coloring on their heads, wings, or elsewhere. The names of the subspecies tend to be descriptive: blue-fronted parrot, yellow-headed parrot, orange-winged amazon parrot. As their natural habitat is thickly grown forests, blunt-tailed parrots are excellent climbers, but awkward at flying and walking. In captivity, they often stop flying altogether.

Parrots were among the first domesticated animals. A helmsman of Alexander the Great was the first to bring live parrots to Europe. One reason for their popularity as pets is their ability to mimic human speech. Parrots have never been observed displaying this ability in the wild. They are naturally intelligent and gregarious, and it is believed that when they are kept in solitary cages they learn to mimic sounds as a way of entertaining themselves.

Legend has it that Christopher Columbus saw a flock of parrots in the air and they prompted him to change his course, thus discovering America.

Melanie Wang was the production editor and copyeditor for *Photoshop for the Web, Second Edition*. Colleen Gorman was the proofreader. Jeff Holcomb and Nicole Arigo provided quality control. Brenda Miller wrote the index.

Edie Freedman designed the cover of this book, using a 19th-century engraving from the Dover Pictorial Archive. Kathleen Wilson produced the cover layout with QuarkXPress 3.32 using Adobe's Gill Sans Condensed and ITC Garamond fonts. Alicia Cech designed the color insert.

Alicia Cech designed the interior layout based on a series design by Nancy Priest. Mike Sierra implemented the design in FrameMaker 5.5. The text and heading fonts are ITC Garamond Light and Gill Sans. The illustrations that appear in the book were produced by Robert Romano and Rhon Porter using Macromedia FreeHand 8 and Adobe Photoshop 5. This colophon was written by Clairemarie Fisher O'Leary.

Whenever possible, our books use RepKover™, a durable and flexible lay-flat binding. If the page count exceeds RepKover's limit, perfect binding is used.

How to stay in touch with O'Reilly

1. Visit Our Award-Winning Web Site

http://www.oreilly.com/

★ "Top 100 Sites on the Web" —*PC Magazine*
★ "Top 5% Web sites" —*Point Communications*
★ "3-Star site" —*The McKinley Group*

Our Web site contains a library of comprehensive product information (including book excerpts and tables of contents), downloadable software, background articles, interviews with technology leaders, links to relevant sites, book cover art, and more. File us in your Bookmarks or Hotlist!

2. Join Our Email Mailing Lists

New Product Releases
To receive automatic email with brief descriptions of all new O'Reilly products as they are released, send email to:
listproc@online.oreilly.com
Put the following information in the first line of your message (*not* in the Subject field):
subscribe oreilly-news

O'Reilly Events
If you'd also like us to send information about trade show events, special promotions, and other O'Reilly events, send email to:
listproc@online.oreilly.com
Put the following information in the first line of your message (*not* in the Subject field):
subscribe oreilly-events

3. Get Examples from Our Books via FTP

There are two ways to access an archive of example files from our books:

Regular FTP
- ftp to:
  ftp.oreilly.com
  (login: anonymous
  password: your email address)
- Point your web browser to:
  ftp://ftp.oreilly.com/

FTPMAIL
- Send an email message to:
  ftpmail@online.oreilly.com
  (Write "help" in the message body)

4. Contact Us via Email

order@oreilly.com
To place a book or software order online. Good for North American and international customers.

subscriptions@oreilly.com
To place an order for any of our newsletters or periodicals.

books@oreilly.com
General questions about any of our books.

software@oreilly.com
For general questions and product information about our software. Check out O'Reilly Software Online at **http://software.oreilly.com/** for software and technical support information. Registered O'Reilly software users send your questions to: **website-support@oreilly.com**

cs@oreilly.com
For answers to problems regarding your order or our products.

booktech@oreilly.com
For book content technical questions or corrections.

proposals@oreilly.com
To submit new book or software proposals to our editors and product managers.

international@oreilly.com
For information about our international distributors or translation queries. For a list of our distributors outside of North America check out:
http://www.oreilly.com/www/order/country.html

O'Reilly & Associates, Inc.
101 Morris Street, Sebastopol, CA 95472 USA
TEL   707-829-0515 or 800-998-9938
            (6am to 5pm PST)
FAX   707-829-0104

International Distributors

UK, Europe, Middle East and Africa
(except France, Germany, Austria, Switzerland, Luxembourg, Liechtenstein, and Eastern Europe)

INQUIRIES
O'Reilly UK Limited
4 Castle Street
Farnham
Surrey, GU9 7HS
United Kingdom
Telephone: 44-1252-711776
Fax: 44-1252-734211
Email: josette@oreilly.com

ORDERS
Wiley Distribution Services Ltd.
1 Oldlands Way
Bognor Regis
West Sussex PO22 9SA
United Kingdom
Telephone: 44-1243-779777
Fax: 44-1243-820250
Email: cs-books@wiley.co.uk

FRANCE

ORDERS
GEODIF
61, Bd Saint-Germain
75240 Paris Cedex 05, France
Tel: 33-1-44-41-46-16 (French books)
Tel: 33-1-44-41-11-87 (English books)
Fax: 33-1-44-41-11-44
Email: distribution@eyrolles.com

INQUIRIES
Éditions O'Reilly
18 rue Séguier
75006 Paris, France
Tel: 33-1-40-51-52-30
Fax: 33-1-40-51-52-31
Email: france@editions-oreilly.fr

GERMANY, SWITZERLAND, AUSTRIA, EASTERN EUROPE, LUXEMBOURG, AND LIECHTENSTEIN

INQUIRIES & ORDERS
O'Reilly Verlag
Balthasarstr. 81
D-50670 Köln
Germany
Telephone: 49-221-973160-91
Fax: 49-221-973160-8
Email: anfragen@oreilly.de (inquiries)
Email: order@oreilly.de (orders)

CANADA (French language books)
Les Éditions Flammarion ltée
375, Avenue Laurier Ouest
Montréal (Québec) H2V 2K3
Tel: 00-1-514-277-8807
Fax: 00-1-514-278-2085
Email: info@flammarion.qc.ca

HONG KONG
City Discount Subscription Service, Ltd.
Unit D, 3rd Floor, Yan's Tower
27 Wong Chuk Hang Road
Aberdeen, Hong Kong
Tel: 852-2580-3539
Fax: 852-2580-6463
Email: citydis@ppn.com.hk

KOREA
Hanbit Media, Inc.
Sonyoung Bldg. 202
Yeksam-dong 736-36
Kangnam-ku
Seoul, Korea
Tel: 822-554-9610
Fax: 822-556-0363
Email: hant93@chollian.dacom.co.kr

PHILIPPINES
Mutual Books, Inc.
429-D Shaw Boulevard
Mandaluyong City, Metro
Manila, Philippines
Tel: 632-725-7538
Fax: 632-721-3056
Email: mbikikog@mnl.sequel.net

TAIWAN
O'Reilly Taiwan
No. 3, Lane 131
Hang-Chow South Road
Section 1, Taipei, Taiwan
Tel: 886-2-23968990
Fax: 886-2-23968916
Email: taiwan@oreilly.com

CHINA
O'Reilly Beijing
Room 2410
160, FuXingMenNeiDaJie
XiCheng District
Beijing, China PR 100031
Tel: 86-10-86631006
Fax: 86-10-86631007
Email: beijing@oreilly.com

INDIA
Computer Bookshop (India) Pvt. Ltd.
190 Dr. D.N. Road, Fort
Bombay 400 001 India
Tel: 91-22-207-0989
Fax: 91-22-262-3551
Email: cbsbom@giasbm01.vsnl.net.in

JAPAN
O'Reilly Japan, Inc.
Kiyoshige Building 2F
12-Bancho, Sanei-cho
Shinjuku-ku
Tokyo 160-0008 Japan
Tel: 81-3-3356-5227
Fax: 81-3-3356-5261
Email: japan@oreilly.com

ALL OTHER ASIAN COUNTRIES
O'Reilly & Associates, Inc.
101 Morris Street
Sebastopol, CA 95472 USA
Tel: 707-829-0515
Fax: 707-829-0104
Email: order@oreilly.com

AUSTRALIA
WoodsLane Pty., Ltd.
7/5 Vuko Place
Warriewood NSW 2102
Australia
Tel: 61-2-9970-5111
Fax: 61-2-9970-5002
Email: info@woodslane.com.au

NEW ZEALAND
Woodslane New Zealand, Ltd.
21 Cooks Street (P.O. Box 575)
Waganui, New Zealand
Tel: 64-6-347-6543
Fax: 64-6-345-4840
Email: info@woodslane.com.au

LATIN AMERICA
McGraw-Hill Interamericana
Editores, S.A. de C.V.
Cedro No. 512
Col. Atlampa
06450, Mexico, D.F.
Tel: 52-5-547-6777
Fax: 52-5-547-3336
Email: mcgraw-hill@infosel.net.mx

O'REILLY®

O'Reilly & Associates, Inc.
101 Morris Street
Sebastopol, CA 95472-9902
1-800-998-9938

Visit us online at:
http://www.oreilly.com/
orders@oreilly.com

O'REILLY WOULD LIKE TO HEAR FROM YOU

Which book did this card come from?

_____

Where did you buy this book?
- ❏ Bookstore
- ❏ Direct from O'Reilly
- ❏ Bundled with hardware/software
- ❏ Computer Store
- ❏ Class/seminar
- ❏ Other _____

What operating system do you use?
- ❏ UNIX
- ❏ Windows NT
- ❏ Other _____
- ❏ Macintosh
- ❏ PC(Windows/DOS)

What is your job description?
- ❏ System Administrator
- ❏ Network Administrator
- ❏ Web Developer
- ❏ Programmer
- ❏ Educator/Teacher
- ❏ Other _____

❏ Please send me O'Reilly's catalog, containing a complete listing of O'Reilly books and software.

Name _____ Company/Organization _____)

Address _____

City _____ State _____ Zip/Postal Code _____ Country _____

Telephone _____ Internet or other email address (specify network) _____

Nineteenth century wood engraving
of a bear from the O'Reilly &
Associates Nutshell Handbook®
Using & Managing UUCP.

POST CARD

BUSINESS REPLY MAIL

FIRST CLASS MAIL   PERMIT NO. 80   SEBASTOPOL, CA

Postage will be paid by addressee

O'Reilly & Associates, Inc.
101 Morris Street
Sebastopol, CA 95472-9902